69889

THE PRINCIPLES

OF

PSYCHOLOGY.

BY

JOHN BASCOM,

Professor in Williams College,

AUTHOR OF

"POLITICAL ECONOMY," "PHILOSOPHY OF RHETORIC," "ÆSTHETICS."

NEW YORK:

G. P. PUTNAM AND SON,

661 BROADWAY.

1869.

Entered according to Act of Congress, in the year 1869,
By G. P. PUTNAM & SON,
In the Clerk's Office of the District Court of the United States for the
Southern District of New York.

BF
131
.F

PREFACE.

It has been a reproach to philosophy, generally and persistently put forward, that it makes no progress, that it lacks established elements, that it is a field of extravagant and contradictory theories. We do not accept these assertions in the unqualified way in which they are thrown out. So made, they are the result of ignorance and ungrounded contempt on the part of those who so easily utter them. So far, however, as these statements are true, they are a common reproach and misfortune, to be removed only by more patient, more protracted, more guarded inquiry. To scorn and reject philosophy as presented under its own, its metaphysical form, subject to its own conditions, is simply to deepen the difficulty, and postpone indefinitely an answer to the most fundamental and central inquiries. If more than the usual number of mistakes have been made in this department, it is because more than the usual obstacles lie in the path of progress. These are not to be removed by discouragement, or by opening ways in other directions. All success to the students of physical science : but each of its fields may have its triumphs, and the secrets of mind remain as unapproachable as hitherto. With philosophy and not without it, under its own laws and not under the laws of a lower realm, must be found those clues of success, those principles of investigation, which can alone place this highest form of knowledge in its true position. The following treatise is at least a patient effort to make a contribution to this, amid all failures, chief department of thought. If asked why I hoped this volume might reward the perusal, I should answer, Not because the system presented is new, but because the statement it here receives is at once succinct and elaborate, is incidentally strengthened by new points, by a consistent maintenance of all that belongs to it, and by the rejection of that which, essentially alien to its principles, only embarrasses it. I trust the Intuitive Philosophy will be found hereby to have gained somewhat of that proof which springs from completeness and proportion of parts.

I have acknowledged my obligations to others in cases in which they have been direct. I here especially express my indebtedness, in the general tone of the philosophy presented, to the eminent explorer and instructor in this field, Dr. Hickok.

Holding my work amenable to thorough criticism, I shall yet expect but little profit from the facile application of previous opinions to detached points ; or from any discussion of the principles involved, less penetrative and systematic than that here presented. I believe this treatise to have the integrity of a system, and to call, therefore, for a joint and complete judgment. To such handling I hopefully commend it.

CONTENTS.

INTRODUCTION.

BOOK I.—The Intellect.

CHAPTER I.

THE FIELD OF MENTAL SCIENCE AND ITS DIVISIONS.

CHAPTER II.

THE INTELLECT—ITS DIVISIONS—PERCEPTION.

CHAPTER III.

THE UNDERSTANDING.

CHAPTER IV.

THE REASON.

CHAPTER V.

THE DYNAMICS OF THE INTELLECT.

BOOK II.—The Feelings.

CHAPTER I.

PHYSICAL FEELINGS.

CHAPTER II.

THE INTELLECTUAL FEELINGS.

CHAPTER III.

THE SPIRITUAL FEELINGS.

CHAPTER IV.

DYNAMICS OF THE FEELINGS.

BOOK III.—The Will.

CHAPTER I.

VITAL ACTION ANTICIPATORY OF VOLITION.

CHAPTER II.

EXECUTIVE VOLITION.

CHAPTER III.

PRIMARY VOLITION, OR CHOICE.

CHAPTER IV.

DYNAMICS OF THE WILL AND OF THE MIND.

CHAPTER V.

THE RELATIONS OF THE SYSTEMS HERE OFFERED TO PREVALENT FORMS OF PHILOSOPHY.

INTRODUCTION.

§ 1. Though a knowledge of the value of a subject is not necessary to its successful pursuit, yet it imparts to our inquiries peculiar zest and pleasure. We shall never fully understand the advantages connected with any science, till we have mastered it; and it is thus natural that each should praise his own favorite pursuit, experiencing daily the enjoyment and power it confers. Nor is this commendation usually, in itself considered, excessive; it is chiefly at fault as it disparages other investigations, in themselves possessed of rival claims. As the fashion of thought in our time is to underrate philosophy, a brief space bestowed to urging its importance will not be misemployed.

We shall not enlarge on the pre-eminent mental discipline it gives, the acuteness of analysis, the steadiness of attention, the breadth of principles. All study imparts more or less of this training, and some are willing to believe that metaphysics bestow an unprofitable subtility of intellect, a gymnastic dexterity of thought; more fit for show than service, more likely to mislead than guide their possessors. There are certain peculiar and pre-eminent considerations on which we would chiefly rest our estimate of philosophy.

The facts which it furnishes are most intimate to our

own actions, to the mastery and ordering of our own thoughts, and to the influence we are to exert over others. It is indeed possible, that there should be healthy and successful intellectual action, a wise play of the emotions and of the moral nature, without understanding them. So may there be physical health without hygiene; yet who will deny an influence of the knowledge of the laws of life in the government of life? To pick up a few facts so personal, so of our very selves, as those which pertain to mind, cannot but be of the highest moment in ordering our action? Indeed, every man who has any claims to general knowledge is a philosopher, however much he may deny it, and however false and limited his conclusions may be. It is not a question whether there shall be philosophy among men; this there must be, if men are to think and act at all; but whether this philosophy shall be a true or false one. Yet we do not wish to dwell on the value even of the facts which mental science gives, their direct practical worth in affording rules for intellectual training, and for influence over others; but rather to point out certain broader relations of philosophy, which make its acquisition yet more imperative.

§ 2. In the first place, no true notion of the dignity of man will be attained without it. If we consider man exclusively in his external relations, in his physical organization, and the ministration of nature to him, though we shall certainly assign him, if we reflect wisely, a pre-eminent position, we shall by no means measure his true worth. The forces and lives of the world grade up to him, and grade down from him; and while he is the highest and latest of living things, he is nevertheless of them, ruling by a superiority, not by a complete separation of nature. The body of man is very perfect; but those other organisms are also in kind marvelous. The brain of man is very large ; but these other brains are large also, and apparently thoughtful. Having traveled in classification all the way up from infusoria, the last strides of progress, great as they are, do not impress as throwing man out of the general range and fortunes of the life of which he makes a part.

As a matter of fact, those whose attention has been most external in its objects, who have studied nature, and man in nature, have held comparatively disparaging views of the rank of the human race. They have often put it in the direct line of development with the life below it ; they have thought it to share its intellectual and moral endowments with the higher animals ; and they have subjected it, in common with all life, to the fatalistic lock of physical forces. Approaching man from below, we interpret him from the types of power we find in nature, we limit his liberty or rob him of it, we expound his moral nature by the law of utility, so obtrusive in the acquisition of physical good ; while we seem to find the germ and outline of his intellectual constitution in brute instincts, perceptions, associations. We are thus as those who contemplate in a statue more the pedestal on which it rests, the marble of which it is made, the measurements to which it conforms, than the living, spiritual power it expresses.

There is no adequate defence against this tendency, no reasoning man out of this grasp of scientific classification, from the position of bimana among quadrumana, from his rank as co-ordinate in structure with the gibbering monkey, the grinning chimpanzee, the brute-headed gorilla, except through philosophy—without reversing the process, beginning at the top and moving downward—without considering that which is internal, and overshadowing with it, transient, external conditions. Suppose, for instance, as the result of such direct, independent inquiry, it is found that liberty belongs to man, a power altogether unique, with no prediction or type in nature; that the moral intuition, the necessary accompaniment of freedom, transforming it into self-poised, responsible life, is equally independent and primary; do we not in these two pillars of personality discover supports which lift the spiritual life into an entirely new region, which cannot be broken by all the blind giants of simple, physical induction that may bow themselves against them? If also it shall appear that the intellectual action of man is throughout different in kind from that of the animal; that we have no proof that the truly rational elements, the regulative ideas of thought, ever enter the lower field of life, ever transform associations into comprehension, then shall we again see, that we have reached a new plane; not the completion of that which is below, but the commencement of that which is above; not to be explained from the earth upwards, but from the heavens downwards.

To estimate man outwardly, physically, is to judge a temple from the exterior, is to decide upon it by the order of its architecture, the bevel of its stones, the greatness of its workmanship, without entering its shrine, seeing its worship, or studying its ritual. So to judge man is as if we should pronounce on the supernatural claims of Christ by an inquiry into his human features and Jewish characteristics, in perfect oversight of the subject matter of the question. Man is to rank according to his spiritual constitution, and that it is the office of philosophy, and philosophy alone, to inquire into. We must go within the mind, see its structure and appliances, before we can know the dignity of the race. If this is denied us, if these portals are locked against us, we can only remain mute till the key shall be brought us.

§ 3. The second great office of philosophy is to furnish a counterpoise, a complement and corrective to the methods of natural science. It is not because we overlook the legitimacy and practical value of these methods, nor because we disparage induction, a chief builder in the temple of knowledge, one that has commenced and is carrying briskly onward some of its most showy and serviceable portions, that we urge the rank of philosophy; but for this end, that the two may be seen to be truly supplemental each to each, that the arrogance of science and its supercilious denials may be felt to diminish the worth of its own services, and so to cut down the scope of human faculties and hopes as to make knowledge itself comparatively trivial and nugatory. It is the nature of the mind that knows, that gives significancy to knowing, and if this term, the one most intimate to ourselves, in which alone we are deeply concerned, is to be excluded from knowledge; if the disembodied spirit is to be left wandering on the further shore in the limbo of things forever uncertain and unknowable, then, indeed, is it a most minute and unsatisfactory gain, that our unexplored and unfathomed powers lay hold for a little of the things about them; a small matter that the stream, rushing on, we know not whither, yields a troubled reflection of the shrubs on its banks.

We claim, that the knowledge that centres directly in mind, in its moral and intellectual powers, and in the social, civil, and religious actions that arise immediately from them, is a full half of all knowledge; and that the methods of reasoning employed in these departments, while very different from the naked inductions of science, constitute the nobler moiety of intellectual life. We urge attention to philosophy, because the sphere of thought cannot be complete without it, cannot be rounded into a well-balanced and stable orb.

If there has been one devolopment more preposterous than all others in the growth of knowledge, that development is Positive Philosophy—a scheme that scouts metaphysics, and yet can do it on no other than metaphysical grounds ; that determines what may be known and what may not be known, and puts among the things to be discarded the knowing faculties ; that uses philosophy to blow up philosophy, and on the ground thus cleared builds up a cobble-house of facts, every one of whose connections must yet be as purely intellectual as those of mental science itself. This is as if the eye, failing to look backward as well as forward, inward as well as outward, should deny the existence of anything in that direction, and affirm the objects before itself to be ultimate, the only resolution of facts into ideas. To save us from such pitiful philosophizing, we need philosophy.

We are, then, in peculiar want of this branch of knowledge, since it is a hemisphere of itself, holding in equipoise the world of truth ; since in it are found new regulative ideas, new laws, new lines of order, and also the tests of the validity of knowledge, and the rational grounds on which the limits of inquiry are established. Patches of truth may be given here and there by science, but landmarks, a synthetic rendering of the whole, can only be secured by the aid of philosophy.

§ 4. A last reason we shall urge for these lines of investigation is, that intelligent, moral action and religious faith must rest upon them. Fortunately, considering the premises from which they start, men are so illogical, that they find no difficulty in believing much which in consistency they ought not to believe, no difficulty in doing that for which their own philosophy can render them no adequate reasons. But in spite of the fact that there is often an interior coherence in action, in the unconscious workings of our constitution, which does not appear in our reasonings, a false, deficient philosophy will, from time to time, come to the surface in unbelief, irreligion, immorality ; the ground will soften under long trodden paths of faith; and many blind pilgrims, plunged into an unexpected quagmire, will fail to reach the farther shore. All the ideas on which morality and religion rest are established and defined in the realm of metaphysics, and to deny us this branch of knowledge, or to treat it slightly, is to put us, in the conflict with unbelief, at such disadvantage that we can never maintain our ground. We may, indeed, shut our eyes, and stand fast; we may stop our ears, and run from the questionings and claims of scepticism; but we cannot maintain our position in quiet and serene conviction, without searching for those foundations of truth found in the discarded field of philosophy.

The nature of right and its obligations, of liberty and its responsibilities, of the infinite in its application to God, as well as the positive and negative knowledge we have of his existence and attributes, are to be established by an inquiry into the phenomena of mind, the truths present to it, their source and authority. To hope, therefore, for morality and religion, and yet to sink out of sight those abutments on which they are to rest, is infatuation. Those do not so hope who wittingly do this work of denial and overthrow,—quite the contrary. Very many of them well understand that their mines run beneath the sacred edifices of religion, the spiritual labors and history of the race, and that, if they can be fully and successfully fired, these will sink, a mass of ruins, into a black, sulphureous chasm. We say, therefore, the intellectual battle between belief and unbelief, religion and irreligion, must be fought, in large part, in the fields of philosophy. The truths of revelation must be vindicated or overthrown by their relation to man's constitution, his powers of knowledge and obedience, and the rational stretch of his hopes.

Simple, then, are the reasons for philosophy, if philosophy be possible. We must abandon ourselves later than all things else, consent to darkness everywhere, if we can only strike a cheerful light at this fireside of our home. Unfortunate, indeed, would it be to lose the reins of power wherewith we guide the forces of nature, but far more unfortunate to miss the right handling of ourselves, and that serene strength which wins the rewards of life.

§ 5. But is philosophy possible? Is there not rather foundation for those many taunts and denials, asserting the endless, hopeless round of conflicting theories, the entire want of progress, the inevitable uncertainty attaching to every conclusion, and all conclusions, in metaphysics? If philosophy be not possible, if there is ground for the scorn and incredulity with which labor in this department is often regarded, so much the worse for us all. Nothing can take the place of philosophy. If we are doomed to ignorance here, our ignorance is hopeless and pitiable. We fail to understand the satisfaction with which some snuff out this light, when they have nothing wherewith to replace it—nothing better to propose than the desertion of this whole region, and a surrender of it to confusion and chaos. The injunction, "know thyself," the revered precept of all time hitherto, thus becomes impossible, and to modern thinkers, ridiculous. Outside of ourselves, we move with patient inquiry; we may feed our senses, and through them the mind; but we harvest home this knowledge, we know not for what ends. We gather facts, ignorant of their ulterior, spiritual uses, as the ox grazes, letting digestion and nutrition care for themselves. We see no grounds for congratulation in such a result. If it must be accepted, it yet remains a painful and sad alternative, turning the key in a door which above all others we would fain open, hiding from us things which most reveal the invisible world. It is as if some one, moiling long and patiently and profitably in the bowels of the earth, knowing how to pick, and blast, and shovel, and sure of the productiveness of those processes, should, hearing of the miscarriages, accidents, and embarrassments of the upper world, begin to deny this region to himself and to others, and to make it the dogma of his life, that there was but one form of sure, safe and remunerative labor, but one unmistakable and positive good, and that was mining. We console ourselves, in view of such conclusions, with their entire falsity, and the utter impossibility of their general acceptance.

Other departments, moreover, besides philosophy, are to suffer from this rejection of the philosophical spirit. The positive sciences themselves require for their successful cultivation something beyond an observation of facts—a classification of resemblances. There is ever kept hovering before the mind some idea of the causes, the concealed grounds and reasons, of phenomena ; and it is this supersensual notion which guides inquiry, directs the eye, and teaches it what to observe. Without this, the classifications of science would come to little more than the child's art in grouping its bits of crockery by size or color or the conceits of fancy. It has been, for illustration, some notion of the nature of light, either as a material emanation, or a movement in a generally diffused ether, that has directed inquiry, instituted experiments, and interpreted facts. Yet there is nothing in philosophy itself more subtile, more impossible of conception, more evasive and evanescent than either of these supersensual conceptions, which have presided over this department, and resulted in most brilliant discoveries. Deny a search into intangible and inconceivable causes, causes that in their inception are purely theoretical, and we lose at once the clew of our labyrinth, and henceforth wander at chance, with no forecast of thought, through its endless passages. Another illustration is furnished by the correlation of forces. Some notion of a hidden equivalence between very diverse phenomena haunts the mind, of a concealed agreement where no apparent agreement exists. This it is which sets the inquirer at work, quickens his thoughts, and leads him to new observations and experiments.

But how vain is it to demand positive, direct knowledge through the senses of this notion itself, so serviceable and indispensable? If we are to banish, as the ghosts of past superstitions, all the disembodied ideas the mind furnishes to positive science, we shall shortly be left without guidance, deserted of these good angels of thought, in whose absence eyes and ears are of no avail. We are in science, no less than in philosophy, constantly reaching and handling supersensual notions, purely mental phenomena; we are ever making them most fruitful sources of farther acquisitions, though certainly with no more full, definite and positive knowledge of their very nature than that we possess of mental phenomena from consciousness. Indeed, the moment we penetrate a very little below the surface, Positive Philosophy is of the same nature with that which it discards, is dealing with causes, forces and reasons which are wholly the offspring of the mind, and the limits of whose legitimate use must be determined on purely intellectual grounds.

Nor is philosophy itself without its fixed, settled facts as generally admitted, and as incontrovertible as those of any science whatever. The laws of association, recollection, attention, judgment, imagination, of the emotions, of responsibility, constitute a large department of knowledge, of accepted conclusions. The principles and precepts therein involved are running hourly through our processes of reasoning, our persuasion, our judicial action, our social opinions. Indeed, no single science, unless, perhaps, we except mathematics, is furnishing so many, so constant, so undoubted guides, both to those who maintain, and to those who deny, its theoretical value, as philosophy, with its adjuncts of logic, æsthetics and ethics. Totally untrue then is the representation, that metaphysics is a helpless medley of contradictory and unverified theories. An appearance of truth is given to this assertion by directing attention from established facts to those skirting and partially explored fields of entological inquiry, of the sources of our mental furniture, and of the authority of our faculties. We might thus discredit the established facts of electricity on the ground of conflicting opinions concerning the nature of the fluid or fluids or physical states which constitute it.

Now it is evident, from the nature of the case, that more of these ultimate questions, more of these points at which direct, sensible knowledge ends, must belong to philosophy than to any other branch. The postulates and definitions of knowledge are conditioned on the faculties of mind, on its necessary action, and to state these in their safe, ultimate, fixed form; to settle where knowing, in all its phases, begins, and to give the reasons and grounds of these statements, is a late and difficult task, and one which should not, by its slow, laborious and partial results, prejudice a department which is highest in rank, as it is most recondite and ultimate in its conclusions.

What act more indolent and unscientific than to jump to the conclusion, that these deepest questions are unsearchable and fruitless—than to turn our back on a region that does not at once yield its secrets? Nor are we without progress in these most obscure directions of philosophical inquiry. In some cases, the true conditions of the problem are better seen—what is to be hoped for and what not; in others, the grounds of attack and defence are shifted. Many arguments and presentations have been exploded, and, though others have taken their place, there has been progress, progress toward an ultimate decision. The battle surges and rolls onward, and is not endless. The doctrine of human liberty is an example of the first sort. A more consistent statement of what it involves can to-day be made than ever before. It can be better distinguished from every form of necessity, and set apart with proper limits, and more defensible boundaries than hitherto. To be sure we cannot *explain* freedom in the ordinary meaning of the word, but we can see why such explanations are not, and ought not to be applicable. As an illustration of the second form of progress, we instance the discussions as to the sources of knowledge; whether among these are intuitive ideas. The doctrine, that experience is the ground of all knowledge, is a very different one in the hands of Spencer and Bain from what it was as expounded by Locke. The later champions pronounce the earlier proofs and defences insufficient. Confessedly then this school has been driven in part from its line of argument. Herein is movement, looking to an ultimate solution of the problem. Though inner lines succeed one another, the city cannot be besieged forever. The grounds of conflict and the balance of strength are suffering daily changes, and though the conclusion may be yet far off, we see that it is slowly prepared for by what transpires about us. This discussion is not simply the dogged reiteration of affirmation and denial, the striking of shadowy forms with immaterial weapons, the wounds of to-day closing against the battle of to-morrow. Quite the reverse; old points are yielded, new points are made; light in turn is thrown upon them, and we move forward toward a conclusion,—move slowly it may be, but as certainly as when the discussion pertains to the nature of heat or light. Reid dogmatically asserted as a tenet of common sense what philosophy ever since has been defending, limiting, settling on rational grounds.

Much work, indeed, remains to be done. The grounds of reasoning are to be more definitely fixed in this higher department; the logic of philosophy to be unfolded, restraining erratic, fanciful movement, bending effort to fruitful results, and urging discussion to a speedy issue.

If the inductive sciences owe so much to a new organum, a new form of logic, and that too to one lacking the strict proof of previous, deductive branches of inquiry, is it not rational to expect that farther modifications of method, a new estimate of the nature and qualities of the proof applicable to the unique and remote questions of metaphysics will be equally productive, will yield fresh fruits to wiser investigation.

§ 6. Before proceeding to the facts of philosophy, I wish to lay down a few of its postulates most frequently violated. First, the mind has direct, intuitive knowledge, which is ultimate, which admits of no farther explanation than that involved in the very act of knowing. To derive all things from something more ultimate, by analogies and resemblance to explain all things, are plainly impossible. The mind must have starting points, and these must be arrived at directly, intuitively. It is irrational not to recogizne the beginning, or to strive to get back of it with an explanation. What these points of commencement are it is the office of philosophy to decide, and to arrest explanation and all effort toward it, when these have been reached.

A second postulate is, that there are different kinds of knowing, each independent of the others, each incapable of affording any light within the field of the others. The various forms of knowing show the various powers of the mind. The independence and diversity of the matter given reveal the independence and ultimate character of the faculties through which it is reached. If one knowing faculty could overlook another, the second would by that very fact be lost or merged in the first; since for the two there would be but one line of perception. We have two eyes, but only one power of sense or sight, and this sense can do nothing, absolutely nothing, to cover the phenomena of mind, of taste, or of smell. The additional and independent action of each intuitive faculty is involved in the very fact of it being a faculty, a distinct power of doing a distinct work.

The reverse statement is evidently equally true, and gives us a third postulate, that we have as many intuitive faculties as we have distinct forms of primitive knowledge. The presence of an idea, a perception in consciousness, must be explained; and if it cannot by analysis be resolved into simpler forms, or by deduction be derived from a more primitive action, it must be accepted as itself primary, and the power to attain it be recognized. The question of elements is not different here from the kindred question in the physical world. Each form of matter ranks as an element, till chemical analysis has resolved it. The classified fruits of knowing imply as many powers of knowing, till the classification can be corrected by a reduction of the number of genera.

A last postulate is, that what is conceded,—avowedly, tacitly, or impliedly,—at one point, must be freely conceded at all points. Processes which themselves assume the goodness of our faculties, must not conclude with a denial or impeachment of their integrity. A doubt must have a reason, a premise, and if this premise involves confidence in the very reasoning by which the foundations of reasoning are disturbed, that doubt is self-destructive. An idea, whose valid possession is denied, must not be allowed to enter furtively into those very processes of thought from which it is professedly eliminated. If it cannot be removed in the mind's ordinary action, it must not be removed in an exhaustive scientific statement of that action.

If these postulates are truly adhered to, we shall cut ourselves off from a great deal of impossible and absurd effort to assimilate one form of knowing to another; from a feeling of dissatisfaction because our analytic inquiries, our logic are brought at length to a halt; from denying all knowledge because it does not assume a familiar and specified form of knowing; and from deceptively using ideas in the very attack which we make upon them, knitting together our reasonings with axioms stolen from an adverse system.

BOOK I.

THE INTELLECT.

CHAPTER I.

The Field of Mental Science and its Divisions.

§ 1. THERE is no branch of knowledge more distinctly defined in its limits than mental science. It lies in a unique realm, cut off from every other,—that of consciousness. All the phenomena of this field in their separation, classification, mutual interaction and dependencies are the subjects of this science and its only subjects. There is thus little opportunity to confound the inquiries belonging to philosophy with those of any other department. Logic and Ethics most nearly approach it; but the one considers abstractly the products or process of thought, and not the thinking powers; and the other, the moral constitution of the mind, and is so far a branch of philosophy, adding thereto, however, an evolution of practical precepts from moral principles.

Anatomy and physiology, on the side of the mental sciences, are most closely allied to philosophy, yet, after all, deal only with the physical conditions and instruments of mental action, and, without the key and interpretation of mental science itself, can cast no light whatever upon it. The facts of philosophy lie in consciousness; here they are to be sought, and every fact therein contained is to be made the subject of consideration.

Consciousness is commensurate with all mental states and acts. It accompanies feeling as much as thinking, and volition as much as either. The only possible way in which a mental state or act can be testified to, is by consciousness; some mind at some time has known or felt it. An event that happens nowhere in space is not a physical event; an act or state that is not found in the field of consciousness is not a mental act or state. There are either facts that are neither physical nor mental, that exist neither in space nor consciousness, but in some unintelligible form in some third, unknown region, or all facts fall under these two divisions; and it remains the criterion of one class that they occur in space, and of the other that they occur in consciousness. A third state is inadmissible as unknown and unnecessary. Consciousness is neither a knowing nor a feeling nor a willing, is neither this nor that mental act, but a condition common to them all, a field in which they appear, in which they arise and make proof of their existence. A consciousness of knowing is necessary to knowing, a consciousness of feeling is necessary to feeling, and of willing to volition; and as these three cover all states and acts of mind, consciousness is involved in the very conception of a mental act or state. It is an inseparable something which defines the nature of the phenomena to which it pertains.

Consciousness gives—we use familiar language, a more careful expression would be, in consciousness is found—the mere fact of a mental state, that it is, and what it is, whether one of thought, feeling, or volition; or a complex one involving two or more of these. It renders phenomena as they exist, not analytically but synthetically, as the eye colors, or the ear sounds. To reach the primary colors which constitute the tint, the separate notes which form the harmony, calls for attention and discrimination. The mere facts of mind as facts are rendered in consciousness, and to be found there and only there by all who meet the conditions of search.

Discussion is had as to the truthfulness of consciousness. There is no ground for such discussion, since the discussion itself involves the thing doubted. Nothing can be better known than a fact of consciousness, since nothing can be known save through such a fact. Consciousness pervades all knowing, all thinking, distrust equally with trust, denial with affirmation. No man ever does doubt, nor can he philosophically doubt, the existence of a present fact of mind. To do so would rob language of all meaning. The only way in which such a dispute becomes possible is by wrongly regarding consciousness as a faculty, giving direct testimony to certain things, instead of something involved in the very fact of feeling, knowing, making them what they are, and, therefore, never present except through veritable, and, for the instant at least, undeniable, feeling and knowing. Whether the thing known has an independent existence, or the thing thought is correct, are quite other questions. The truth of the testimony of one or more of our faculties to the various things declared by them is a scepticism by one step less central and less absurd than the distrust of consciousness. In this there is no show of rationality. There is involved in the one act an affirmation and denial of the same thing.

§ 2. The facts of mind are confined then to the field of consciousness, and there they are to be sought. In this search, as has been often observed, there are peculiar difficulties. It is with most an unusual effort of mind to direct attention to interior phenomena. External objects have been the chief subjects of consideration, and to turn the sight of the mind on itself is an unfamiliar and delicate process. It is like an effort to reveal to the eye itself, its own chambers, by casting in light and by adroit reflection.

Neither are the several phases of mind observed as transpiring, but as remembered. In the very act of thinking, the mind is so occupied with the subject matter of thought as not to make the process itself the object of attention. Now memory is at best but a dim and obscure vision, and especially so of internal states, which less draw the mind's eye than the objects and facts which are the occasion of them. If natural science were to proceed by the memory of things, seen at periods more or less remote, its progress would be comparatively uncertain. Nor can the phenomena of mind be restored perfectly at pleasure, and thus the recollection of them freshened. This is more possible in thinking than in feeling and volition; yet even in thought, for its natural and full flow in a given direction, the mind must be disengaged from conflicting states and considerations, and be left to the unobserved and spontaneous action of the associations and impulses peculiar to the mental movement.

This inability to hold directly the state considered before the mind, as the plant or mineral is watched and retained by the eye, is connected with another difficulty, that no one can join us in our investigation with the directness and certainty which pertain to other inquiries. The object before the mind of each observer is hidden from the other, may not be of exactly the same character, nor looked at in the same direction. This confusion of objects and observations is most perplexing. It is as if the eye were turned a little askance, and the movement and the blow, therefore, directed at the shadow or image before it, and not at the very thing itself. Much skill and time are thus consumed between different observers in drawing attention to exactly the same facts. They often, through the deceptive effect of agreeing words, seem to have attained this result, when they have not attained it, and thus fall into inextricable confusion and contradiction. The feebleness of direction and construction is akin to that experienced, when, by the sense of touch alone, groping in the darkness, we strive to understand the parts, proportions and relations of even a familiar room.

It is also incident to this search of consciousness, that no one observes more than the phenomena of his own mind, and those too of a comparatively recent period. It is difficult, therefore, to determine how far a peculiar balance of faculties, as individual habits and associations, may have modified the mind's action, giving prominence to certain forms and connections of thought, and obscuring others. This fact also embarrasses us in deciding how far the mind's later convictions are due to protracted association, and how far to native, inherent tendencies or powers. Is the normal, adult mind in its forms of action the fruit of growth, or are these forms native and indispensable to it? The consciousness of the child or of the savage, so far as these questions may there seem to find an experimental answer, is beyond our exploration.

Another embarrassment in philosophy, though not peculiar to it, is the blended way in which its facts are presented. Not only do thought, feeling, volition unite in one state, diverse and conflicting feelings struggle for the mastery, and, in the simplest judgments, are interwoven perception, memory, reasoning, imagination, intention, and the subtile effects of association, rendering analysis a difficult, yet an indispensable condition of success. Separation of this obscure character, with phenomena in themselves evanescent and fluctuating, requires the utmost skill and tension of mind.

Another obstacle to success to be mentioned are the peculiar deficiencies of language in this department. Language, always an essential, is here a chief instrument, of investigation. It is the precision of the word employed, that separates and holds fast the faculty, element, or relation designated. In natural science, objects exist apart, though not named, and hence do not lose their identity, are not so merged in the ebb and flow of shifting phenomena as to escape all observation. The very sense of existence is largely due in mental facts to a clear, specific, generally recognized name; since we handle the states of philosophy exclusively through their names, and without these, readily lose all traces of them. Moreover these names are applied somewhat in the dark. It is by description and suggestion that we are taught what the internal states are to which given words are set apart. The word is the same, but the internal fact which explains it is, in every single case, different, that is lies in a different mind, and must be hit on as the thing meant by the sagacity of that mind. We are as one who puts together a complicated machine by a printed description, and directions before him. Careful observation is required to determine the parts referred to, and failing of this, all is confusion. Yet in this illustration the parts are fixed, separate, with a permanent, independent existence; while the parts of a complex, mental state admit of various divisions, or may disappear altogether, like some rivet in the dust of the shop. To attach words, therefore, to their objects; to make the two so that there shall be no escape for either, is a delicate and uncertain process. The ambiguity of words embarrasses all forms of statement and reasoning, but is never elsewhere the source of so much idle discussion and fruitless inquiry as in philosophy.

A further obstacle presented by language is, that it comes to mental phenomena saturated with the imagery of the external world. Words are born amid sensible facts, and thence transferred to the mind. They come, therefore, to this new service with the images and associations acquired in the old. They subserve a popular, familiar use only the more aptly for this reason. It is when they are made the subject of careful analysis, when they are treated as the exact expression of the thing named, that their physical root and relations reveal themselves disastrously. The mind reaching this interior analogical thread of interpretation is pleased by it, and overlooks the fact, that investigation is thus sure to be led astray; to be turned entirely from true mental phenomena, and to be sent wandering among their shadows and reflections in the external world. Thus, from the very beginning, every discussion concerning liberty has been embarrassed, and in most instances has miscarried, through the application to motives and desires, in a figurative sense, of words begotten amid the necessary connections of physical things. These half-reclaimed servants, when closely questioned, have betrayed their low relations, and in so doing have lost to liberty its high, ethereal form. Like its household, it has been thought to be mud-born.

The last difficulty is allied to this, and arises from the uniqueness of the department. It refuses to receive illustrations from the analogies of matter; or rather it refuses to accept as the exact types and counterparts of its own facts and dependencies those of a realm at the farthest possible remove from it, at the very nadir of the sphere of being. Yet the mind, familiar with certain processes, certain forms of explanation, certain couplings of thought, is uneasy and dissatisfied with all others, is only content when it has put new matter under the old law, the new wine into the old bottles. Unable to hold it in these stiff, inflexible casements, such a notion as that of the infinite perplexes and vexes the mind, simply because it is not the finite, and thus stands opposed to its other forms of knowledge, and is excluded from them. Equally is it annoyed with liberty for not yielding to some analogy of necessity, some interpretation drawn from the physical world; for not taking upon itself, in a subtiler way, the iron-bound connections of matter; and with right, because it will insist on being final, and refuses to be merged in any other form of good whatever. To accept a new department—so new and so novel as this of mind when contrasted with that of matter—as new, to lay aside prepossessions, and to commence again with simple intuitive convictions, the axioms of this field, involves a sore conflict, and the more a conflict in proportion as the inquirer has gained great victories of knowledge in the material world, and dwelt long amid its methods of action. This is probably the gravest of all the obstacles to philosophy, and the more so because it is generally entirely overlooked or forgotten.

§ 3. While the phenomena of mind are to be obtained directly, and only directly, from the mind itself, there are very important indirect auxiliaries of inquiry. Language is one of the prominent of these aids. Language, as the product of the mind, as the external, visible trace of the mind's movements, reveals of course the forms of its action, and, in the designations of mental phenomena, a part at least of the facts of the interior world. On disputed questions of analysis, also, the inherent, spontaneous, general convictions of men are betrayed by the words they use; and a distinct designation is so far proof of the general recognition of a distinct idea. That certain words are always and everywhere floating in popular speech indicates that the thoughts of men find rest in them, something valid, sufficient to steady and sustain the mind as for the moment it lights upon them. These traces of the mind, indicating its own spontaneous convictions, that which is actually woven into the web of its thinking and feeling, must be included in every sound theory of philosophy, and furnish the suggestions for its construction.

Of the same nature exactly, though not as easily accessible or explicit, are the facts of daily life and of history. The shadow of the mind is cast upon them, and we may reason thence to the powers and capacities they indicate. A theory which utterly confounds, as do some metaphysical theories, all the convictions of daily life, and makes the facts of history and those of philosophy rest on utterly diverse conceptions, so much so that no region seems so startling, remote or even preposterous as this metaphysical dream-land to the very beings who are said to inhabit it, by that fact reflects on itself extreme improbability. History must be felt to be, and found to be, the very shadow, the close and intimate reflection of that inner life which is revealed to us by mental science.

Another aid to philosophical investigation is found in an inquiry into the instruments of the mind, the physical organs which it uses; and into the incipient and rudimentary development of intellectual action shown by animals. We are thus able to give more correct weight to the purely physical element, and to separate more intelligently the lower, nervous, and instinctive forms of animal life from true, mental powers. While not underestimating the secondary and inferential aid thus to be rendered to philosophy, we think that extravagant and absurd expectations, of the results of investigations primarily physical, have been entertained. One might look at a brain till he was blind, and, without the interpretation of the facts of consciousness obtained by introspection, his observations, as initiating a science of mind, would not be of the least avail. To suppose that the divisions of mental faculties can be found either on the outside or inside of a skull is preposterous. Passing the experimental proof so fully given by Hamilton, that no such connection as that sometimes claimed between certain powers and certain localities of the brain can be shown to exist, we insist, that even if the fact of such a connection were proved, we should still as much as ever need an independent philosophy derived from consciousness. These bumps are not labeled in the human subject. They contain in themselves no suggestion of the purpose subserved by the portion of the brain beneath them. The observer must have an antecedent idea of certain mental powers, and be ready to attribute one or other of these to the prominence under his fingers. Afterward he may confirm the act by observation. This first condition, however, failing him, the bump under discussion might as well be a protuberance on a potato as a projection on a human skull. The one, in and of itself, as a mere prominence on a round body, makes no more declaration of ideality, benevolence, language, than the other. Suppose we have made from consciousness a wrong division of powers, what is there to hinder us from transferring these errors to our map of the cranium? Nothing; they will rather inevitably thus reappear. The chart that is to guide us must be made out before we can begin to outline and number and name the divisions of our plaster bust, and equally also before we can attribute a faculty to a locality in the living subject. The absurd classification of phrenologists; such faculties as combativeness, philoprogenitiveness, secretiveness, are sufficient proof, if farther proof were wanting, of this inability to find the invisible action of the mind in the visible form of its instrument. All the aid given to philosophy by an external fact is inferential, not direct; and that invisible faculty or force which is thus to be reached, on which our conclusion is to landed, must be given, in the only possible knowledge of its nature, by consciousness. The analysis of mental phenomena shows, that firmness is the complex result of various, and of different, mental states, and no locating of a supposed faculty so called in one or another portion of the head can alter, or throw light on, these facts. The singleness of the name and locality imparts no new singleness to the mind's action, marks no division of its faculties. The invisible cannot be seen through the visible. Each must be determined independently, and the connections between the two established by experience. It would be as rational to suppose that the letters contained in the word *will* should of themselves convey to every mind the notion of that power, as to suppose that a prominent eye should reveal the existence of a faculty called language. Regarding consciousness, then, as the only field of the science, whether reached inferentially, or directly under the interpretation of the light it itself furnishes, we pass to the general divisions of mental phenomena.

§ 4. The leading divisions of the faculties of the mind, so generally accepted since the time of Kant as scarcely to demand further explanation or defence, are those of knowing, feeling, willing; the intellect, the emotions and the will. The desires are by Kant and Hamilton included with the will. They belong rather with the feelings. Desire is employed to designate a state of feeling toward a certain object or objects. We find things differently, related to our happiness; we cease, therefore, to be indifferent to them; one object or line of action gets a hold upon us; we are drawn toward it, and this continued state we call a desire. Language sustains this decision. Desires are constantly spoken of as feelings, never as thoughts or volitions; the words in the first case are used interchangeably, not so in the second. We apply the same adjectives to them as to the feelings. We say of a desire as of an emotion, that it is strong or weak, consistent or changeable, intense or feeble; and sometimes, as in the case of avarice, speak of it as becoming a passion. Our desires, also, may be directly opposed to our volitions. We greatly covet a certain possession, but our pride constrains us not to ask for it. We wish the pleasure of a given action, but through fear determine not to perform it. A state of desire, like every state of feeling, is antecedent to volition, and may or may not find play in subsequent choices. As a desire it may arise and pass away emotionally, like envy or jealousy or sympathy or love, and find no expression in action, awaken not the will at all. It may either meet with acceptance by the mind, or suffer rejection by it. Desire, then, should be included in the field of the emotions, where it arises, and spends its power. It does not, in the fact that it gives occasion to the will for activity in providing for its gratification, differ from other feelings. These also, as long as they last, are springs of volition.

§ 5. An attempt has been made to farther divide the department of will, into choice and volition. A color of plausibility is given to this division by distinguishing between initiatory volition and executive volition. The first is termed choice, the second volition. When two diverse lines of action are contemplated, and the mind is as yet undecided between them, the desires have free play, the sense of moral obligation is present, and the conflict awaits a definite setlement by a choice between them, a fixed determination in favor of one or the other. We sometimes, at this point, use the word choice out of the meaning which should attach to it as pertaining to volition. Thus we say, "My choice would be this line of effort," though we actually accept and pursue another. Choice is thus made to express a state of desire, not one of will. The word choice, however, in its use in the third department of mental phenomena, expresses an explicit termination of all vacillation, a close of deliberation by an act of will in favor of this and in rejection of that.

The case thus being closed by a specific and peculiar act, there remains a longer or shorter series of efforts to be made in reaching the object proposed, in accomplishing the career marked out. There are no definite limits in analysis to these intermediate acts. Our division may extend to each muscular movement, or it may stop short with each specific undertaking. I propose to build a house; the number of distinct physical and intellectual efforts involved in the project are indefinitely great; and while they are all under the control of the will, we hardly have occasion to place a distinct volition back of each one of them. The will has the power, by a few explicit volitions, to direct the current of the vital powers in a single channel of expenditure. A walk once entered on, the movement becomes in a large measure unconscious, and the mind is left at liberty to pursue any line of action it prefers. The voluntary and involuntary play of physical members differ not so much in the manner in which they are sustained, as in the way in which they are initiated, and in the fact that the one is momentarily open to modification, and arrest.

The distinction between a choice and a volition, then, seems to be found in their position in reference to an end, rather than in their intrinsic character. The one is initiatory of a line of action; the other sustains and completes it. The one is primary, the other subsidiary. The one is determinative and governing, the other executive. The first gives character to an action, the second sustains and develops that character. The one is immediately free, the other mediately so, through its dependence on the first. The division thus sinks into a classification of volitions, and removes neither choice nor volition from the phenomena of the will. Choice, as an act of will, does not include the deliberation and the play of feeling from which it proceeds; but only that final art by which they are brought to a close, and the powers of the mind made to unite in a line of effort. Volitions are the secondary impulses of will, by which its primary impulses are completed; they are the subdivisions and prolongations of that power, which is born of choice. The ball is driven in a given line, but receives accessions of force, and changes of direction, as the exigencies require.

§ 6. The relation of consciousness to the three forms of mental action is the same. Sir William Hamilton seems to have regarded its connection with knowing as somewhat peculiar. While he speaks of it as the condition of all mental phenomena, he says, "Those of the first class, the phenomena of knowledge, are indeed nothing but consciousness in various relations." The complete and expansive statement is rather that consciousness is the condition, and equally the condition, of all mental acts and states. It is merely through a deficiency, or peculiar use of language, that it seems to be more intimately connected with knowing than with feeling. To know a thing, and to be conscious of it, are used as interchangeable expressions; and, hence, we have come to regard consciousness as a kind of knowing, or as an act of knowing, and not merely and purely the condition of such an act, that which permits knowing to be knowing. It is not strange, that a constant condition of an act should, in language, take the place of the act itself. Through this interplay of the words conscious and know, we are able to say, "We know that we feel." "We know that we will;" though we can with only doubtful propriety say, "We feel that we know." "We feel that we will," and cannot at all say, "We will that we know." "We will that we feel." This use arises, we apprehend, through a peculiar connection in the language employed of consciousness with knowing, and thus a transfer of the word know to both feeling and volition. Consciousness is no more an act of knowing than it is one of feeling, and is a condition in exactly the same sense and way for the one as for the other. We know in consciousness, we feel in consciousness, we will in consciousness; and consciousness is neither an act of knowing, nor of feeling, nor of willing, but a condition of them all. Consciousness is not a something, a faculty, a light, which reveals acts, independently of knowing, feeling, willing, to the mind; but that which makes an act of knowing to be one of knowing, of feeling to be one of feeling, and volition to stand forth as volition. Mind, by virtue of its own nature as mind, does and suffers what it does and suffers, consciously under this simple, peculiar, and inexplicable condition of being aware of its own acts, a condition which is no more allied to one act than to another, to one state than to another; but is common to each in its indivisible nature. A feeling is not a feeling and a knowing that we feel; a volition a willing and a knowing that we will, but simply and singly an emotion and a choice, under the essential condition of such acts, to wit, consciousness.

§ 7. Two allied inquiries arise in this division of mental phenomena. Are there any mental phenomena below or outside of consciousness? Are the states of mind, the acts ot consciousness, consecutive or intermittent? Sir William Hamilton, and many other metaphysicians, recognize unconscious modifications of mind, we think without sufficient proof. The conclusion is too purely conjectural to command our consent. Mental and physical phenomena are cut broadly and deeply apart by the fact, that the one class transpires exclusively in consciousness, and the other as exclusively out of consciousness. The last are actual or possible objects of some organ of perception, are somewhere located in space, and thus open to the outisde action of mind, its action through senses; the first are within the mind, evincing their existence exclusively by their effects in consciousness. Not to exhibit anywhere, to any actual or supposable organ of sense, any phenomena, is, in the physical world, not to exist. Existence is affirmed only on the ground of some effects, however subtile, in sensible objects, and directly or indirectly in organs of perception. We never hear of physical facts above or below space, beyond all possible tests, all possible forms of perception; since such phenomena would be utterly unable to manifest this existence, to give any proof to it. The very notion of physical being arises from that of physical effects, under suitable circumstances open to observation. Thus also should mental phenomena be regarded. There is likewise only one known field for these—consciousness. All, aside from physical facts, that transpires outside of this, is necesarily unknowable. An alledged fact, which is to be found anywhere as a fact, has but two avenues through which it can make itself known, the senses and consciousness. These are the sole means by which we take cognizance of any class of phenomena. To assert, therefore, the existence of other modifications or changes than those which respond to these two methods of knowing, is to affirm some third field, wherein events transpire whose nature is utterly unknown to us, and of whose being we can at most have only an hypothetical and inferential knowledge.

Some strong, some imperative reason should be given for the acceptance of phenomena—phenomena, not the basis merely of phenomena—utterly unknown, and from the nature of the case unknowable. By what principle are those unknown modifications, if thought to exist, classified as mental facts? Something it would seem should be revealed more distinctly as to their character, before they are assigned to this class rather than to that of physical facts. If these unknown modifications are acts or states of mind, are in any way phenomena of mind, we ought to have provision made for them in our classification of mental facts. The division would then run thus: the phenomena of knowing, of feeling, of willing, and a fourth class different from any of these, and composed of certain unknowable states, acts, conditions, or whatever you please to call them, of which we have no direct consciousness, and can say nothing by way of explanation. States, then, of mind may transpire of which the mind itself knows nothing, and which furnish, neither in the field of thought or of forces, any direct proof of their existence. The argument for their being is thus of the most naked and inferential character.

If it be said that these modifications are modifications of the mind itself, and not of the nature of actions, of phenomena, I think it must be granted, that they are thus conceived wholly under the analogy of material changes, and that if they are shown to be, and to belong anywhere, it is in the physical, and not the mental world—in the brain, the instrument of the mind, and not in the very mind itself. In this last, we know, and can know, of no organic changes. Its own acts, states, constitute the sum of our knowledge concerning it. Nor are we hereby rid of these alleged modifications as phenomena; nor of the consequent need of giving some clue to their mode of existence.

We are thus brought to the fundamental difficulty of this view, that it tends to confound the broad distinction between mental and physical facts,—especially between mental facts and those of physiology, those which pertain to the brain and nervous system. No matter what relations exist in the brain itself, or what changes take place in it, an observation and knowledge of these, is no part of mental science, and do not necessarily, do not alone, give a clue or explanation to any one of its facts. The organic functions and dependencies of the brain, are matters of as distinct, and purely physical knowledge, as those of the liver, and no changes here can reveal to us the nature of a mental state, or of the powers peculiar to the mind. We can no more find the mind in the brain—because this is the organ of thought, than we can the life in the heart, because this is the chief organ of life; or than the ancients could have searched it successfully for the affections, because they regarded it as the seat of the feelings. Listen for a moment to the words of one of these modern philosophers, who reject consciousness as the field of mental science.

"Not only is the actual process of the association of our ideas independent of consciousness, but that assimilation or blending of similar ideas, or of the like in different ideas by which general ideas are formed, is no way under the control or cognizance of consciousness. When the like in two perceptions is appropriated, while that in which they differ is neglected, it would seem to be an assimilative action of the nerve-cell, or cells of the brain, which, particularly modified by the first impression, have an attraction or affinity for a like subsequent impression; the cell so modified and so ministering takes to itself that which is suitable, and which it can assimilate or make of the same *kind* with itself, while it rejects for appropriation by other cells, that which is unlike and will not blend."—*Maudsley's Physiology and Pathology of the Mind, p.* 17.

It is difficult to treat with respect explanations like these. Is the brain the only organ whose cells take to themselves "that which is suitable? that which they can make of the same kind with themselves? Why then do not the liver, the kidneys think, and unite like things in thought, by resemblance? No one thing is more separate from another, than is cell-action from thought. To speak of the two as the same is to use words for ideas. Who, by observing the one, could come to a knowledge of the other? One might watch at his leisure the operation of Morse's telegraph, and, unless his previous knowledge furnished him the solution, made nothing evident, but his own vacant mind. Yet the connection of this contrivance with language is far more mechanical and obvious than that of the brain with thought. The affirmation of subconscious phenomena is especially objectionable as playing into materialistic philosophy, as confounding the distinction between physical and mental changes, and referring real or imaginary modifications of the brain to the mind, as if the two were equivalent.

But the views of Hamilton are not intentionally open to this objection ; let us briefly consider the reasons he gives for the acceptance of unconscious modifications of mind. The first of these is the extraordinary power the mind sometimes shows of recalling events, and even unintelligible sounds, as those of an unknown language, long after every trace of them seemed to have passed from the memory. "Extensive systems of knowledge may, in our ordinary state, lie latent in the mind beyond the sphere of consciousness and the will ; but in certain extraordinary states of organism, may again come forward into the light, and even engross the mind to the cxclusion of its every day possessions."

In this argument we simply meet the old difficulty. How does the mind remember? How does it store up knowledge with no apparent store-house, accumulate mental vigor with no mental muscle wherein to lodge it, gain sharpness, precision, ease, with no underlying structure, in which those qualities may be thought of as inhering?

That memory shows unusual power under certain abnormal conditions of mind does not essentially alter the character of that power, nor introduce new states into the problem. Physical strength is not different in kind when exhibited in an astonishing degree by a maniac, from what it is in ordinary states of body. An ordinary act of recollection involves the whole question, involves neither more nor less than an extraordinary one. These queries—How does the mind remember? How does it subjectively acquire and retain power?—we must submit are unanswerable ; questions which receive no light whatever from any supposed modifications of some supposed substance of the mind. If such modifications were granted, we should understand not in the least how they were equivalent to acts of memory, or productive of them — we should simply have two inexplicable things instead of one. The tendency to ask and answer such questions arises from the physical world, where we expect no change of powers without some of structure. The early solution given to this problem of memory, that certain films escape from objects, and are laid away in a secret store-house of the mind, is just as good philosophically as the latest; and sprang from exactly the same false tendency to carry the analogies of matter into mind. The form of mental action is not revealed to us, and we have no clue to it except this false one of reasoning from things and processes totally unlike those of mind; bringing the interpretation of physical phenomena to intellectual facts. We reject the explanation of mental power furnished by unconscious modifications of mind, because it is really no explanation, making the subject not the least clearer; because these modifications themselves are wholly hypothetical; and because they are inferred by analogy, from a field remote from the subject in hand, and alien to it.

The second proof offered, is allied to the first. It is drawn in like manner from the analogies of the physical world. The minimum object which the eye can perceive may be conceived as divided into halves; neither of these will be objects of perception, yet each of them must make a distinct, though unconscious impression on the organ of vision, in order that the conjoint effect may be perceptible. We have, then, the first conscious state in sensation secured by effects themselves unrecognized. Hence springs the inference, a conscious state of feeling or thought may be preceded by unconscious states as its conditions. We object to the analogy. The eye is a physical organ, lying between the object and the perceptive power. There may be in it, action too slight to reach the mind. In the case which this fact is brought to illustrate, there is no analogous middle term between the mind and its own action. The question is, whether its own, its veritable, acts and states are always known to the mind? Now these actions are not occasioned in some intermediate substance by a foreign cause, and taken thence by consciousness, or overlooked by it, as the case may be. There is no such medium between the mind and its own acts. External, physical conditions, there doubtless are; but these constitute no part of the mind itself. Keeping the inquiry itself clearly in view, Does the mind know all that the mind itself does, all that transpires in it? it will be seen that the above analogy casts no light upon the subject. If the theory is, that external forces act on the substance of the mind, or, to put the same thing in appropriate specific terms, that nervous energy animates the brain, and that a certain amount of this influence is necessary to constitute thought, and does constitute it; while less amounts, though of the same nature, transpire without consciousness, then indeed there is an analogy in the cases, and the argument too so far holds; but we have reached out and out materialism. The theory on this basis offers no more explanation of the problem, How does a pure act of judgment or of memory take place, than would be found in the study of a piece of mechanism, a power-loom or an electrometer. The brain is indeed more immediately the condition of the mind's action than any other part of the body; but the brain, the body, every machine and instrument it uses, are the conditions to one or more of its activities, and no one of them constitutes the very substance, the very nature of those activities.

A third argument is found in acquired dexterities, as those of the equilibrist, or the musician. It is asked: How shall the separate acts involved in the rapid performance of the musician, each of which was originally preceded by an act of volition, be explained, when established skill has banished from sight this directive power of the mind. One philosopher answers, "The movements of mind remain, but take place too rapidly for distinct observation and memory." A second replies, "they remain, but remain as acts or changes below consciousness." Before we attempt to judge between these opinions, it may be well to inquire for the proof, that these impulses of mind remain at all. We believe that the supposed difficulty arises from overlooking the nature of the connection of the mind and of the body. Much of the nervous, executive play of the body, never passes under the cognizance of the mind, does not penetrate the region of consciousness, is purely automatic. Some of this action, on the other hand, which is usually self-sufficient, is yet open to the arrest and modification of the mind. Of this character is the process of breathing. Few will claim that an act of mind is back of each inspiration and expiration, though we can at pleasure shorten or deepen, quicken or retard the movement. I may find myself breathing in a manner that is inadequate or injurious. I may for weeks laboriously strive to enlarge and deepen the play of the lungs. I may succeed, and the improved method become habitual with me. Will it be claimed, that henceforward my inspirations are all voluntary, each preceded by an act of mind? I think not. The improved process is as automatic as the previous one, and no more requires subconscious mental acts for its explanation.

There are still other physical movements more constantly voluntary, more rarely involuntary. We thus speak of them as voluntary acts, and seem to regard them as under the exclusive impulse of the will. There is no good reason for this. The fact that I walk whither I will, and modify my movement as I will, is not a sufficient reason for requiring a distinct, mental act, conscious or unconscious, back of each muscular movement made in passing over each rod of the road I am pursuing. The will, as it were, by one volition, belts the automatic powers, and these run on till they are again arrested or redirected. If the play of the nervous energy to and from the nervous centres is sufficient to secure motion without consciousness of any mental action whatever, as in the case of the heart, is it not equally capable of continuing a motion the will has established? If we analyze each voluntary motion, so called, into the most single, simple, muscular movements of which it is composed, and place a mental act back of each, we have an absurdly complex result, and one not in the least testified to by consciousness, nor required by the known conditions of the problem. All the powers of life are not mental, and a great share of the labor of living is done by forces with a strength and movement more or less, as the case may be, independent of intellectual control.

In acquired dexterities, volitions are, as in the case of respiration, required for a time to establish and confirm the automatic movement, but this, once settled, is able to sustain itself by a purely vital power, a play of nervous energies without direct or constant support of the will. The difficulty of the question seems to have arisen from not marking the degree in which vital phemomena are independent of mental action.

A last argument for unconscious modifications of mind, is found in the association of ideas. Links of association, it is said, are frequently omitted. The mind passes from number one to number five or eight in a train of connections without distinctly recalling the intervening steps. How does this happen? Does the mind move through the entire series, though too rapidly for memory? or does the unbroken thread lie below consciousness, there traversed by the mind? The last query is thought to indicate the true solution. But is there any sufficient reason for shutting us up to these alternatives? Is it so certain that the mind never makes a leap, that it cannot associate five with eight directly, omitting altogether six and seven? Is not this also an act and a method of association, as much so as that which originally united the ideas marked five, six, seven and eight, respectively? The very fact that these four have thus stood together, is a new and a second law of connection, and may at times supersede the first law. Six scholars stand before me in the recitation room. This fact of itself, no matter by what previous connections occasioned, is a fresh ground of association, and may cause the memory on the presence of one, to recall any of the remaining five.

Take the case of acquired meanings. A word may have stolen from application to application along an obscure path of resemblances, of subtile connections, till it has reached the twentieth meaning. How many of these successive uses any one mind shall recall in employing the word will depend in part on knowledge, and in part on the frequency with which the word recurs.

The last meaning may be the only one suggested to the majority of minds in the majority of cases, though the previous ones and their connections may be known to them, in whole or in part. The word becomes at length a literal term in its twentieth meaning, attached in this signification directly to its object; though there lie between the first use and the present application nineteen images, each of which has been carried in the imagination, imparting to the word a figurative force for a greater or less length of time. What is to hinder the mind's going cross-lots? Nothing: association itself prepares the way for it.

The explications offered by unconscious mental acts involve facts more obscure than those explained. This movement under the surface of consciousness, is in itself a most perplexing riddle, a strange something we know not what. Nor, if it is granted, do we at all understand how it can, or does change its nature, and suddenly issue in a movement within consciousness. The supplied links in this theory are of an unintelligible nature, and do their work in an unintelligible way. The whole result is more perplexing and obscure than if we accept the naked phenomena. and suppose the mind to pass from idea to idea, now by a more direct, now by a more circuitous route, able to do the first, because it has done the second. The facts presented in consciousness are more manageable by themselves than when surrounded by suppositions, which involve phenomena unknown and unknowable. The dip of the thread of connections below consciousness is a loss of it for all practical and explanatory purposes in chaos and night. If it re-appears in the realm of knowledge, it comes like a ghost from Hades, in a mysterious method and an inexplicable guise.

The connection of this idea of a subconscious region with materialism plainly appears in Lewes' *Physiology of Common Life.* He affirms: "that all nervous centres in action, give rise to *Sensation,* and thus furnish elements to the general *Consciousness.*" Thus we are made to be conscious of all the muscular and involuntary movements that take place in the body. This strange affirmation is thrown into the very teeth of consciousness itself, momentarily affirming the reverse truth to us all, on the purely *a priori* grounds, first, that a similarity of ganglionic structure in these nerve-centers implies similarity of office; and second, that constant, physical impressions must be made upon them, and hence, must enter consciousness.

"Every such excitement of the sensitive organism must be a sensation. These sensations will neccessarily be very various, as the organs excited, and the exciting causes, are various; but they must all be sensations, they are all active states of the general property of sensibility. *Ergo,* they must all be elements of consciousness." Thus this author so thoroughly identifies physical with mental states, that having established the first, he out-faces the mind itself, and declares that they must be consciously found in its record. This is only a bolder movement in the one general direction, since it pretty much annihilates the distinction between conscious and subconscious phenomena, and brushes lightly aside any testimony the mind itself may offer, as to anything that is, or is not, passing within it. If there is any mockery, any ridicule of consciousness more extreme than every other, it is this affirmation, that every peristaltic motion of the intestines is a phenomenon of mind. So one mind at least classifies its activities.

§ 8. We have dwelt at length on consciousness as including the entire range of mental phenomena, because thus only can we adequately define the field of mental science, and keep it forever distinct from all physical inquiries. Physiological facts are of incalculable interest and value, but are perfectly distinct from philosophy. Each branch is capable of independent development, nay, must receive it, and neither is as obscure as the connections between the two. Only by a double light on either hand, the mind being made known to itself, and the brain and nervous system being carefully inquired into, can we hope to trace obscurely and slowly the connections, or rather the dependencies of the physical and spiritual worlds; even then reaching everywhere ultimate facts beyond our solution. Metaphysics, with all its erratic and fanciful reasonings, never gave explanations more absurd and inadequate than those sometimes rendered of intellectual phenomena from a study of physical organisms. The assertion that the brain secretes thought, is the crude form out of which, with more subtile and obscure phraseology, these impotent reasonings from matter to mind arise.

This premature and preposterous union of the two realms,

or rather absorption of the one by the other, is greatly aided by the admission of a region below consciousness, a region in some way attached to the mental field, though not fairly located in it. The mind thus allies in conception its phenomena to those of the physical world, taking place under a blind play of forces, and then readily unites them to nervous and cerebral action. Hypothetical, unlocated, unknowable facts are thus made to furnish a passage between the two departments; to give inlet to lower physical causes, whose service it ostensibly is to explain, but which really obscure and destroy, intellectual and spiritual powers.

We reject this region of subconsciousness as unexplored and inexplorable, either by the inner or the outer eye ; as furnishing no ground for induction or safe deduction ; as necessarily a region of myth and fancies, offering no solid explanations which can be subjected to any form of experience. Let positive science give us its positive facts, established with sufficient inquiry, located in the brain and associated organisms—facts as material and sensible as those of brass or iron, oxygen and hydrogen, heat or electricity, and as physical facts we will recognize them ; let philosophy declare what the common consciousness can verify, and its statements shall be accepted as at least of equal value and validity with those which creep into the mind through the eye and the ear ; but let neither form of investigation bring alleged facts from a region which it itself puts beyond the entire range of our critical faculties. Consciousness presents a distinct, a complete and independent field. On it no purely physical inquiry can enter, and in it philosophy can lie intrenched beyond the power of any form of ignorant or jealous scepticism. The students of Positive Philosophy, ready to desecrate this sanctuary of our spiritual nature, will, like the blind man of Sodom, weary themselves in vain to find the door.

Mental Science will also be aided, by this divorce of the

unknown from the known, the conjectural from the established; in bringing its own doctrines to a more decided test; and in expelling some of those dogmas, which, unintelligible, yet possible to a bold and blind faith, have hovered about it, and given it a superstitious, visionary, and unphilosophical appearance. Of this nature is the assertion, that one may sin below consciousness, or the belief that sin is transmitted from parent to child. If all the acts and states of mind are conscious ones, then, of course, all moral phenomena must transpire in the light.

§ 9. The second preliminary inquiry referred to—Is the mind always consciously active?—is closely allied to the one now answered—Is the mind ever unconsciously modified? A negative answer to the second inquiry would seem to prepare the way for a positive answer to the first. If no movement or modification or phenomena of mind transpire below the surface, then we should anticipate, that the continuous existence of the mind would be productive of continuous activity above the surface, and that some phase of thought, feeling, or volition would be ever transpiring. The second question of course contemplates a modification of mind in the nature of an action, or an induced change of state, and not at all the admitted fact, that the mind increases in power. The subjective method of this increase is beyond present explication; we are simply not to figure it under a material form, as if it were a substantial change. If, on the other hand, we say with Sir William Hamilton, that there are unconscious modifications of mind, we have prepared the way for denying its constant, conscious activity; since some moments of being, at least, would seem to be sufficiently accounted for by the transpiring of these subconscious facts, and the existence of such facts would prepare the way for their hypothetical occupation of the mind in periods of external repose. Yet, Sir William

Hamilton answers this question, justly we believe, in the affirmative. The mind is always consciously active.

The reason which most avails in bringing us to this conclusion is one which will probably have little weight with most minds. It is of an *a priori* character. The only proof of existence is some form of phenomena. Existence without phenomena is unevinced, unintelligible. Matter that should manifest neither active nor passive effects anywhere, under any conditions, would cease to meet our idea of matter, would be non-existent. Now the sole known phenomena of mind are those of consciousness; and to suppose a total arrest of these leaves the mind, for the interval, without the proof or the form of existence. We may figure, in some vague way, under the analogy of matter, some passive state or power as belonging to the mind, and maintaining for it a phenomenal existence during the hours of sleep; but here again we are in the region of pure hypothesis. We know nothing of mind save as the source of certain activities, and if these are gone, the only grounds on which we ever predicated its existence are gone. To suppose it capable of existence in a passive state, is a pure supposition, altogether beyond knowledge, and made so easily tenable only by analogies, carelessly caught up from the physical world. We believe, therefore, in the constant activity of the mind, as the only state under which we know it at all, or, in consistency with what we do know of its nature, can at all conceive it. The notion of total rest leaves the mind as mind without any possible manifestation or proof of existence, to any being under any circumstances. The only known phenomena of mind are removed, and with them pass away the evidence of its present being.

Urging, however, no farther this consideration, we believe the strictly inductive proof sufficient to render the conclusion, that the mind is always active, at least probable. As it is dwelt on at length by Hamilton, we shall treat it briefly. The chief difficulty to be overcome in the affirmation, is the admitted fact, that the memory does not retain and report the movements of the mind in hours of sleep or of syncope. How strong is this objection? Much the larger share of the thoughts and the feelings of yesterday have entirely passed from the mind, and yet we readily believe in their existence. We have no doubt of the continuity of thought in our waking moments; yet we arrive at the conclusion more from our present experience than because we can recall one in ten thousand of the feelings which have passed through the mind in the last dozen years. Now the impression of dreams, when these are known to have occurred, are of a much more evanescent character. At the very instant of waking, we may be able to recall them, and yet lose all hold on them in a few moments. We also know, that in proportion as sleep is sweet and sound, these impressions of the night are fleeting, and must be caught almost in the very act of transpiring, or they are wholly lost. It has happened to many, perhaps to most, to awake in a dream, and to take delight in the images left by it, and yet after another hour's sleep to be unable to restore them.

The memory also, above all our faculties, seems to be especially affected by physical conditions. Fatigue and nervous exhaustion for the time being greatly diminish its power; some forms of disease erase its impressions in whole or in part, while the weakness of age first betrays itself in this faculty. Since, then, physical conditions so obviously and directly modify this power, it is but natural to expect, that so great a change as that from wakeful activity to sleep might decidedly affect its action. The thoughts which pass through the mind in revery or abstraction, often leave very slight traces. Suddenly startled from such a waking dream by a practical claim, we can scarcely, the moment after, recall what it was which so occupied us. These facts are sufficient to overcome the antecedent improbability of continuous mental action, arising from the defect of memory. and to leave the way open for proof.

The most obvious facts which go to establish the constant activity of mind are dreams. The memory does testify to a large amount of movement in hours of sleep, not to be distinguished by external signs from other periods of repose. Some habitually dream: that is the play of imagery, the dumb show in the hours of darkness, the spectral troop of the sportive thoughts passes and repasses within the scope of mental vision, and the person, on waking, remains mindful of this fleet, flitting assemblage—of this under-current of his thoughts escaping the control of the senses and the voluntary life. Now, though others rarely dream, that is, rarely recall these shadows of the mind, leaving no more visible traces on the external life than do the clouds that fly through the heavens on the earth, which they darken for the moment; this fact goes but a little way to weaken the presumption, that they are not very different from their fellows; that the rehearsal of dreams is only a little more interior and close locked in the one case than in the other. This supposition is strengthened by the fact, that the habit of recalling and relating dreams is said to confirm the tendency to them, and to deepen their impressions.

The nature also of dreams is a proof of their continuous presence. There is shown in them a certain freedom, yet also a certain weakness of the mind not found in the waking moments. The intellectual powers are plainly divorced from the usual restraint and guidance of the senses and the voluntary activities. Nothing seems monstrous, that is unnatural. The most incongruous events are accepted with perfect composure. The laws of nature are largely set aside, and the mind binds together, with its own fanciful connections in its own fanciful creations, the events that arise before it. The inner wheels are ungeared from the outer world, and revolve in their own rapid and irregular way. This fact goes to show that the senses are in full repose, while the mind retains this wild, free, sportive, untiring activity.

In dreams, also, the will, through the rest of its physical instruments, seems utterly powerless. Flight, however urgent the apparent necessity, is impossible. No personal exigency is met with physical prowess and strength. This seems to arise from the fact that the will finds itself thwarted by the inert, sleeping body, and not inducing its wonted effects in this torpid mass, throws back on the mind fear, faintness, and a sense of hopeless failure. Sometimes, indeed, the effort it puts forth is so great as to run, like an electric shock, through the muscles, and the awakened body is landed at a leap, stark and astonished, on the floor of the chamber. These facts all indicate that physical repose is accompanied with mental activity, and not simply that sleep is partial and disturbed. Such a state, indeed, affects the character of dreams, and deepens their impression, and thus aids us in recalling them ; but does not seem to be their cause.

A third fact looking to the same conclusion is the familiar one of talking in sleep, though the person on waking retains none of the impressions which occupied the mind. In such cases, mental activity is fairly shown to exist without corresponding recollections. The dog even will bark in his sleep, tickling the motor nerves with some tantalizing image of cat or rabbit.

Allied to this is the fourth, more general proof furnished by somnambulism in all its forms. In these cases, the mind acquires a partial control of the body, and, while leaving the senses at rest, guides and stimulates its muscular powers. The wonderful precision and daring with which this is sometimes done evince great calmness and activity of the faculties, enabling them to reach results impossible to the frightened, swimming senses. Of this character are those familiar instances in which the somnambulist passes through positions of great peril without failure or disturbance. A student in my own college class had been greatly interested and perplexed by a difficult problem. He could not hit upon its solution. He retired to rest, and, in the night, rose in his sleep, and wrought it out on the board in the room. There, to his astonishment, he found it in the morning, the whole labor having left not the slightest trace in the memory.

A fifth fact looking in the same direction, is that testified to by Sir William Hamilton, and open to any one's verification: "I have always observed that when suddenly awakened during sleep, (and, to ascertain the fact, I have caused myself to be roused at different seasons of the night,) I have always been able to observe, that I was in the middle of a dream. The recollection of this dream was not always equally vivid. On some occasions, I was able to trace it back until the brain was lost at a remote distance; on others I was hardly aware of more than one or two of the latter links of the chain; and sometimes was scarcely certain of more than the fact, that I was not awakened from an unconscious state."

One more fact remains of very general prevalence confirmatory of those now given. The mind is found to exercise a certain measure of watchfulness over the body in hours of sleep. We sleep, as popular speech has it, with one eye open. Any thing unusual, though slight in character, arouses us, while familiar sounds pass unheeded. There is evidently a sentinel posted, who reports at once anything alarming, while he suffers ordinary events to pass unchallenged. We see something of this even in the torpor of intoxication. The mind under an unsuccessful effort to arouse the body on the approach of danger, and, if the danger is extreme, sometimes sobers the man at once. We assign the mind a specific duty. We lay upon it as a task, that it shall awaken the body at a given moment. The mind is frequently disturbed, and made nervous by the imposition, and arouses the vexed body in a tentative way half a dozen times before the hour arrives; or, better trained and more familiar with its service, it leaves the repose unbroken till the moment has fully come.

These and kindred facts of observation seem sufficiently to establish the constant activity of the mind, and to render it certain, that this invisible agent of invisible phenomena has a continuous and manifested existence, whatever the condition of its factor—the body, may be.

CHAPTER II.

The Intellect—Its Divisions—Perception.

§ 1. THE first great class of mental faculties are those of the intellect. When we speak of faculties, we mean the different ways in which the one individual mind acts, rather than a combination of distinct powers under the analogy of our physical organism. The forms of knowing are treated first, not because they necessarily arise first,—feeling doubtless precedes them, and chiefly occupies consciousness in the first months of life—but because, in the activity of mind, they prepare the way for emotion and choice, and chiefly determine their form. The knowing are the receptive processes, and give material to the feelings and alternatives to choice.

The intellectual powers have been divided into three principal classes; the sense, the understanding, and the reason. The first furnishes the direct facts, the forms of existence which the mind contemplates, whether of the outer or inner world. The second carries on and sustains the processes of reflection concerning these, elaborating them into knowledge, experience. The third furnishes those necessary ideas under which only the movements of a rational mind can go on. We shall not pause to speak of these divisions, as all that we have to say under each of them is requisite for their perfect comprehension. We proceed to treat of the first of these classes, that of sense.

This term is somewhat awkward, but as it has already been used in this connection, we avoid, by its retention, one great evil of metaphysics, a perpetually shifting nomenclature. The sense includes two, and quite diverse sources of knowledge ; the power of perception, and the immediate cognizance which the mind has of its own states. Under an image, but very partially applicable, they may be spoken of as the outer and inner eye of the intellect.

§ 2. In perception we shall not, as is usually done, include all the senses. A portion of these seem primarily avenues of feelings rather than of percepts. When the sensation is manifest, lying in the organ, and contemplated there as an occasion of pleasure or displeasure, the sense is evidently one of feeling, rather than of knowing. Though we may make the peculiar character of the odor, the taste, the pain, a ground of inference as to its source, and thus of knowledge, this fact does not destroy its primary connection with the sensibilities, the feelings. Nor is the fact that an odor, a flavor are, as it were, a form of knowing, a knowing that cannot be otherwise arrived at, a ground of classifying these sensations with the intellectual faculties; since the same is true of love, sympathy, anger. The perplexity arises, as has been already intimated, from the fact, that every feeling involves consciousness, and to know, and to be conscious of knowing, a thing, are constantly used as interchangeable expressions. As consciousness belongs necessarily to thought, feeling and volition, it is not in this common condition of their existence, that their differences are to be looked for ; but in the nature of that existence, consciousness being conceded. All then, that abides in the organ as a distinct, local sensation, an incipient, or a positive pain or pleasure, is a matter of feeling, rather than of perception, and should be classified as a portion of our emotional nature. With this distinction in view, we have but two unmistakable organs of perception, the eye and the ear. Even these, under certain conditions, may give rise to sensations. The light may become so bright as to be painful ; the sound so loud or so sharp as to be disagreeable, that is organically disagreeable, and thus these senses serve for the time as avenues to feelings rather than to perceptions. The pleasures that enter the eye and ear in painting, sculpture, music, not being organic, but mental, do not interfere with the purely perceptive action of the senses.

In perception, matter of knowledge, or of subjective emotions simply, is, through the medium of the organ of sense, brought to the mind. It is only by reflection, observation, that we know that the eye is the means of sight, or the ear of hearing. Neither of these organs, in their healthy state, give any direct indication of their office, or excite us by any passing sensation in the performance of it. To this fact our language conforms, and we speak of perception, an acting of the mind, through, rather than in the organ employed.

The sense of touch seems more mixed than any of the others. It declares its locality, and lodges its results as distinct feelings in the finger-ends. Its sensations should, therefore, be primarily ranked with the feelings, and it be regarded as an organ of feeling. Indeed, this conclusion language seems unmistakably to indicate, and, in designation, we have passed over with the same word, *feeling*, from the external sense to the internal emotion. Touch, however, approaches the two higher senses, in the fact that its sensations are made almost exclusively the ground of inferences rather than of enjoyments, and when highly developed, are clear and ultimate in the information imparted, and almost wholly overlooked as forms of feeling. The blind doubtless cease almost entirely to contemplate the agreeable and disagreeable in touch—indeed the tactual character of these sensations, and find in them a direct, unconscious medium of knowing. Under such circumstances, the sense is one of perception rather than sensation.

§ 3. Taking the eye as the type of the intellectual senses, we ask, What do we see? Most multiform and perplexed have been the answers to this question, and most fatal, and, to the common understanding, preposterous have been the conclusions drawn from them. It is no part of our purpose to dwell on these either by exposition or refutation; but simply to state what we regard as the just view, and with passing indications of its bearings to leave this to displace them. The nature of this view, and therefore its grounds, are so much involved in our idea of the intuitive action of the mind as to turn upon this fundamental feature of philosophy. The full reasons of our conclusions cannot therefore at once be spread out, but will be slowly made up as we present the entire furniture and action of the mind. The separate parts of our structure can show neither their full strength nor fitness, till the whole is finished.

In the first place, the eye as an organ of perception deals only with color, the ear only with sound. The sources of these colors and sounds are known only inferentially. It is a necessary belief arising under the notion of causation, that these organs, that any organs, can become means of cognition only through these effects which have been wrought in themselves, and that unaffected they can be the medium of no knowledge. Effects not only demand causes, but causes efficiently present in them, interpenetrating them. The last, the immediate cause is inseparable from the effect. Now light and sound are the agents, and the only agents that reach these organs, and it is a matter of experience, of observation, that perception is immediately dependent on these agents as they penetrate into and work their changes on the organs of sense. Each organ is mechanically, obviously fitted for the action of its own agent, and every interference with these internal adjustments, these means of transfer, destroys perception wholly or in part. While, therefore, our necessary beliefs demand an immediate effect on the organ of perception, experience clearly points out the agents of this effect, and the contrivance by which it is wrought.

The purely intellectual character of sight, the extent to which the eye is a simple, unconscious, translucent medium of the mind, is shown by the number, delicacy, variety, and furtive character of the judgments inextricably involved in vision. The earlier years of life are evidently busily employed in learning to see, not in the scientific, but in the familiar use of the word. Only objects of special brilliancy, or near at hand, or united with sounds, are able to arrest and hold the eye of the infant. Slowly does it learn to distinguish the mother's face when at a distance, or to give direction to the eye, or separation to objects, except as one or other of them is forced obtrusively on the attention. These facts harmonize with the further recorded fact, that the eyes of one couched in mature life, seemed to report all objects under the analogy of touch; that is, as directly in contact with the organ of vision. These spaces, greater and less, which the educated eye now reveals; this opening up and spreading out of the universe before it, this unsearchable depth, this heignt this breadth, are not the products of direct vision, but of vision modified by innumerable judgments, and mingled with them. The most of them we form unconsciously, and learned to make early in life, their accuracy and ease being increased by every day's experience. How many things come in to determine our estimates of the distances of surrounding objects, the clear ness or faintness of colors, the depth of blue cast upon them by the atmosphere, their apparent size, intervening objects and the muscular adjustment of the eyes in their perception. The nearness or remoteness of objects is exclusively determined by these considerations, and is not at all a matter of direct sight. Most have probably experienced, in some moment of relative abstraction, an exaggerated or false impression made by some object or objects, seen, but not observed, and marked the instantaneousness with which these flashed into their true form upon the first voluntary, distinct direction of the eye toward them. The relative position and size of objects are also almost wholly a matter of judgment; the eye itself only records their angular separation. It reduces them to a map-surface, and leaves their relations and distances unrecorded. Angles, not lines, are contemplated by it. The distances outward from the eye, and hence laterally also, are wholly a matter of conjecture; of experience.

To these judgments are to be added those which reveal forms, which turn on light and shade, and from these data arrive at the most complex surfaces. We thus see that the pure visual data of sight are very meagre, and bear no more resemblance and intimate connection to the world in which we live, than do the canvas and the paints thereon, as canvas and paints merely, to the landscape represented. This saturation of a sense by the understanding, this inflation of a single drop by the breath of rational thought into a brilliant sphere, and the acquired ability to do this as child's play, are the noticeable features of this, our highest organ of perception, quite distinguishing it from such an organ as that of taste, from which with smack, pause and reiteration, we reach one or two uncertain conclusions.

The ear is akin to the eye, though considerably below it, in the number of judgments its habitual use involves. The direction, distance and source of sounds are plainly learned by experience; though in most cases we hardly separate the mere phenomenal fact from the judgments on which our knowledge, our conclusions depend. To these are to be added all the variety of feelings expressed by intonation, and unconsciously derived therefrom, and also that representative power of articulate sounds instituted in language, yet through familiarity employed and interpreted without thought. Here again the under-play of the understanding is very great, exploding a single ictus of sound, like a thimble of powder, into a death-warrant, or opening the gates of blessedness by the key of a monosyllabic assent. Thus does the mind work up the crude material, the physical nutrition of an organic susceptibility, into the daily food and the special feasts of the soul.

The point of most philosophical interest in these senses is the approach we make to a more exact answer to the inquiry: What do we perceive? Is it something external to the organ? or, is it something subjective to it? or is it subjective to the mind itself? If, in the word perception, we include all the mind's action therein, its direct and its inferential knowing, then plainly we perceive something external to the eye, external to the mind. If, however, by perception, we mean only the arriving at those simple intuitive data, around which these judgments cluster, and which they construct into the well-ordered and complete vision of mature life, then the mind perceives that only which is subjective to itself, and knows directly no more about the intermediate organ it uses than it does of the external object which is the joint, final product of its perceptive, reflective, inferential powers. The first spontaneous answer of philosophy has been, the direct perceptive action of the mind is confined to the circle of its own activity, to consciousness; and probably no other answer would have been sought for, had not the conclusions drawn from this earlier statement, led to a reconsideration of it. These conclusions have been idealism, and have compelled those who have wished to establish the independent existence of the external world, and have had no other means at hand to do it, to re-analyze perception, and find therein a valid objective element. Overlooking the inferences of the mind, they have given it a direct knowledge of matter.

The proof of idealism runs thus: 1. "We cannot know things in themselves; all knowledge is subjective; it is confined to unseen states and changes.

2. "If this is so, then still more is what we name the objective, only a state or change of us as subjective, it is a *mere* fiction of the mind so far as it is regarded as a beyond, or a thing in itself.

3. "Hence we do know the objective; for the skepticism can only legitimately conclude that the objective that we do know, is of a nature kindred to reason, and that by an *a priori* necessity we can affirm that not only all knowable must have this nature, but also all possible existence must. Self-conscious intelligence must be, according to its very definition, subject and object in one, and thus universal."

Hamilton has striven to break this charmed circle of the mind at the point of perception, affirming that a real objective element is directly recognized therein. He says, "we have no reason whatever to doubt the report of consciousness, that we actually perceive at the external point of sensation, and that we perceive the material reality." "The total and real object of perception is the external object under relation to our sense and faculty of cognition." "Suppose the total object to be twelve, that the external reality constitutes six, the material sense three, and the mind three; this may enable you to form some conjecture of the nature of the object of perception."

Is there any good ground for the very general and very stubborn conviction that the mind cannot, by way of direct apprehension, act on anything external to itself; or are Reid and Hamilton right in regarding this as a pure assumption.

It is very difficult and very important, in a discussion of this character, to be aware of the physical images which cling to our words and mislead the thought by material analogies. In and out, where it is, and where it is not, are expressions applicable to matter rather than to mind, and we must not in this case confound the intellect even with its instruments, the brain and the nervous system. The effects which take place in these are one thing, and what enters consciousness as a purely spiritual product, a thought, a feeling, an inner experience, is quite another. The connection between the two, an affection of the organ of sense and an affection of the mind, is unknown, and for the present at least insoluble. They are as wide apart in kind as any two known things can be, since the one is physical and the other spiritual, classes of phenomena for which we have found no common term. There seems some plausibility in the notion of external perception, when we contemplate the organism of any one sense, as that of the eye. The light enters. A sensible, visible effect—visible to another eye—is provoked on the retina. To this compound effect, to which two agencies are contributing, the eye and the light, it may seem reasonable to regard the nerve as sensitive, and therefore to suppose it to take cognizance of the immediate presence of a foreign agent. If, then, we could identify the perception of the mind with this condition of its organ, there would seem to be in it also a direct knowledge of one force at least, that of light, alien and external to itself.

But even on this supposition, farther reflection would modify our conclusion. In purely physical causation, the cause, though entering into the effect, is not as a cause recognizable there. Indeed it seems probable that there is not invariably the same transferred force in one series of effects as in another, and that in some results the prime agency quickly disappears. A ball is struck by a bat, and set in motion: after the ball has parted from the bat how much of the antecedent fact could be found in the subsequent one of independent motion? How far would the second phenomenon directly disclose the first, or what common term or force could be detected in the two? The force is not discernible aside from the results it occasions, and antecedent effects are not given in subsequent ones. Suppose the same ball to be observed falling under the influence of gravitation. How far would this new cause be discoverable directly in this new phase of movement? Again, chemical action is initiated by a rise of temperature; water is instantly frozen under certain conditions by a slight jar; the brain is quickened by a full stomach; in these and a thousand other cases of causation, what portion of the cause is in the effect, to be found there as a part in a whole, as the numbers 6, 3, 3, in the sum twelve. Evidently in a purely physical effect it is impossible for us to detect the cause as a cause; as a second, primary, alien agency, entering into and constituting a distinguishable part of the new, simple, single state before us.

We perceive phenomena only, not the underlying forces, not the very causes; these, and the antecedent facts they may have occasioned, are matters of inference and of experience exclusively. If, then, the phenomena transpiring in the eye were, as they are not, identical with those of the mind, it would be impossible that these should include a knowledge of the very cause, and even less possible that they should include a direct knowledge of antecedent, external phenomena reached only by inference through this hidden, unsearchable force or cause. We may direct attention in this discussion to two things: the very cause or efficiency which necessarily co-exists with the effect and sustains it, and the immediately antecedent phenomenal effect, more often spoken of as the cause. The first of these is not discoverable in the eye, since no causes, as causes, are, or can be directly known. To know phenomenally the very cause, would be to make that cause a phenomenon, that is an effect, that is not a cause. Pure being, causal being, the being or force that lies back of effects, of phenomena, cannot be known perceptively as a result. To affirm this is to deny causation, and make a phenomenon its own cause.

The second of these, to wit, the immediately antecedent, outside effect, cannot be perceptively found and known in the eye, for the obvious reason that it is not there. If, therefore, we were to direct the attention to the eye, the organ, alone, and identify its states with those of the mind, we should still be unable directly, perceptively to discover anything in it but its own phenomena, which are neither the outside object, nor do they contain any cognizable portion of it. We are not to regard the eye with the facts that transpire in it as at once inseparable from the mind and external to it. If its changes are the changes of the mind, then all that is to it outside is equally so to the perceptions. So truly subjective, then, is even the organic state of the eye in sight, that were this the thing revealed in consciousness, we should still not be able to separate or distinguish the external element, "six," in the sum twelve, and know it directly as a foreign agency. The phenomenal six alone should we perceive, and still be compelled to infer hence the causal six supporting it.

But when we pass, as we should, the condition of the organ as itself unknown to the mind and outside of it, and contemplate the true immaterial content of consciousness, the case is, if possible, still plainer. Perception as an act of mind does not reveal to us the instrument of sense employed, or the state of that instrument. The connection between a mental state and the physical state which accompanies it, is mysterious and unknown ; it is not so much as hinted at in the very act of perception, in consciousness. For aught that we can see, the last might be very different from what it is, and the first remain the same. Indeed, that there are to sight and hearing accompanying physical states, what these states are, and even where they are, constitute facts which require to be learned from experience. Even in advanced life we do not always recognize at which ear a given sound chiefly enters, and tentatively test the question by turning the attention, first in one direction, then in the other. The content of consciousness, then, is not of such a nature as to reveal in perception the states of the retina, or of the auditory nerve ; or whether there is in them more or less of foreign action. These changes are sunk foundations on which the visible structure rests, but are not in the least disclosed in their nature by it. They are the sub-marine cable, neither declared in its length nor its depth, nor in the mechanical, nor electric conditions of its structure, by the messages sent and received at either terminus. To introduce causes into consciousness, that they may be there directly known, is either to assert their supersensual and immaterial character, is to grant the assertion of idealism : "we do know the object, and therefore it is of a nature akin to thought;" or, it is to break down the fundamental distinction between mental and physical phenomena, affirming that both transpire in consciousness, that the physical facts of the brain are the spiritual facts of mind. Yet having made this inadmissible concession, we are confronted with the facts, that consciousness does not of itself indicate whether the brain, or the heart, or the bowels, are the seat of thought; whether we see with our fingers or our eyes; and the farther fact, that causes, as causes, are never discoverable even in purely physical effects.

The assertion, then, that we cannot directly know things in themselves, follows inevitably from the two assertions: consciousness is the sole field of perceptive knowledge; no material phenomena, as material, can appear in consciousness, interpentrated, so to speak, by it. Consciousness covers all intellectual knowledge, and excludes all else; lays down a line of demarcation impassable either from within or from without, cutting apart matter and mind. This conclusion we believe all experience confirms, and that no one would have thought of denying it, save under the pressure of certain difficulties to be evaded, and certain conclusions to be reached.

§ 4. How far pure idealism, that professedly knows only mind, is entitled to these assertions which we are ready to make in common with it, is a question of more doubt. We, in our position, arrive at them by a knowledge, an inferential knowledge, both of matter and mind, by an experimental discovery of their mutually impenetrable character. If we were, as idealism asserts, in every way debarred access to matter—to matter as believed in by the masses of men, it would certainly not be so plain, how we could come so universally to form a distinct, uniform and controlling idea of its character, and be able also to affirm, that this most omnipresent and fixed of our notions is, in its essential features, a mere figment of the brain. Why a series of physical conceptions which is removed by the very nature of mind from even the bare possibility both of knowledge and being, should nevertheless be the most uniform and universal of mental states, is not explained by idealism. How a form of thought, necessarily false, comes to be a fixed product and characteristic of mind, how if happens that we continually talk, think, and act in reference to matter, matter which by the constitution of the mind, is beyond all its forms of knowledge; how science and philosophy come to so utterly differ from each other in their beliefs, are mysteries which must ever to the straightforward practical thinker reflect the highest improbability on idealism, and leave it among those strange, remote conclusions, which when not directly disproved are too far off to disturb the orbit of our daily life. When philosophy subverts knowledge, instead of expounding it, and denies the validity of he most settled, familiar and unavoidable judgments of the mind, it assumes an anarchical character, removing the foundations, if not of thought, yet of conviction.

§ 5. We believe the true doctrine of perception to be, that the state of consciousness therein, the knowing, is purely subjective both in action and object, indeed that the action and object are inseparable. To perceive a color, is to put forth a complete, primary, simple act of knowing, complete in that something is known; primary in that no farther explanation can be forced upon it, the act standing in its own light, apprehensible for what it is in itself; and simple in that it is incapable of successful analysis. On the occasion of such a perception, the mind, of its own interpreting action, under the notion of causation, infers an external source of the impression, which, as a necessary, and certain, and uniform conclusion, becomes to it as valid as any that it ever makes. Its validity, like the validity of all mental acts, is referable to the clearness and constancy with which it is made and repeated. The ground on which we accept any truth is the distinctness and reiteration with which the mind affirms it. We reach, then, the external world not directly by perception, but indirectly, inferentially, along a bridge of thought, whose farther abutment our rational nature supplies, and whose connections are established by varied and repeated, and protracted experience. Shifting the figure we strike the shore with the grapple of causation, and by this guy we swing.

If asked why the mind supplies the idea in connection with one mental state, that of perception, more than with another, as that of thought; how it knows where and when to fling into the air its coil of rope, that it may thereby be lashed to the physical world, the answer comes: It is the fruit of varied and protracted experience. A sensation is found to be a new, distinct, sudden, independent state. As such it demands explication in an outside cause. A thought is a consecutive, evolved, dependent product, that can be renewed in the mind at pleasure, and by this fact find explication through the mind itself. The various senses also, in their diverse yet independent reports, mutually aid and guide the mind in this reference of sensations to external causes. Impressions in distinct organs are found always to accompany each other in certain forms, under a fixed order. Thus experience is constantly disclosing the character of phenomena, and the mind rapidly learns to distinguish those inwardly dependent on its own action, from those dependent outwardly on foreign agents. This class it cannot, from its own constitution, leave without this causal reference and exposition.

The confusion which sometimes overtakes the mind in perception, illustrates its method of education, and the manner in which it is commenced. A pressure is felt across the forehead, as if the band placed upon it had been drawn too tightly. We cannot tell with certainty whether the impression is due to this, or to the astringency of a fluid with which the fillet was saturated. We test the point by raising the hand, and determining whether or not mechanical force is present. In the absence of this, we refer the feeling to the condition of the nerves. Again, we seem to hear a sound, as the anxious parent the crying of her child-

She cannot at once decide whether the impression was the suggestion of her own thought, or the actual effect of the supposed cause. The attention is more carefully directed, the phenomena that enter the mind from without, being discriminated from the mere play of fancy; and by this more complete separation of its own action from the action of other agents the point is settled.[1]

§ 6. It has been thought, and much has been made of this point, that a denial of direct perception is an impeachment of the veracity of our faculties, or, as it is expressed by Hamilton and others, of consciousness; and that the way is thus logically opened to universal skepticism. Idealism is certainly not a denial of the facts of consciousness. Perception as a fact of mind, is accepted, and the first exception taken, is as to what perception is, what it gives us. Now the veracity of consciousness is only involved in the mere fact of perception, the mere rehearsal and acceptance of its mental phenomena, not at all in the nature and validity of its supposed revelations. Idealism does, however, set aside a general belief of mankind, and so far tends to skepticism. Even this accusation does not hold against the view of perception now presented. The general belief of men in an external world is maintained, though a careful analysis shows the grounds of the conclusion to be somewhat different from those at first accepted. The accusation against idealism is not, that it shows a general opinion to be groundless, but that it affirms simply and nakedly a general and necessary belief to be deceptive; that is the reiterated and constant action of the mind to be delusive. We may, on like grounds, pronounce the axiomatic conclusions of the reason unreliable. These are nothing more than its inevitable convictions.

The affirmation in which the unaided powers of all men agree, which they spontaneously and inevitably make, is the existence of an external world, the opposition of matter to mind, a reference of a portion of our inner experience, to outer sources or causes. Whether this conclusion is direct, intuitive, or involves one or more of the simplest acts of judgment, most men have never so much as inquired, and have therefore no convictions concerning it. It is doubtless a matter of surprise to most persons, to find, on inquiry, so many judgments mingled with the simplest act of sight. These had been overlooked, and the act of seeing regarded as more full, explicit and immediate than it is. Language favors this concealment of obscure, rapid judgments, and we are said to see the form of a sphere, when we merely infer it. Yet there is no ground for a distrust of man's faculties, because they are formed to act in ways and proportions not perfectly understood by those who accept results, with no investigation of methods. To tell a man that the unlikeness of the images of the same object in each of his two eyes, is one of the grounds from which the impression of nearness is received, may interest and surprise him, but does not so shake his confidence in his own conclusions, in the reliability of the mind's action, as when he is told that the external world, in which he has so fully believed, that he has never so much as thought of its existence as a matter of belief, is a mere creation of the mind, one portion of its own acts being thrown into opposition to another portion. The one assertion arrests and throws back in confused, eddying currents, the whole stream of intellectual action ; the other merely shows that analysis reveals more elements in mental phenomena, than those at first caught sight of. There is no reason why the statement, that there is a simple judgment, an act of inference involved in a belief of the existence of matter and of mind, should be regarded as any more skeptical, any more destructive to the faith to be reposed in our faculties, than the generally accepted doctrine, that sight includes many judgments, dependent on protracted experience. The assertion of Hamilton, "that consciousness gives a knowledge of the ego, in relation and contrast to the non-ego," even if it were readily intelligible to all, would hardly, I think, be regarded as a satisfactory statement of a general and unwavering belief, when contrasted with the statement, there is found that in consciousness, from which we directly and inevitably infer the existence of matter and mind. Most would doubtless regard the two statements as open to consideration, as lying alike in the line of the common belief in the external world. Indeed, to say that the mind is conscious of itself, is conscious of matter, gives a shock at once to thought, and to language, and is far from being that explicit, indefeasible statement of the common faith, which all at once recognize.

The exact grounds of the general belief, is certainly open to inquiry, and one statement which accepts its validity is no more exposed to the charge of a denial of the integrity of the human faculties, than another. Indeed the spontaneous conviction of the existence and nature of external objects involves many judgments besides this one of causation. I see the apple before me. My present impression is—the steps of my past experience being unanalyzed, that I see it to be round, to be red, to be three inches in diameter and at a distance of three feet. How does this impression agree with what Sir William Hamilton says is the real object of perception? "Through the eye we perceive nothing but the rays of light in relation to, and in contact with the retina." Who ever perceived them, or came to so much as a knowledge of them, without diligent scientific inquiry? Light, as the fruit of much research, is found to be a form of motion, and this motion to affect the retina; but no man ever knows the existence of the retina, or of the undulations of light therein, save through an inquiry into eyes other than his own, and a careful investigation of the physical world. What is here asserted to be the sole object of perception, the mind never perceives, but only employs it as a submerged, unknown cause through which it arrives at its own knowledge, to wit : a red apple of a given size, and position. In this final product of perception, there are contained innumerable judgments, and it should certainly be no surprise to find among them, this one of outside existence. That the spaces of the world are inferentially given, is entirely in keeping with the fact, that those of a painting are, by the previous habit and impulse of the mind, supplied under suitable suggestions of light and shade.

The crude material granted to the mind seems to be a subjective impression of redness, of certain extension and various shades. From this, by the aid of muscular and tactual experience, and the help afforded by the color and relations of surrounding objects, it constructs an apple and assigns it independent existence in a definite locality. This it now does instantly, like a flash of light, though it has acquired the power of doing it slowly, by much and forgotten experience. The intuitive, primitive, intellectual elements are wholly unlike this final physical result, this tissue of judgments, these data of sense inter-shot with a few firm threads from the shuttle of reason. Indeed, no instance in our later knowledge, in which an entire system of principles is evolved from a few facts, more evinces the astonishing power which belongs to the mind, than does this simplest, earliest, most common case of reasoning, that of perception.

That color is known as the motion of an ethereal medium on the retina, or that there is any connection of the two, or knowledge of the one in and through the other, are statements not intelligible even, till science by secondary inquiries has made them so. The transfer of motion at one sense into vision, at another into hearing, and in the brain itself into thought, are inexplicable transformations, whose terms we only know by independent investigation, and even then fail of their connection. To suppose that any portion of this knowledge comes directly in perception, is the most obvious and violent perversion of experience.

If we were directly cognizant, and only cognizant of the content in the organ of sense, cognizant of it for what it is, and where it is, physically, there would be no opportunity for deception or oversight in matters of perception. A force acting on a machine tells, and must tell, for exactly what it is. The effect is direct and inevitable. So would it be in perception. We should never make a ghost of a stump, or overlook altogether the objects whose images are actually on the retina; that have actually caused the light to impinge with customary power on this sensitive medium. It is because the mind gives a frightened attention, or no attention, inadequate interpretation, or no interpretation, to these objects, that perception is distorted, or fails altogether. The mere physical effect in itself alone is nugatory.

It is said that those whose eyes are distorted, use either one or the other as they choose, directing the attention, the perception, to the right or the left as convenience requires, the impression in the neglected organ going for nothing; and we all of us evidently take up and lay down at pleasure the physical effects on the retina, using them as means of vision only when the mind is at leisure to do so. These facts show, without doubt, that perception is deeper than the organ of sense, is by no means identical with the appropriate action therein, nor is sure to follow it. It is, then, no impeachment of the veracity of our faculties to inquire into the exact mode of their action, nor any the more so because the inquiry discloses unexpected results.

§ 7. A farther error connected with the doctrine of direct perception is the division of the qualities of matter into primary and secondary. The list of primary qualities is differently made out by different philosophers. Extension and solidity are generally recognized as chief among them. The criteria of these qualities as compared with secondary qualities are that matter cannot exist without them, and especially urged by Hamilton, that in the primary qualities perception is peculiarly direct and clear, "the objective element predominates," "matter is known as principal in its relation to mind." The distinction between primary and secondary qualities seems in these tests to be in part untenable, and in part of an uncertain character, and to arise from an oversight of those necessary intuitive ideas involved in the very existence of matter.

Extension should not be regarded as a property of matter, and if so regarded is not, in the form in which it exists concretely, a necessary property. No portion of matter is necessarily of one size rather than another. The actual quality of extension, if it is to be so termed, is as variable as any other quality. The only universality in this attribute more than in other attributes of matter is found in the fact, that all matter must exist in space, and hence under the one form of extension. Space, extension, is a necessary condition of matter. Without it, those qualities, properly so called, which constitute matter, cannot have a being. It is involved in their manifestations, that they occupy some portion of space, and this primary quality, so called, is only this essential condition for the existence of matter. We might as well say that duration is a quality of matter, as to say that extension is such a quality; since no form of matter can exist without occupying, or extending through, some period of time, more or less.

Nor is the second criterion any more satisfactory in its application. If there is any one direction in which the mind acts with a sense of establishing and defining its own data, it is this of extension. Odor, taste, color, are what they are, directly through the nature of the outside cause; but the form of a body is arrived at through meagre grounds of judgment unfolded by the enlargement and corrections of protracted experience; while the notion under which alone their evolution can proceed, that of space, is furnished entirely by the mind. Let the full action of intuitive ideas be recognized, and primary qualities in their peculiar significance will disappear. Perception, instead of being unusually direct and immediate in extension, is more than elsewhere indirect, enlarged by inference. A knowledge of the forms of bodies involves an unusual number of judgments, whether arrived at by muscular movement, or the eye, or the two conjointly.

Solidity, as a primary quality, is open to a like form of criticism. That which must in this discussion be understood by solidity, is very different from the notion which the word ordinarily conveys; it is the impossibility of complete compression, complete displacement. A gas is in this sense as much a solid as a piece of steel, since, when properly confined in a cylinder, it is found to exclude the piston as certainly as the most solid substance. Compression cannot proceed to all lengths. A resistance accompanies pressure, and an increased and insuperable resistance remains as the final result. Without this ultimate resistance to foreign matter, this capability of occupying space to the exclusion of other things, whatever may be the signs of force present, as in gravitation or electricity, we withhold the appellation of matter. Here again any given degree of incompressibility is not necessary to matter, but only that there should be some degree of it, and some degree of incompressibility is necessary, as involved in the occupation of space. Only so can space be filled and held possession of. The general necessity, then, is evolved from this general condition of the existence and recognition of matter, that it shall be a space-filling force, that it shall have a permanent substratum to its phenomena.

As then the necessary connection of extension with matter arises from the idea of space, so that of solidity arises from the *occupation* of space, the idea of a local, fixed cause, the source of fixed phenomena. That the forces which lie at the basis of matter may in some cases penetrate each other, as in the union of two gases, and may in others entirely exclude each other, as in the contact of solids, are facts to be learned by experience. The very notion of matter, however, is that it involves a local cause or force, and if a cause or force, that it has some means of showing itself as a force, some power of exclusion, some solidity. The notion of causation, therefore, assigns a measure of resistance to matter as a necessary condition of its phenomena. A specific measure and kind of force is a quality of a given form or kind of matter, and involves the fact of resistance or solidity when the matter under appropriate conditions is subjected to pressure.

If it be said that the distinction between primary and secondary qualities is valid, since solidity necessarily involves force, the substratum of matter ; answer is made, that no actual, that no specific form of force is necessary to matter, but only some form of force, and that this is as necessary to color, to flavor, to odor, when these are present, as to solidity when this is shown. Solidity, or resistance, or more strictly still, the sense of resistance, has no permanent existence any more than odor or color, demands like them for its manifestation appropriate conditions, and does no more than they do, in demanding as a condition an external force. If, then, we speak of the effects matter is capable of producing as the qualities of that matter, odor, resistance are such qualities, but neither of them are constant ; both are occasional, and conditioned to fitting circumstances ; both of them imply that which is permanent and necessary. From taste as from touch, we may infer an external, local cause, a cause that must hence occupy space, be a space-filling force, at least to one sense, which is the entire conclusion derivable from resistance.

If it be said that the circumstances are in all cases possible under which the quality of solidity may be drawn out, while those which disclose odor are peculiar to a few bodies, we answer, this is a question of experience, is far from being proved, and, if established, could bring with it no sense of necessity, differencing the two cases. Bodies which yield no odor under one form, may under another. Odor seems to involve chemical change, and it might be found that every substance would yield it under fitting chemical conditions. This is a question to be decided by protracted and varied experience, and however decided, could only be the ground of an empirical, and not of a necessary division of qualities.

Take such a secondary quality as that of color. It seems antecedently probable, that all bodies have color. Some gases are apparently colorless, but so is the atmosphere in small volumes. Experience and theory would lead us to expect that the most diffused force in sufficient volume would affect the transmission of light. On the other hand, who has ever tested all the forms of matter as to resistance under pressure? Certainly not metaphysicians. The distinction between primary and secondary qualities resting on this basis would be purely empirical, of no metaphysical significance, and till inquiry of a thorough and searching character should have been instituted, of a doubtful nature.

This then cannot be the sufficient and prevailing ground of this distinction, but we must look farther for something thought to inhere in the very nature of matter, necessary to it and betrayed by solidity, by every primary quality. This necessary something we accept, and believe the notion of it to arise under the intuitive idea of cause and effect;

but also believe, that this notion is revealed, called forth, as certainly by odor, by color, by taste, as by pressure; and that we inevitably put back of each of these subjective effects, a permanent force called matter. This permanent force is necessary to the notion of matter, and is as appropriately reached by one sense as by another, by one effect as by another; indeed, is indicated by any sensation which betrays an external world. The qualities which find entrance through one organ, have no more right to be called primary, that is fundamental, than those which enter at another. If the sense of muscular effort were wanting, we might still be able to arrive at the idea of matter; though its alleged primary quality should not be directly recognizable by us. We should then understand color and flavor as indications of a local force, apprehensible by sight and taste.

The second criterion more signally fails than the first in its application to solidity. Far from matter's coming most directly and fully in contact with mind through solidity, in many instances it is only in a secondary, inferential way, that this quality is at all arrived at. A gas makes no impression on the muscular system, offers no obstacle to movement, calls forth no sense of resistance, till closely confined; and then by that very confinement is put beyond direct contact with any organ of sense. We are left wholly and most obviously to infer the resistance, the solidity of gases, from the fact that the piston cannot, in the cylinder containing them, be forced perfectly down to its bed, and recoils as the hand is lifted. Surely perception is not more immediate and full here than elsewhere; on the contrary, there is no perception of the point at issue, the solidity of the gas, but only a judgment to that effect. Even the solidity of a solid directly handled is inferred from the muscular effort expended in the attempt to crush it, and only admits of an estimate by an indirect method.

This doctrine of primary and secondary qualities, maintained by so large a variety of philosophers, is of interest, chiefly from the way in which it has grown out of the errors, or betrays the errors, held by them ; and yet more from the indication it gives of an unconscious influence of truths not formally recognized. Thus, Locke speaks of the "inseparable" nature of extension as a quality of matter, while declining to accept the antecedent necessity of space as a condition of matter, and a knowledge of matter. Herein he grants to matter the necessity which he has denied to mind ; whereas by necessity can only be meant something which the *mind* inevitably affirms, a union of things which it sees to be indissoluble. No matter how often things are practically connected, unless the mind can so far penetrate that connection as to see the one to be involved in the other, their dependence would not seem to be a necessary one. Yet this father of materialism speaks of inseparable qualities, when experience in many cases had neither seen, felt, nor in any way tested their existence. Why this inference, this judgment of universal, of necessary extension and solidity ? Because of a conviction latent in the mind through its intuitive ideas, a conviction independent of the complete expansion of experience.

Hamilton, again, looking at this division of qualities through the doctrine of direct perception, jumps at the conclusion that primary qualities are those more immediately revealed, whereas inquiry shows that solidity, the most undeniable of them, is often wholly unapproachable to any form of direct perception, and is arrived at by reasonings from sensations which arise indirectly from the object of experiment. The staff so quickly clutched at has become a broken reed. Thus philosophers furnish undesigned and most valuable proof to an adverse theory, by recognizing and striving to use in a disguised form the truths which it proclaims, and assigns their true position. The acknowledged necessity of primary qualities is not in *them* but in that *intuitive action* of the mind which they call forth. Necessity which every philosopher seems ready to introduce at some point, is born not of experience, but of men's thoughts ; not of matter, but of mind.

We briefly sum up the conclusions arrived at. Extension is not a quality of matter, but its antecedent condition, and owes the sense of necessity that accompanies it to the necessary idea of space. The same reason that makes it, would make duration also a quality of matter. The actual form or extension of bodies is contingent and inferential. Solidity, or the power of exclusion, is a quality of matter, and owes its necessity to our idea of the nature of matter, an idea arising under the notions of space and of cause. It differs not from odor, color in implying a permanent substratum. Every quality of matter, every sensation and perception involves this, though they mutually deepen and confirm it. Solidity, a sense of resistance, is felt to be more necessarily involved in matter than odor and taste; that is, that a permanent force should make this impression on an organ of sense, seems to us more certain than that it should impart a flavor, because, in experience, we almost exclusively use this constant and convenient test of its presence. This, however, is an empirical distinction, arising from the nature of our senses, of an uncertain character, and of no particular importance. Solidity always involves inference, often rests entirely thereon, and is not therefore directly perceived. The distinction then of primary qualities, while covering important points in philosophy, in its common form breaks down. These qualities are not more directly perceived than other qualities; they are not in contrast with them nor known to be more necessary. If we reason from the quality to the substratum, each implies this, and the necessity is common and complete. If we reason from the substratum to its qualities, no individual quality is seen to be necessary, neither any kind nor class of qualities as hardness, color. We cannot so penetrate the nature of the cause as to antecedently declare what its action will be. The greater constancy of one quality over another is learned by experience ; the intrinsic necessity of that constancy, if there be any, is unperceived. A local substance perfectly penetrable, yet having odor, color, and flavor, would doubtless be regarded by us as matter. If we lacked the sense of pressure, this fact would cut off the action of the quality of solidity upon us, but not necessarily that of the other qualities of matter.

Our general doctrine of perception is then confirmed by this distinction of qualities so universally made. Purely subjective effects are attributed with different degrees of ease, frequency, certainty to external causes ; and this attribution is confounded with the perception which gives rise to it. The perception is subjective, and is expanded, transformed into an objective world under intuitive elements and empirical inferences. As we open the painting on the canvas into the landscape, so we expand instantly, unerringly, habitually, the inner suggestions of the sense, into the reality of the outer world.

§ 8. Consciousness, or the inner sense, the remaining means of a direct knowledge of phenomena, requires but a brief notice. Our chief difficulty in conceiving this source of knowledge, and in speaking of it, is found in the language we are compelled to employ, and the confusion already occasioned by it. Self-consciousness, or consciousness, or the inner sense, is not a method of the mind's action, is not a faculty of perception. These words are used by us simply to express the fact that the mind knows what it does know ; that its states, acts, experiences, are necessarily open to itself, not by any direct effort or attention on its part, but by virtue of the very fact that they are its own states. We cannot readily speak of this knowledge which the mind has of its own phases of activity, without seeming to imply more than we intend; to imply an explicit form or faculty, or means of knowing. What we wish to draw attention to, then, as a second source of phenomenal matter, is the familiarity of the mind with its own thoughts, feelings, volitions; and hence its power through memory to make them objects of attention, inquiry, analysis. Indeed by these powers primarily is philosophy established, the phenomena of mind separated into their elements, and the laws of their combination discovered. Consciousness furnishes only the bare data of mental facts, the perceptions, thoughts present, and is nôt in the least responsible for their accuracy. Its verity is only involved in rendering them as they are, that is, as they lie in the mind. Whether we perceive what we think we perceive, whether we know what we think we know, that is, the objective justness of our mental action, these are quite different inquiries. The subjective state is all that is revealed in consciousness, and this is revealed by the very nature of mind. Concerning it, there is no opportunity for skepticism in the very moment of its transpiring; later the question is one of of memory.

CHAPTER III.

The Understanding.

§ I. THE understanding includes all those mental activities by which the data of sense are wrought into knowledge; indeed every intellectual power which is not intuitive. They are memory, imagination, and judgment. The first condition of rational activity is perception, some object given to the mind toward which it may be moved, with which it may occupy itself. The second essential condition is memory, by which perceptions, thoughts, gain continuity, are united into one experience, are made ready to pass over to conviction, to be woven into the fabric of belief. Without memory our conscious states would be separate, incommunicable, save by direct sequence, with no more reciprocal play, unity, and growth, than belong to particles of sand. Memory is involved in the coherence of intellectual life, as much as the constant inter-action, the mutual and permanent influence of its organs are included in physical life. Memory is the power of recalling the phenomena of consciousness. The experiences of the past are restored to the mind, by this faculty, with a recognition of their previous existence. Like all primitive powers, it has its own simple, unique action explained only by experience. The words retaining, recalling, may, through the force they have acquired in physical connections, suggest the idea that some impression of the objects remembered is held in the mind, and again restored to its observation ; or that some trace or result of the first act remains with the mind, waiting renewal in memory. Indeed, looking more at the material suggestions and illustrations of mental phenomena, than at the simple, primitive, inexplicable character of the act of recollection itself, some have inquired, whether the very thing first known is the object of memory, or whether the mind is occupied with some image of it? We might as well inquire whether the artist's conception of a painting is the very painting itself, or an image of it? It is certainly not the first, nor even the second in any other than a figurative sense. When I say that I recollect an event, my language is about as intelligible as it can be made. There is in it a direct appeal to the interpretation of every one's experience, furnishing like simple, separate, original acts. In memory a new impression of the event is present, accompanied with a knowledge of its previous presence.

It is merely a futile struggle with physical images, the misleading effect of physical analogies, which prompt us to inquire with an analysis more cunning than cognizant of the true conditions of mental experience, Whether, as our language seems to imply, we actually remember the very object that has passed away, or, whether some impression of it is restored to us? Each act of memory, is a primitive distinct act, efficient in itself for its own independent and peculiar end; is moreover purely subjective, though often involving a knowledge of the objective. Memory is not a repeated experience; it is the cognizance of a previous experience without repetition. The renewal of awakened action in the brain, if it could be shown to accompany recollection, would be no explanation of it. Of a like character are all the explanations of memory, which spring from purely physiological facts. Whatever may be the effect of thinking on the brain, the connection of these physical changes in a physical agent, with the act of memory, is wholly unintelligible. I might as well explain the recollection of a sword-wound, by the presence of a scar on the body, as by any changes effected at the time in the brain by the suffering then experienced. That a scar constitutes memory, is as apprehensible as that a modification of a nervous tissue, or substance, is memory. It is a fact, that memory, like other intellectual powers, is dependent for its exercise on the conditions of the brain, but why, or how dependent, are queries beyond the circle of knowledge. The vital play of nervous fluids along nervous lines is one thing, the action of the mind a totally different thing. The one is learned as an outside fact by outside observations, the other as an inside fact by consciousness. The synchronism of the two is an interesting point, but one for the present, barren in philosophy.

That memory is more dependent than our other mental powers on physical states is generally believed, though we may be easily deceived in the grounds of this judgment. Memory is readily and quickly tested in its strength. A straight-forward, categorical question betrays at once its weakness. We observe, therefore, failure at this point, more certainly than at others. In moments of weariness the memory fails us, but so, evidently, does the judgment. Obstacles seem disproportionately great, the occasions of fear unusual and pressing. In old age, memory is said to be the first faculty that shows decay; yet the old man, withdrawn from active life, naturally first discovers his failure here. It requires occasions of judgment to disclose the deficiency of judgment to others, while to ourself, these failures are not betrayed from the very fact that the judgment, as weak, does not detect its own weakness. On the other hand, a dozen events every day expose inevitably and unmistakably the defects of memory. Moreover the things chiefly forgotten are those of recent occurrence, a fact accounted for by the want of strong feeling, clear perception, and energetic attention. Diseases that weaken the memory by the destruction of brain-tissue, are especially unfavorable to the recollection of events that occurred in the periods immediately previous to the sickness. Remote events may be retained with distinctness, while those of intervening years are wiped away. These facts go to show that physiology is not prepared, I will not say to offer an explanation of the phenomena of memory, but even to point out with certainty and fullness the changes in the brain co-incident with the changes of this power. A general dependence of all our powers on the vigor of this, their common instrument, is the brief summation of its knowledge. Language like the following, conveys no intelligible idea: "All that has so far been said respecting the different nervous centers of the body cannot fail to demonstrate the existence of memory in the nervous cells which lie scattered in the heart, in the intestinal walls, in those that are collected together in the spinal cord, in the cells of the sensory and motor ganglia, and in the ideational cells of the cortical layers of the cerebral hemispheres."—*Maudsley's Physiology and Pathology of the Mind, p.* 182.

What a famous stroke of explication—"ideational cells!" What a liberal distribution of recollection from the sole of one's foot to the crown of his head! Surely forgetfulness is inexcusable under such endowments.

§ 2. There are other theories of memory not so crude as these physiological ones, yet as deficient in proof, and resting back almost equally though somewhat more subtlely on physical analogies. Of this character is that one elaborately and repeatedly enforced by Hamilton. He affirms "that an energy of mind being once determined, it is natural that it should persist, until again annihilated by other causes. This in fact would be the case were the mind merely passive in the impression it receives; for it is a universal law of nature, that every effect endures as long as it is not modified or opposed by any other effect. But the mental activity, the act of knowledge of which I now speak, is more than this; it is an energy of the self-active power of a subject, one and indivisible; consequently a part of the ego must be detached or annihilated, if a cognition once existive be again extinguished. Hence it is, that the problem most difficult of solution is not, how a mental activity endures, but how it ever vanishes." Is not this notion of the necessary persistence of force, of activity, referable exclusively to physical forces? What is the proof of its applicability to mental action? The facts of mind inquired into on their own basis, seem to indicate quite the opposite conclusion. He proceeds: "If it be impossible that an energy of mind that has once been, should be abolished without a laceration of the vital unity of the mind, one and indivisible,—on this supposition, the question arises, How can the facts of our self-consciousness be brought to harmonize with this statement, seeing that consciousness proves to us that cognitions once clear and vivid are forgotten? The solution of this problem is to be sought for, in the theory of obscure or latent modifications. The disappearance of internal energies from the view of internal perception does not warrant the conclusion that they no longer exist." "All the cognitions which we possess, or have possessed, still remain to us—the whole complement of all our knowledge still lies in our memory; but as new cognitions are continually pressing in upon the old, and continually taking place along with them among the modifications of the ego; the old cognitions, unless from time to time refreshed and brought forward, are driven back, and become gradually fainter and more obscure. The mind is only capable at any one moment of exerting a certain quantity or degree of force. This quantity must therefore be divided among the different activities, so that each has only a part, and the sum of force belonging to all the several activities taken together, is equal to the quantity or degree of force belonging to the vital activity of mind in general. This obscuration can be conceived in every infinite degree, between incipient latescence and irrecoverable latency. The obscure cognition may exist simply out of consciousness, so that it can be recalled by a common act of reminiscence. Again, it may be impossible to recover it by an act of voluntary recollection, but some association may revivify it enough to make it flash after a long oblivion into consciousness. Further, it may be obscured so far that it can only be resuscitated by some morbid affection of the system; or finally, it may be absolutely lost for us in this life, and destined only for our reminiscence in the life to come."

The view, whose salient points with large omissions are here indicated, is purely theoretical, is beset with internal difficulties, and is unable to explain the phenomena that call it forth. It is purely theoretical, for its alleged facts all lie in the unapproachable region of sub-consciousness, whose existence is not established, much less the details of its phenomena. It is vexed with difficulties of its own, greater than the difficulties it is brought forward to remove. It rests on a physical idea of force, but cannot consistently carry out that idea. If no force, no activity can be lost, how shall an act of mind fade out of consciousness? What is this fading away, if it be not a loss of force? Or, again, if the mind have but a given amount of force to bestow, and each act takes a portion, how long will it be before its stock of power will be exhausted? Or, if this power is divided up into a multiplicity of acts, and previous acts therefore are weakened in their impressions, does not this imply a withdrawal in part of activity, attention, interest, from earlier actions, and if a partial withdrawal is possible, what renders complete removal impossible? Again, what is meant by recalling an obscure cognition? Is it simply infusing more power into it, deepening the action already present, or, is it a new act of mind by which we direct attention to it, and bring it to the light? Must this new act also, in turn, subsist forever, still farther sub-dividing the power of the mind? These and many like questions are pertinent to this semi-physical theory, and show it to be unintelligible, not to say preposterous. It has no coherence and completeness in itself.

Nor does it explain the difficulties which the facts of memory present, and which call it forth. Indeed, these phenomena are every way more comprehensible than the solution of them here offered. The act of recollection, resuscitation still remains, and is certainly no more intelligible because we suppose somewhere, in some out of sight region of the mind, is lurking a previous act, which this new one fastens upon and brings forward. What relation do these distinct co-existing acts, the recalling and the recalled, the captor and the captive, bear to each other? How do they together constitute memory? Recollection seems to be as single, simple, pure an effort of mind, as perception or thought in the first instance. There is no occasion, because memory is an act of *recollection*, to put either in the mind or out of the mind, in an independent self-existent form, the exact thing recollected. A dead man can be remembered as easily as a living one, a defunct thought as readily as one that has not passed away. Indeed, we do not see why any other needs to be recalled. So far as the act has not passed from consciousness, it calls for no reminiscence; so far as it has, it is lost to the mind, and the power to restore it involves the whole mystery. These words, restore, recall, resuscitate, are not to be allowed to mislead us by their physical imagery. The state recalled exists alone, exists anew in the primitive, simple, inexplicable act of memory; a movement of mind as much of its own kind, and with its own force, as the first act of perception; and as independent, save that the occasion for it is found in the existence of previous states of consciousness. If acts of mind could be shown to be fire-flies passing from light into darkness, and darkness into light, with patient and inexhaustible alternations, it might be to the purpose; but if there must still be a distinct act of recollection, either to go in search of other acts and restore them, or when they are present to remind us of their previous presence, such an act involves the entire difficulty, and to be really anything, it must be a fresh handling of an old topic, differing from the first in that the mind knows it to be a second state of consciousness, and subject to the conditions of such a state. To re-experience sensations and recollect them, are quite different things. Much is written concerning the last, which at most would be applicable to the first only. A peculiar, primitive power is present in memory as in every other act of mind, and as a simple act, it admits and calls for no explanation. To foist on such states of consciousness, ultimate and complete in themselves, cumbersome, conjectural analogical explanations, is to make the simple and plain, complex and obscure, is to darken counsel with words. If we would let memory alone, it would be more intelligible. To create difficulties by the introduction of physical analogies into a field alien to them, and to seek their explications by a farther importation of imaginary states, is a palpable violation of the principle of original, simple induction in each department of inquiry. It is a most vicious *a priori* method, disguised under the form of analogical, experimental investigation.

§ 3. We need to distinguish memory from certain things with which it is in result allied. Association may restore facts to the mind with no direct effort of recollection, indeed, in hours of idle revery, with scarcely a distinct observation of their previous presence. This indolent flow of thought, mingling past, present, future, blending the real and the fanciful, submitting itself to the native cohesion of events and desires, is remembering, precisely as it is thinking. It is neither the one nor the other, consecutively, tensely, clearly; but is merely a succession of mental movements, holding on to each other, under a feeble impulse of pleasure, by accidental connections of thought, memory, fancy, acting the part of nimble servitors in this feast and repose of the desires. Association in large part rests upon memory, yet this easy natural movement of the mind, in certain trails of imagery, of thought, of recollection, which have been established by previous experience, serves to disguise the action of memory which underlies it. A certain sequence of impressions may be the result of many previous examples, yet directly recall no one of them, when, in the lazy flow of thought, the mind, the fancy, passes this way, using once more groups of conceptions which the entire past life has been combining. Much therefore rests upon memory in which its action is so far from being prominent, that its presence is hardly discerned. Much is thought to be original which is not so, because the memory has restored it stripped of the time, place and circumstances of its acquisition.

Habit, incorporated into the body, an education of the muscles, an immediate connection of sensible nervous impressions with action, involuntary movement voluntarily established, a permanent union by repetition of certain states with certain acts, often closely unites itself with memory. Words which have been very frequently uttered in a fixed order, can be repeated with a rapidity and slightness of attention which hide the act of memory. We are said to recite them by rote. There is here doubtless muscular training as well as recollection. The facility gained in any lengthy process by repetition, is of this double character. The memory itself, however, seems in most cases to require the lapse of a certain time, and a certain frequency of recurrence, to make its action rapid and spontaneous. We readily repeat in the morning, what was recited with difficulty the evening before, and few can acquire a piece for easy, accurate rehearsal in the period immediately preceding its delivery. The same effort, scattered through several days, is far more effectual.

The growth of the mind is also to be distinguished in its effects from the action of memory. Mental phenomena are so blended, that the predominant is by no means the exclusive element. Later movements of mind are not mere counterparts of earlier ones. A better grasp of premises, and more insight into them; conclusions more complete and decided belong to the thinking powers, as they are strengthened and enlarged by use. This fact of growth is an ultimate one. We know it, and through familiarity it seems simple to us without our understanding its grounds. It is something more than memory. We are not merely wiser, with more acquired knowledge : we are stronger, able to make an increasingly effective use of what we know. Memory and growth are very closely related. The accumulated stores of the mind are the condition of its expanded action, and this increased action gives new significance to its acquisitions. It is not easy to say how far present soundness and shrewdness of judgment are the product of increased strength, and how far of increased knowledge. Our reasoning powers, by easily evolving conclusions from premises, by renewing, rather than by recalling previous processes of thought, may closely resemble the memory in their action. We may seem to recollect an argument, to remember a proposition when in fact we are merely tracing again the steps of reasoning of which it is constructed. Historical facts also, as our information is enlarged, cluster together, and are held in the mind with less tension of memory than while they remained comparatively few and scattered. A knowledge of their dependencies enables us to reach one from another, to mingle reasoning with memory, and hold the entire group by the double ties of deduction and recollection.

Memory is the simple power of recalling the past in our intellectual experience. We have no occasion for the double division of a conservative and a reproductive power. We know nothing of any conservation save as we choose to infer it from reproduction. The first, without the last, can give no ground of inference, even, wherewith to establish its existence. Reproduction is the only process that comes under our observation. We do know that the mind recalls its previous states, but how this is done, or whence these states come, are inquiries either impossible of answer, or impertinent to the subject. Indeed, the tendency to ask them, we regard as an unphilosophical one, pushing back of simple ultimate action, and this under the analogies of the material world. Of course those who enter on the wholly theoretical ground of the manner of the mind's possessing its phenomena, may find occasion for a theoretical, conservative faculty, to do the theoretical work assigned it. Of the presence and action of such a faculty, we directly know nothing, and find its existence a matter of inference.

If then we confine our attention to actual phenomena of mind, and believe it quite as intelligible that the mind should repeat states in the interim unexistent, as to recall states that have passed by, sunk down into subconsciousness, hidden themselves, in some reservoir region of defunct ghostly impressions, we have only occasion for one, to wit: the reproductive faculty. What becomes of a thought after we cease to think it, of a feeling after we cease to feel it? From what quarter of the universe do they return to us when recollected? are inquiries whose only gleam of meaning comes to them from material fancies. A power, that should simply hold without being able to recall facts, would be an odd power, a power not powerful enough to show its own existence, an activity too indolent to give the least scintillation wherewith to indicate its whereabouts; a ridiculous and gratuitous faculty.

§ 4. The two qualities of a good memory are strength and quickness. These are by some said to be separable, to exist in various degrees in different persons. Is not this conclusion somewhat akin to the double division of the power, and does it not arise from not directing attention exclusively to the action of memory? A strong memory is a quick memory, and a quick memory is so far forth a strong, retentive one. We sometimes fully recall things which at first we could not remember, the mind struggling with obscure recollections till the facts one by one come to the light. This result is only partially the fruit of memory; it is largely reached by reasoning, by closely questioning the facts that are retained, and making them witnesses for the recovery of the remainder. When the reflective, philosophical habit of mind predominates, memory may have the appearance of retentiveness without celerity; but it is an appearance rather than a fact. The weakness of the memory is covered by the strength of the elaborative faculty, and results are at length reached which the memory vouches for, but could not alone have plucked from oblivion. The action of simple memory is aided by other powers and facts of mind. Our reminiscence fails us, and we strive to grapple the lost fact by inference. We say it must have been so and so, because these were the preceding causes, and these the accompanying circumstances. A clue thus given to recollection, the detached fact lays aside its disguise, comes forth from its hiding-place, and confesses itself found. Or the mind keeps in the region of the lost fact. It directs its attention to every resembling or adjunct object, hoping by the thread of association to restore to consciousness the furtive event. The mind thus, in the weakness of memory, avails itself of the logical cohesion of thought, betakes itself from one position to another, lingers in the neighborhood of the lurking impression, to see if from some vantage of ground, from some sudden disclosure, the memory may not again seize it. This, however, is not recollecting, it is trying to recollect, bringing other powers and attitudes of the mind to the assistance of memory. Such a memory is neither strong nor quick.

Memory presents different phases of power. Some persons recall one class of things easily, other persons another class. Some have a verbal memory, while others are very deficient in this respect, finding it perhaps much easier to retain figures than names. The idea alone is treasured by one mind, while the exact expression is borne away by another. These variations seem chiefly due to different degrees of strength, and the different degrees of interest attendant on diversity of powers. The memory that refuses to retain the precise language is relatively a feeble one, while the thought itself is lodged in the mind as much by the force of the truth, by logical connections, by the interest of the statement, as by mere recollection. The power of recalling words, especially proper names, is a chief test of the strength of memory, since these, detached from all connection, are thrown as a dead weight on the mind. Weakness of memory may sometimes exist in connection with considerable ease in the retention of figures, since a mathematical habit of mind and general interest and power in this department may concentrate attention on its data, and increase the ability to retain them. The diverse forms are chiefly to be ascribed to diverse tastes and habits, and the interest and attention which accompany them. A tendency once established toward a given pursuit, reacts strongly on all the faculties engaged in it, making them peculiarly vigorous and effective in that direction.

Though memory looks for aid to all those mental powers which unite and correlate ideas, it is by no means dependent on them. The most vigorous and characteristic efforts are almost wholly independent of association. It is when its native direct strength fails, that association comes prominently forward. If the memory could act always with entire vigor, it would pick up at random, by any arbitrary, momentary law, the facts of past experience, not collocating them by any of the accepted connections of thought. This, in cases of rare power, it freely does. A person has been found, who, after a single rehearsal, could relate thousands of words thrown promiscuously together, could repeat them backward, could rccite every fifth, sixth, eighth word, could deal with them exactly as if they lay before the eye. Herein is the perfect, the typical power of memory, and it derives no assistance from association. Even when the influence of association is most manifest, it is only the order of the conceptions which can be accounted for by it, not their actual recollection or restitution to the mind.

The power to do this work still remains simple and primitive. We need, therefore, no doctrine of latent states to account for the remote character of two facts reported by the memory; nor a belief in a great crowd of thoughts, always present to the mind, of only a small number of which we are distinctly conscious, in order to explain the celerity with which memory produces an appropriate event, or matter pertinent to our state of mind, or to the argument in hand. The conception that the memory has already partially evoked from limbo a great crowd of facts, and is moving among them as so many personæ dramatis, making ready by various laws of association to produce the next fit player on the open stage of consciousness, entirely transcends the facts, is no more intelligible, is not so simple, as the statement nakedly accepted, that memory, under the suggestion of a direct question put by a stranger, or at the intimation of the thoughts with which the mind itself is occupied, can directly reach and repeat pertinent previous experiences, and thus enable us to regain, without constantly maintaining, former phases of activity. In most of the connections of association, there is no potency whatever wherewith to restore a missing member, except as memory gives them that potency. Many of these connections are only an application to the objects recollected of those general, regulative, intuitive ideas, from which these, no more than the facts themselves, can wholly escape. If I recall every fifth word in a list of names, I do indeed locate them in space, or in time, in order to distinguish which is fifth; but this arises simply from a necessary law of mind, and by no means establishes a link, an association between these words, explaining my power to recall them, or, why I recall them. The connection has been accidentally, externally suggested to me, and by an efficient act, an act of memory, I am able to apply it, to discern the fifth word, and bring it to the lips. There is here only one of those tenuous threads of connection which must lie between all things under the general, inclusive ideas of the mind; and it is not in the least explicable of the power by which I thread upon it these detached, separately complete facts. Memory underlies association, more frequently than association memory. I may be aided in recalling an event through the connection of causation, but the relations in time and space, are made effective associations only through memory.

Strength of memory depends much on original endowment, though this faculty is as readily cultivated as any of our powers. It comes to do what we patiently insist on its doing. The acquisition of a few names in botany or in ornithology may at the outset be very difficult, yet in the end memory may retain many hundreds with comparative ease. In extemporary discourse the line of thought comes by practice to be recalled with scarcely an effort ; yet when the occasion has passed, it at once and entirely slips from the mind. To insist early and strenuously on the tasks assigned the memory is necessary to its efficiency. Yet in spite of cultivation, there will be very striking differences in this power. Some will retain lengthy discourses, after one or two readings, while others can scarcely repeat with accuracy the shortest production.

A powerful memory is a great aid to other faculties, though its strength does not seem necessarily connected with the strength of any portion of our intellectual endowments. Memory is liable to usurp the office of reflection, and to overshadow the native growth of the mind with the luxuriant products of other intellects. Indeed, there come these compensations to a memory comparatively weak, that we are thrown back more habitually on our own resources ; that the thoughts find free play, the statements of others on the same subject, and their methods of treatment not being vividly present ; and that we make all acquisitions minister to the vigor and growth of thought, to its nutritive processes rather than to those formal possessions which are held in a somewhat lifeless way in the memory. We are thus compelled to enlarge and develop our resources by consumption and redigestion rather than by retention. Yet with a truly vigorous mind, that cannot be overborne and burdened by the thoughts of others, a strong memory is a most valuable power.

§ 5. The second faculty belonging to the understanding is that of imagination. By the imagination we mean the power which the mind has of presenting to itself vividly all phenomenal forms. Whatever has assumed, or is capable of assuming, this phenomenal character, whether in the external or internal world, is an object of imagination. A landscape, a melody, a state of consciousness, a character may all be imagined, that is vividly presented to the mind under their own appropriate forms. As sight is the most full, elaborate and distinct of the senses, giving many particulars, and cutting them apart by sharp outlines; the pictures which arise under this form of perception are especially clear and impressive, and hence have given the name imagination to the faculty which paints them, and have furnished the general type of its action. Nothing however seems unapproachable to the imagination which is capable of phenomenal existence, that is, of appearing and hence reappearing in consciousness. Thought, let it be observed, enters the imagination as it enters consciousness, merely as phenomenon. The moment we begin to think, that is to judge, we renew thought as a fact, and do not restore it as an image.

Imagination is simply a general, representative power, and cannot therefore work alone without working at random. The powers which direct it, which employ it in their service, are memory, appetite, fear, desire, the æsthetic and the moral taste.

By its aid we restore vividly, that is under a living form,

the past; we intensify the present, filling it with the imagery of pleasure; we reach toward the possible, the future, in a higher conception of achievement and character. Imagination is so blended with memory in a portion of its action, that we should hardly separate the two, were it not for other fields independent of recollection on which it enters. It, like memory, is instrumental, and waits the use and guidance of other faculties.

§ 6. A theory of the imagination accepted by philosophers so diverse as Hamilton and Bain, is expressed by the latter in these words:

"*The renewed feeling occupies the very same parts, and in the same manner as the original feeling, and no other parts, nor in any other manner that can be assigned.*" (The Senses and Intellect, page 344.) "The imagination of visible objects is a process of seeing. The musician's imagination is hearing, the phantasies of the cook and gourmand tickle the palate." (Page 352.)

The statement of Hamilton is not so unqualified, and to that degree less objectionable. Both of them, however, go much beyond our knowledge. When a statement so purely theoretical as this explicit, italicized dogma of Bain's, is made the foundation of a complete explanation of the faculty involved, an explanation resting entirely upon its truth, we see that metaphysicians of the old school are not the only ones who can put foot in air, and mount to the stars. An act of imagination and memory thus becomes with the latter another—as indicated by the clause, "nor in any other manner"—unmodified perception, lingering or reawakened in the organ of sense.

The proof of their explicit assertions, is found by Bain and Hamilton in the fact, that the organs of action are evidently affected by the images present to the mind in imagination as they would be by the objects themselves, only in a less degree, and that with a loss of any of the senses the power of imagination disappears in a corresponding direction. The examples adduced under the first argument are of a kind not leading directly to the conclusion in issue; but are quite as explicable on other grounds. "A dog dreaming sets his feet a going, and sometimes barks." "Some persons of weak nerves can scarcely think without muttering—they talk to themselves." "Anger takes exactly the same course in the system, whether it be at a person present, or at some one remembered or imagined." Suppose our fancies to be pure intellectual acts, independent of the senses, and should we not expect these results? The nervous flow outward on the active, related powers would naturally be secured, though the senses were quiescent, if the intermediate, active state of mind were present. These examples furnish no proof, that the organs of perception are affected, and are the source of this tendency to movement.

Farther examples are quoted from Müller. "The mere idea of a nauseous taste can excite the sensation even to the production of vomiting." We think the more correct statement would have been, the mere idea of a nauseous taste can produce vomiting. In this form, it loses all pertinence as proof. The active results follow from the idea, the action in the brain, and not from the sensation. We do not in such cases suppose that we taste the disgusting food, but only that we conceive its taste. "The mere sight of a person about to pass a sharp instrument over glass or porcelain, is sufficient, as Darwin remarks, to excite the well-known sensation in the teeth."

Now the setting of the teeth on edge, is an effect of nervous action, and may as fitly follow that action when coming in connection with the imagination, as when occasioned by the senses. The fact that fancy affects the nervous system, and hence the muscular system, in a manner alien to that of the senses, no more proves the identity of imagination and sensation, than a fright at a ghost, proves the existence of a ghost. These examples do not reach deep enough to do the work required of them. They only show the results to be in a manner the same, whether the object be imagined or perceived, whether the initiative is from within or from without: whereas they ought to show the organs of sense so affected in what we call imagination as to be a sufficient cause of the effects which follow. Against this, mental and physical experience testify. We distinguish easily between acts of imagination and perception, both in the character and locality of the activity. We observe, also, that the action occasioned by the images of fancy in others, is slight and ineffectual when contrasted with the results of real perception.

Neither do we find that that which paralyzes the organ of sense, necessarily and immediately destroys the power to imagine objects which enter through that sense. A deaf Beethoven can compose music, a blind Milton, blind by disease of the nerve, can write an epic. That there should be a slow decay of the imagination in connection with the early loss of a sense is natural, almost inevitable. The requisite material ceases to be presented to the mind; present possessions, impressions, fade out, and the objects of the remaining senses usurp the place of the lost sense. The doctrine, as stated above, would require that blindness, when an affection of the nerve, should be followed by the instant and entire loss of the images of visible objects. The facts signally contradict the theory, and the theory fails. The blind man deals with all the imagery of the eye, walks the streets, and uses, to the full, the language of vision. Indeed, in the strict form in which it is stated, this dogma approaches an absurdity. If I imagine a visual object on the retina of the eye, "in the same manner" in which I see it, my imagination should be confined to the open eye, and be identical with objects actually seen. Otherwise it must be conceded, that in one case the agency affecting the retina acts from without, and in the other from within ; in itself a grave difference. The imagination of feelings, tastes, odors, should also be as clear and decisive as the conception of the objects of sight. Quite the reverse is true, a fact entirely intelligible, on the ground that imagination is an intellectual power, independent of the organs of sense ; as the intellectual element decidedly predominates in sight, while the lower senses are single and emotional in their character, and thus yield less matter to the fancy. We take a certain pleasure in drawing attention to the airy strides of one who so thoroughly sympathizes, as does Bain with Positive Philosophy. Having ourselves no theory to sustain, not having set to ourselves the task of preparing the way for the insensible growth of intellectual out of physical phenomena, we can accept the impression of consciousness, that an act of imagination is one of imagination, quite distinct and distinguishable from every form of perception, clear or obscure. We feel no more interest in discussing imagination under perception, than perception under imagination. In honest induction, we can take what we find. Nor is the intelligibility of our philosophy any the less in thus regarding the mind as an independent first cause of its own action, than in filling it with echoes, and mild vibrations, and the lingering, trembling, sobbing, swelling cadences of sensation, as of a harp, unable to part with the harmony that has once run along its strings. These transferred, translated analogies are the most inexplicable of all explications. Mind and matter present plain phenomena, each in its own way cognizable ; but mental movements that are semi-physical, and physical movements that rise into and are productive of thought, have no organ whatever for their apprehension. Seen with the eye, they become purely material ; known by consciousness, they become at once and completely transcendental. Two things known as unlike, each by its own faculty, are far better known than when affirmed to be alike, with no basis or common ground, or common origin for their comparison.

§ 7. Whatever is thought of the nature of imagination, its influence and office are not doubtful. It is a great intensifier of emotions. Acting under the impulse of desire, it brings vividly forward the means of gratification, and kindles the passions into a flame. The mind, occupied by furious lusts, becomes, till imagery is displaced by reality, the lodgment of a Tantalus. Unreal phantoms provoke the eye, stimulate the appetites, and, in the grasping, sink back into tormenting shadows. The mind is consumed momentarily in the red heat of its own passions, which it can neither quell by authority, nor quench by indulgence. Misery in all forms uses the imagination as a means wherewith to irritate and exasperate itself. Discouragement and fear evoke troubles beyond the reality. Not only is the ship battered by the waves about it—the vista of a yet more angry ocean is opened up, and it plunges on from shock to shock, the heart sinking in despair more in view of what is to be, than of what is. Disappointment aggravates the evils it suffers, by exaggerated pictures of the good to have been attained. One feels the heat of the desert, and thinks of cooling streams.

On the other hand, pleasure owes its hilarity, its intoxication very much to the imagination. It spreads the rosy blithesome atmosphere of the present to the very horizon, and makes the distance gorgeous with a play of light, beyond what approach will verify. The eccentricity, the boldness, the poetic inspiration, the enthusiasm of the mind find expression and play chiefly in the fancy. By it we cease to be roadsters along the regular route of existence; we dart ahead, or fall behind, or turn to the right, or to the left; we rise upward, tread paths of air, and return only at intervals to the actual, where the foot-sore senses and judgment are plodding on.

It is evidently this faculty that is yoked to the car of the mind in sleep, and wheels it, in ranging fashion, through possible and impossible scenes, through weird imagery, recollections interlacing fancies in strange and monstrous guise. The very fact that the senses find such complete repose in sleep, while the imagination is so bold, dashing and wayward, would seem to indicate that the action of the two is far from identical. The same is true in reverie, in day-dreaming. The mind closes its senses, takes out these airy steeds of fancy, throws the rein on their necks, and gives itself up to the luxury of motion along ways in which the friction of ruts, the jar of collisions, the retardation of mud are not experienced.

The imagination also, greatly aids our thoughts. The judgment and the fancy, are frequently regarded as faculties somewhat opposed to each other in their action. The ease and certainty of the first, in some of its most severe and logical processes, depends very much on the clearness and precision of second. In solid geometry, in many branches of the higher mathematics, in mechanics, in astronomy, a first condition for the ready and safe movement of the thoughts, is a clear conception, an unwavering image of the solid, or of the objects and their relations, involved in the problem. If the subject of contemplation cannot be easily evoked, and quietly held in the field of imagination, the judgment is at once at fault in establishing its connections, and gropes in the darkness, like one blindfolded. Scientific inquiry also, classification, the tracing of analogies, the observation of resemblances, are greatly aided by a vivid imagination, presenting distinctly to the mind a large circle of objects. The memory is but very partial in its action without this faculty, and the mind, in the

U OF M

weakness of representation, is compelled to take up objects singly, to the oversight of dependencies which might furnish the key of success. The imagination, then, is as essential to philosophy as to poetry. The difference lies in the two cases, not so much in the number of objects presented, as in the manner and purpose of consideration.

Most immediate and powerful is the influence of the imagination on action. The pleasures, disappointments, regrets, admonitions of the past, keep company with the mind in that living way which makes them effective counselors through this faculty; and, as the wisdom of the present is chiefly the gleanings of the past, our immediate purposes its ripened conclusions, the pictures of the fancy are as the reflectors which gather the otherwise diffused, fugitive light, and pour it all in on the working-point. But it is in the ideals of action and character, which are always distinctly present in noble minds, and hardly wholly disappear even with the lowest, that the most constant and valuable function of the imagination is seen. Through a conception of that which is more desirable in ends, more skillful in means, more wise in action, more graceful and winning in method, more pure and holy in purpose, more benignant and beautiful in presentation; imagination furnishes an embodiment of the truth nearest us, becomes an angel of light running before us, guiding our steps, scaling for us every steep of excellence, dropping back upon us words of encouragement and hope. To be destitute of an ideal, is to want the best motive of effort, is to lose direction, is to lack momentum, is to be dead, passively preyed on by the forces that have clutched us. Evil and death admit this inertia, goodness and life do not; and an imagination that looks out on fields of light, that opens vistas into the paradise of hope, becomes an essential to all high resolve and cheerful effort.

§ 8. The strength of the imagination, aside from original

gift, depends on exercise. This faculty cannot fail to be called forth ; the point of interest is chiefly the direction and degree of its employment. When made to minister to the judgment chiefly, it seems to be somewhat overshadowed by that graver power, and its action oftentimes appears to be less than it really is. Philosophy may be as impassioned as poetry. When, on the other hand, the fancy is left to construct its imagery at the beck of desire, bound down to no useful artistic end, it leaves the mind extravagant in its conceptions, wayward and fickle in its purposes. Persons characterized by the unguarded, ungoverned action of this faculty, are inefficient and visionary. The most perfect and exclusive training of the imagination, is found in the fine arts. Here it is put to its boldest, yet most restrained and governed efforts. The sense of the beautiful calls it forth, and guides it, and the combined vigor and poise of its action, yield the highest works of art, the statue, painting, cathedral. The energetic exercise of our intellectual power, especially elicit this faculty. All forms of expression seek its lustre.

There is, in this connection, a very misleading use of the word conception, to which we wish to draw attention. That an idea is conceivable or inconceivable, is constantly brought forward in philosophical discussion, as a reason for its acceptance or rejection. There are other uses of the word to which we shall revert later, but the use which connects conception with imagination, and calls that conceivable which can be imagined, and that inconceivable which does not respond to this faculty, is a frequent and deceptive one. As the imagination deals only with the phenomenal, to say that a thing is in this sense inconceivable, is only to say, that it is not of a phenomenal character, not presentable in its essence under a phenomenal form. This may very well be, and yet the idea be one that is to find acceptance. It may be offered and urged as one that is not phenomenal, but is of a direct, intuitive character. To say of such an idea, that it is inconceivable, is simply to restate what is avowed, indeed, insisted on concerning it. It is the essential character of an inner intuition, that it should not be an object, or like an object, of experience, and therefore not capable in the fancy of assuming this form. In this sense of the word, the truth of a judgment even is inconceivable. The act of judging is conceivable, the objects to which it pertains are conceivable, but the truth itself of the judgment is inconceivable. If it were so, we should require no judgment. The act of conceiving or imagining, would be sufficient, and would include in itself the entire process of reaching the truth. The judgment is superadded to the imagination for the very reason that new matter is and may be amenable to it. Not to be able to conceive a thing, is simply not to be able to imagine it, and the field of imagination is, in the outset, put down by us as a limited one. When, therefore, we are by claim and concession talking of that outside of their field, the assertion is not pertinent, disproves nothing, that the subject is inconceivable. Of course it is; if it had not been, we should not have offered it as an intuitive notion, a necessary and universal idea, but as conforming to our observation. The true stroke of overthrow directed against such notions as that of liberty, of the infinite, would be they are conceivable, and therefore of a phenomenal character, not deeper nor more necessary. To say of such ideas, that they are inconceivable, and therefore not true, is to make that a ground of inference for their non-existence, which is in fact the result of their peculiar and permanent character. The blind might as well say, colors have no existence, because they are neither tastes, odors nor sounds, nor are they conceivable as such.

§ 9. The third power of the understanding is judgment. This is, in some sense, the most fruitful and important of all our faculties. To it, the others seem especially to minister, and, in connection with it, to fulfil their purpose. By the judgment we thoughtfully handle, we rationally combine and use the material furnished in perception and intuition. It is that action of the mind, by which the phenomena of sense are taken up into the light of reason, there interpreted in their necessary relations, and presented as a system of things. The judgment is the power by which we unite subject and predicate under some appropriate regulative idea. The exact meaning and force of this language may not at once be obvious, but will be unfolded by farther discussion.

Abstraction, generalization, conception, synthesis, analysis, are all processes of thought, requiring no farther, no peculiar power, beyond those now mentioned.

They are the results, the accompaniments, the attendant methods of judgment, judiciously employed. The faculties of perception are not left to perceive all things promiscuously and indiscriminately. The judgment does not judge blindly, satisfied with the link of each copulation, no matter whether it lies apart, or is united into a chain with others. This power is set at work in the service of certain impulses, and works therefore consecutively with selection and rejection, with directed and conjoined effort towards the desired results. Separate judgments are thus thrown into trains of reasoning, and those judgments sought—which can be made the parts of such a train. Those objects are considered, and those qualities in each objects which are, in the present connection, points of interest. Agreements are sought as links of thought, to the dismission of differences. Thus we have abstraction, the separation of one quality or relation in attention from every other; conception in its limited sense, the uniting of several qualities under one generic and specific word, to the exclusion of individual distinctions; generalization, the detection of one quality, one form of action, one relation in many diverse objects; synthesis, the union of parts in a whole; analysis, the separation of a whole into its parts. These, then, as the various methods and fruits of a fertile judgment, require no farther attention in a discussion of faculties, but belong to logic, which treats of the laws of thought, of the several forms of activity which the one power, the judgment, assumes. The extent of field, the complex results which belong to this faculty, are evinced by the fact, that a distinct science is set apart to it, and the laws of thinking or judging are discussed in a separate and complete form, as logic.

§ 10. Before proceeding to speak more fully on the exact office of judgment, I wish to draw attention to one or two erroneous views becoming increasingly prevalent concerning it. Says Sir William Hamilton, "Consciousness, necessarily involves a judgment; and as every act of mind is an act of consciousness, every act of mind consequently involves a judgment. A consciousness is necessarily the consciousness of a determinate something, and we cannot be conscious of anything without virtually affirming its existence, that is judging it to be. Consciousness is thus primarily a judgment or affirmation of existence." These assertions are much too broad, especially so for the philosophy of Sir William Hamilton; that we directly know the object of perception as external. All matter in consciousness may become a subject of judgments; if it is thought about, it must become such a subject. But there is no absolute necessity that it should, to the judgment, be made an object of attention; that this faculty should play upon it; that it should more than quietly flow through the organ or sensation without producing any action of mind beyond simple perception. To say that mere, pure perception is a judgment, that "consciousness is primarily a judgment," is an affirmation wrong in form, since consciousness is the condition of mental action, and not the action itself; and erroneous in idea, since it virtually merges all mental acts or powers in one. If perception is primarily a judgment, so is feeling, so is memory, since out of each of these acts, by the same method, a judgment can easily and instantly be concocted.

Perception as perception is distinct from judgment, and may exist without it. There is nothing in the one, which necessarily involves the other, which is covered by it; though in the rational mind the one gives constant occasion to the other. Moments of perception may be moments in which objects come and go with no thoughtful attention directed to them; they are left to expire in the sensual impression they are for the instant making. In the case of the brute, is not this the habitual attitude of mind, the field of consciousness occupied with sensations with no reflection on them, or interpretation of them? Why speak at all of the power of perception, if, in later analysis, we purpose to resolve it into judgment? What may instantly spring from an act and the act itself are very different.

What also becomes of Hamilton's doctrine, that "perception affords us the knowledge of the non-ego at the point of sense," under this farther assertion, that "consciousness is primarily a judgment or affirmation of existence." Is such a judgment involved in the perception of an object? If so, we have not the doctrine of direct, external perception, but rather the view given by us of the necessary, inferential existence of the outer world. The two views would be identical, save that we do not affirm, that each single perception compels, or in that sense involves, the formal or actual inference to real, outside existence. It only gives a ground or occasion for such conclusion, which may, or may not, in a specific case, be made. If, however, we do perceive simply and purely "the non-ego at the point of sense," then that act of perception or of consciousness is not a judgment, does not include one as its primary element; or the distinction between judgment and perception disappears, and we infer, and do not in the ordinary sense perceive, the existence of the external world. If an act of perception, as such, gives us, the "non-ego," we find no occasion for an act of judgment to do the same thing.

The actuality and externality of the phenomena are already present as a fruit of perception. Does not the difficulty lie here, that Hamilton has given to perception a task impossible to it, and then, in later analysis, for a moment forgetful of previous assertions, has made it to involve a judgment, thereby easing it of its burden, though at the same time losing the distinction between these two acts of mind?

A very limited and objectionable statement of that in which judgment consists, has been much dwelt on by Herbert Spencer, and distinctly enunciated by Alexander Bain. "What is termed judgment," says he, "may consist in discrimination on the one hand, or in the sense of agreement on the other: we determine two or more things either to differ, or to agree. It is impossible to find any case of judging that does not, in the last resort, mean one or other of those two essential activities of the intellect."—*The Sense and the Intellect p.* 329. Says Hamilton: "What I have, therefore, to prove is, in the first place, that comparison is supposed in every, the simplest act of knowledge: in the second, that our factitiously simple, our factitiously complex, our abstract, and our generalized notions, are all merely so many products of comparison: in the third, that judgment, in the fourth, that reasoning, is identical with comparison."

That resemblance, or, stated on both sides, agreement and disagreement, is the sole ground of connection between subject and predicate in a judgment; that comparison is the only act of mind involved in reasoning, is a conclusion quite consonant with a philosophy that derives all the data, the conditions, the material of thought from the phenomenal world, from perception and consciousness; but is wholly at war with a philosophy that accepts those ideas which illuminate facts, and makes them intelligible subjects of thought, as of supersensual origin, furnished by the mind itself, as adjuncts of its comprehending powers. If we deal purely with phenomena, we can only compare them, discover and assert their agreements and disagreements. If, then, we do more than this in judgment, this limited statement should recoil against the system that puts it forth, whose ultimate and consistent product it undoubtedly is. That all judgments do not rest on resemblance will appear in the analysis of the action of the mind in predication—in the office which thought performs.

We believe a judgment always to involve the direct or indirect application of a regulative idea to the phenomena included under it, and this is its peculiar feature and occasion. Using an undesirable word, judgment is the rationalizing of sensations, it is completing them in thought, through those ideas which the mind furnishes in making them objects of rational contemplation. The full force and proof of this statement cannot be easily seen, previous to a detailed statement and establishment of these native forms of thought; yet a little analysis may render it intelligible. Every single perception admits of a statement, a judgment, which is the product of the first action of the thought upon it. This statement has no two perceptions to deal with, and therefore no ground for a comparison between them. It is simply an application to the phenomenon of a regulative idea. The finger is pierced. A single, sharp feeling is present. We say, it is painful; a judgment which, restated to give its substance distinct expression, becomes, pain is. Here the specific experience is taken under the general notion of existence, and we call the result a thought, a judgment that may be offered to another mind. Between the idea of existence, and that of pain, there is no resemblance, for I could have as readily affirmed it of a pleasure, of a color, an odor. This judgment, the type of a large class, a step by which any experience whatever receives a form of statement, and becomes an intellectual product, is bringing to a phenomenon one of the regulative, formative notions pertinent to it.

But I might have said—The pain is one. The pain lasts. The pain is here. In each of these cases, I should have brought forward a different idea, and affirmed its application in a given form to the sensation. Now, if these ideas are themselves previous sensations, then the doctrine that resemblance forms the substance of every judgment holds good, but not otherwise. If for instance the idea of duration, of time, be entirely distinct from the whole, and every part of the sensation that evokes it, and is ready to be furnished by the mind to each of twenty or twenty thousand sensations, that endure in order that they may singly or collectively be made intelligible in this relation of time, then this judgment—It endures—is one whose predicate and subject are totally distinct in kind, received through diverse powers, and united in another relation than that of agreement, by a third power. In this example we suppose a mastery of language, which does indeed in its acquisition imply comparison. This fact, however, does not weaken the analytic proof, since we can suppose the judgment to be present without the words to express it, or a present mastery of words independent of the training which leads to it, is essential to it, though not to the very act of judging. The belief which identifies comparison and judgment, must make the notion of time derivable from a number of sensations; something in the sensations themselves, rendered discernible and comprehensible by repetition. It would thus follow that a single sensation could not be made the occasion of a judgment, since there is in it no opportunity for comparison. It is a unit. The mind has nothing to bring to it, and it abides barren in the organ of sense alone. The feeling could then no more be said to exist, than it could to be unusually intense, since both assertions are alike relative. How Hamilton, who has given his authority to a statement so alien to the intuitive philosophy, would dispose of the fact, that the mind puts a single perception in the form of a judgment, a point he especially insists on, going so far as to say, that perception necessarily involves judgment, is not evident. In the first act of perception, there is no material present to the mind, between which to institute the comparison said to be involved in the judgment, itself involved in the incipient perception. To initiate such a movement, he would be compelled to make his comparison between the pain and the idea of number, the idea of time, the idea of space, the idea of existence, and affirm at this point a resemblance, a complete abuse of the word comparison. The objects compared are unlike in kind, belong to alien fields, and do not admit the notion of similar and dissimilar. In fact they must admit similarity if either, since the two are coupled in a conjunctive judgment. Only as we regard the time, the unity, the existence, as in some way in and a part of the sensation, and also in and a part of the other sensations present to the memory, can we make these judgments examples of comparison. That these ideas cannot be thus directly discovered as parts of sensation, as Spencer, Mill, and others affirm, will be further seen in a later discussion. In this first class, then, of judgments, which are statements concerning single perceptions, states of consciousness, it is evident that a regulative idea is united to a phenomenon, and the content of the lower organ, so to speak, taken up into the intellect. To this class also belong those judgments in which the same idea, existence, place, time, number are affirmed of several phenomena.

§ 11. Another form of judgment unites two distinct objects under a regulative idea. Of this character is the statement, This apple is like that apple. Under the notion of resemblance, two objects, the products of distinct sets of sensations, are united. Here the thought-process consists in bringing the two together under a comprehending form or rational notion. It is to this kind of judgment, that Bain and Spencer would analyze all thought, omitting even here the essential feature of the act, that a notion is found, is intuitively seen by the mind, under which the movement goes forward. A sensation is complete and independent in itself, and does not necessarily lead to any farther state of mind. This it may or may not do, according to its connections, its relations. In reflex action, so-called, an inward current, that never affects consciousness, is followed by a physical force, by an outer motor current. This inward movement may, by its results, that is as a sensation, enter consciousness, and may thence go forth in certain, involuntary, automatic action ; or, as a sensation, it may be taken into the processes of thought, be merged in the intellectual movement, and reappear, if it reappears at all, as a voluntary act, a new and independent impulse. Now the sensations occasioned by the presence of two apples, may simply and directly, as in the case of a brute, draw forth action ; or they may become the occasions of thought, and the inquiry be instituted, whether they are of one kind, or of different kinds. For the first result there is necessarily present appetitive senses ; for the second, rationalizing power, which is no other than the power to furnish an idea, in this case, that of resemblance, under which an inquiry can be instituted and a judgment formed. It is the exact office of the judgment to apply discriminatingly in reference to an end, these notions to the objects before the mind. The sensations, as sensations, are complete. They are not halves; they are not uneasy, nettlesome, looking out for mates; nor adhesive, linked, dragging something after them; nor are they dove-tailed into thoughts, making their succession inevitable. They might lie forever perfectly quiet, nothing coming of them, were it not for the appetites below them, into which they sink by physical connections; for the eye of reason above them, into whose realm of thought they rise, by the dropping down upon them of judgments, through tentative inquiries prompted by its own perception of invisible, unheard, unfelt relations. This working up of sensations, this vitalizing of them in processes of thought, needs solution as much as the activity of chemical elements previously dormant, when heat is applied.

We know an object as red, as sour, as fragrant, through our respective senses of sight, taste, and smell. A judgment has nothing to do with this knowledge. The first object received in any sense imparts to it, calls forth in it, a form of knowing, in itself ultimate and inexplicable. When we meet with a second object of a like kind, we have no new sensational knowledge; yet we have an occasion of a judgment, which we did not have, as regarded the quality, the flavor, or odor, or color in the first case. We say of the two, They are the same. Now, how happens it that the second sensation has in it more than the first, to wit, this occasion of a judgment?

As sensations they are alike; one is no more stimulating than the other, should yield no more than the other.

The solution lies in the fact, that the mind is able to furish an idea, that of agreement and disagreement, infusing rational order and relations into a plurality of objects, and brings it forward for immediate application, on this, the first occasion. Here the judgment finds its function and office to run between phenomena, and marshals them under notions. Of phenomena alone it could make nothing. It must have its men, and its plan of rank and regiment, and then it can construct an army.

Of the same character are the judgments, This is higher than that, This event more recent than that. In each case, objects of perception are thrown into relation with each other, by means of a regulative idea. Many, accepting the intuitive nature of the idea of space, would easily recognize the character of the judgment, This house is nearer than that mountain, who would yet fail to see the transcendental element in the kindred statement, This stone is like that rock. Evidently the mind furnishes the ground of the judgment,—the idea of the relation, as much in the one case as in the other. The present division of judgments includes all acts of classification, and is a most numerous one.

The statement, This action is right, may sometimes be one of classification, assigning the act by its form to a kind or class previously recognized as right. More frequently, however, it is a judgment of the first class, in which a single act is stated and interpreted under an intuitive notion The notion right, is not perceived, organically seen in the action; but brought to it, put as a form upon it, discerned as a spiritual factor in it. If it had been redness that had belonged to the object, the mind must needs have waited for a second, third, fourth instance before it would have said, This is red : and then the assertion would have been one simply of classification. The perception gives the quality, and the judgment remains quiescent till, by repetition, it is called to the act of classification. In the case of the right action, however, the action enters through the senses without this quality, simply and nakedly as an action, and the reason bringing forward a farther idea for its explanation as the act of an intelligent and free being, the judgment at once finds play in applying it, and says, It is a right action. This it might do should the mind never know another, if this act in its motives and consequences remained plainly before it. In the first class of judgments, one limb of the predication rests in the phenomenal, the other passes over into the purely intellectual, the transcendental. In the second class, both abutments of the arch press back on phenomena, but the spring and crown of it rests in the air; the connection strikes into and returns from the region above.

There is a third class of judgments of which the expression, The heat melts the wax, is a type. Here, under the notion of causation, we grapple by a judgment that which physically exists, yet never directly enters the phenomenal world. The mind walks as one who travels on a morass, the points of support are hidden a little below the surface. The foot, under the quick suggestion of the eye, and the inference of reasoning, dashes at the more stable ground, which it never sees, and is yet able to find. The mind could not move, did it not believe in causes, yet it never sees a cause, or knows one save through the effects constantly attributed to them, safely expected from them. It is not sufficient that the mind should weave the visible into a firm fabric of order by invisible connections it alone can grasp; it is made to stand, and must forever stand, and all it beholds stand with it, on invisible, intangible supports of power, whose existence it can verify by no sense, and must leave with its own assured conviction. Deny these supports and it must yet seek for them, and believe in them, and talk about them every moment of its life. These judgments by which we spread the phenomenal over the actual, by which we search out the streams of force, and feel the under-flow of divine power, are among the most constant and radical of any we ever make. It is evident, however, that they do not rest in resemblance merely, since the cause is never in any way phenomenally known, save through its effects, and therefore furnishes no hold for a comparison. Of course we mean the actual cause, and not the phenomenal cause, that is the effect just previous to the effect under consideration. We mean the very heat, and not the taper, which is itself in its visible form an effect, and not a cause. In the third form of judgment we unite the sensible and the transient, to the insensible and permanent, through a pure intuitive movement of mind. What was understood to be, also understood in relation to other things that are, is now referred to hidden sources or causes. It is then the general office of judgment to unite the phenomenal and the intuitive, the perceptive and the purely intuitional elements of mind in the rational apprehension and use of the former. Reasoning is the interlock of these judgments, a chain of these conclusions by which remote points are united, and discloses therefore no new power.

§ 12. Before passing from the judgment, we wish to mark a second use of the word conceive, leading to further obscurity. By a statement, that an idea, for instance that of infinity, is inconceivable, is sometimes meant, that the judgment cannot grapple it, that it cannot be wrapt about, log-chained with logical relations, worked up as material in the processes of thought. Very well; the judgment deals with the phenomenal under ideas, and therefore a notion not phenomenal, and not calling for the interpretation of a farther idea, is not material for the judgment. The judgment ought not to be able to handle it; if it were able, a phenomenal element would therein appear, destructive of its pure emotional character. The query still remains, however, whether such an idea may not be validly presented to the intuitive power set apart for its apprehension, given to perform this service? The inconceivability of a thing may be proof of its nature, though not of its reality or want of reality.

We are now able to see something of the relation of the understanding to the entire mental furniture, and also of the three powers which compose it to each other. The understanding plays between the intuitive parts of our nature, the physical perceptions on the one hand, and the spiritual intuitions on the other. With no absolute, final comprehension of either, it interlocks them, and comes to a definite knowlege of their relations. This knowledge of connections seems to us more satisfactory than that of qualities in perception, or of ideas in intuition. We try to make a color, an odor, the notion of existence, an object of reflection, and can do little or nothing with it. As simple and primitive, it eludes those relations which we are so diligent in establishing between objects, and the mind, perplexed by its inability to fasten and weave the web of thought, is ready to feel that there is here no real knowledge ; forgetful that an organ of sense gives a new and final form of knowing. All knowledge is good and adequate, if we know enough to recognize and accept it. The understanding furnishes us a knowledge of relations.

The judgment, like a busy shuttle, flies between the loose, parallel, independent lines of phenomenal being, bears with it the interlying thread of intuition, and shortly weaves all into a firm, coherent fabric, a system of things. The steadfastness and permanence of the work are secured by memory, while its brilliancy, the vividness of its coloring, arise from imaginatton. We thus seem to see some reason why these faculties, and no others, are called for. The judgment, under the eye of reason, knits together facts into relations, which makes them significant and intelligible, which shows them to be a system of things, the memory stands by to proffer the facts, and store the fabric ; while the imagination dips again in living colors, these shadow products of the mind, as the sun saturates the cloud with its own hues.

CHAPTER IV.

The Reason.

§ 1. We have now reached an action of mind, a faculty, whose existence is strenuously denied. Most able and thorough thinkers, patient inquirers within the field of philosophy itself, with a host of scientific investigators, who bring with them predilections and reasonings suited to other departments, regard this furniture of intuitive ideas as wholly fabulous, as an unnecessary assumption in the explanation of phenomena entirely intelligible without it. Yet there is in philosophy no point of more importance, of more wide-reaching influence than this ; and that, too, not merely in the department itself, but in its social and moral and religious bearings. It is vain to strive to disconnect social and religious issues from mental science. The institutions of society, and the commands of God, have man for their subject, and neither their defects nor their excellences can be understood without a knowledge of his nature. Indeed, the very character of those notions on which duty turns—of right and of liberty—are here brought under discussion ; and also the validity of those conceptions and that reasoning on which the existence and government of God repose in our thoughts. The past attachments of our nature, its present powers and future hopes, are all involved in these investigations of philosophy, and more especially in that branch of them which settles the original endowments of mind, and the degree of its dependence on the external world. Indeed what is meant by the external and internal worlds, and whether either or both of them can furnish a valid proof of their being, are inquiries that are now to find settlement, or to be left unsolved doubts, unexplained fears, ultimate mysteries, drifting athwart the mind, restricting its spiritual vision, and displacing its cheerful surface-life with the shadows of deep, despairing clouds.

Yet these discussions are as subtile and perplexing as they are important; and moreover are looked on by patient plodders amid facts—most influential and servicable men —as hopeless and futile. They regard these labors as the mere money-maker would regard another expedition to the North Pole. The whole region, to the purely scientific mind, seems one of chimeras, not dire only because increasing wisdom enables us to laugh at them. Ghosts are always unproductive, and to men, ridiculous. The only touch of kind sentiment that the student of natural science has on this subject, is the regret that so many are still found to waste a hope or a fear on such airy existences; are yet unwilling to confront daylight with open eyes, instead of owling in invisible regions for invisible things. In these fields of difficult and abstruse inquiry, we shall need to work our way slowly and patiently, confronting our adversaries fairly, ourselves convinced of the importance of the truths here hidden; sanguine as to the power of the mind to push and answer the questions most intimate to its own destiny, and repelling the scorn of ignorance with the silence of settled conviction, knowing that if ours or another's keel shall ever touch the distant shores of truth, shall ever add to the hemisphere of matter that of mind, the question, Who are fools? will be easily settled.

The ideas in dispute have received various designations. They have been termed innate ideas, regulative ideas, intuitive ideas, *a priori* ideas, and also have been regarded as forms of thought, entirely independent of the objects or matter of thought. Some of these are very faulty methods of expression, especially if adhered to as complete in themselves to the exclusion of other methods. Indeed, no one word or expression is perfectly applicable to any one of these ideas, and the relation of the mind to it; much less is such a word sufficient to characterize all of them, varying as they do, intrinsically, and in their connections with the phenomena explained by them. One seems to inhere like a quality as right in action; another to be a condition, as space to the objects in it; another to be the manner in which the mind regards the things to which it applies, as number in connection with the objects numbered. No single expression, therefore, can be analyzed, no particular words tortured to disclose more exactly what is meant by an intuitive idea. In each case the relation itself must be contemplated, and the word be crimped to the fact, rather than the fact be learned by the word.

We do not understand by this doctrine of regulative ideas, that the mind finds in itself a notion as a realized mental product, and applies this to the product before it; nor that there is in thought certain forms, directions of movement, from which it cannot depart, and under which it works up the material brought to it. We understand rather that in the facts, on the occasion of the facts, the mind, not the senses, discerns relations by which it is able to explain them, to think concerning them, and this by means of certain rational elements which it brings with it, or finds evoked under its own direct apprehension by the conditions of the problem before it. Nor do we affirm that these notions come necessarily and at once to every mind on every occasion intrinsically fitted for them; but that they each and all do find, sooner or later, an occasion on which they do arise, and that there is in them a furnishing by the mind itself of other and higher material of thought than the senses alone can supply. In other words, there is in the intellectual handling of the facts of the world revealed in perception and consciousness, a new power of mind, which we term the reason, furnishing rational ideas and grounds of procedure, and enabling the judgment to operate on the otherwise limited, stubborn, irreducible sensations present. The existence and office of a portion of these ideas all philosophers admit ; they are at variance only as to their source and nature—a variance which leads to the denial of the remaining and most essential ones. The notions of space and of time, traced to an empirical source, prepares the way for a denial of right and liberty in their transcendent character.

We shall now proceed to take up these ideas one by one. both to establish the whole class and each member of it singly. In doing this, we shall not hesitate to repeat the argument in each case, so far as it presents any new features. The general doctrine of intuitive ideas is maintained if any one of them holds its ground, though for its successful and thorough application, the exact number and nature of these notions must be known.

§ 2. The first of them is that of existence. This has drawn forth less discussion than some others, and does not therefore afford the best ground on which to meet the opposing views. The affirmation is, that in the presence of sensations, perceptions, the mind comes at some moment to say, These are ; or involving another idea, that of causation, to say, The object occasioning them is. When this act of mind does take place, there is proof in it of a double activity aside from that of the judgment—an activity furnishing the perception, and a second activity supplying the predicate. Can the judgment be made without both of these conditional activities? Can the three be resolved into two, or one? We answer, no. The judgment can do nothing with a naked sensation. It is to this higher faculty, lumber without tools. The sensation can yield nothing but mere feeling. Feeling, as feeling, is complete in itself, and may as well repose in the organic structure of an oyster, as in that of man. The judgment alone can add nothing to that which it is to handle ; for if it does, you therein assign it a double office, that of reason and judgment, that of calling forth the predicate, and of coupling it with the antecedent.

A sensation and the notion of existence involved therein, or better, evoked thereby, are very different. I see no reason why the one may not be experienced indefinitely without, in and by itself, giving rise to the other. Indeed we, with our rational powers even, are constantly enjoying or suffering sensations without affirming, or thinking of, their existence. This notion is present only as the mind from time to time is brought directly to contemplate them. There is no latent judgment of their existence in clearly experienced, but not definitely thought of, sensations, in any other sense, than that the mind may, at any moment, have its attention directed to them, call them before itself for contemplation, and then be led to affirm their existence, under this mode of regarding them. A cloud is above the earth, and the mind may so decide at any instant : but there is no latent decision to that effect in the simple act of seeing a cloud, only the possibility of one.

As the opposite view has not here received that complete and exhaustive statement which we shall find of it, under space and time, we cannot, to the best advantage, controvert it. We merely remark, that it seems to confound the sensation with the idea. This it does partly perhaps through the ambiguity of the word consciousness. It is not an unusual or very harsh form of expression to say, I am conscious that the odor exists, while the affirmation, I smell that it exists, is obviously inadmissible. Yet for philosophical purposes the last expression has all the breadth that can be allowed the first. Consciousness only reports the sensation, is as broad as the sensation, and this is fully expressed in the verb, *smell*. We are not then conscious of the being of an odor, unless we smell that being. The words *conscious*, *consciousness*, have so enlarged their meaning as to be regarded as the ground of that which is known, when that knowledge springs from a judgment, and is thus referable to an indirect not a direct, a reflective and not an intuitive faculty. We are conscious of the existence of a sensation in no other sense than that we are conscious of the sensation, and also of the intuition and judgment by which existence is referred to it. These three acts are separate sources of separate elements in the joint product, This odor is. Consciousness is nothing in itself, nothing additional, but is the common and pervasive condition of each of these acts as of every act of mind. No knowledge can be referred to consciousness which is not farther, more explicitly, referable to some given, specific power of mind, and the act of mind yielding the notion of existence is the one here insisted on, the reason.

Says Bain, "The sum total of all the occasions for putting forth active energy, or for conceiving this possible to be put forth, is our external world." (*The Senses and the Intellect, page* 380.) In this and the accompanying passages, the sensations of resistance, rather than the suggestions and interpretations of those sensations, are kept uppermost, and thus the action of the reason concealed under that of the senses and the judgment. "The occasions" are rather occasions to the mind, and thus become the conditions of a knowledge not found in the simple energies of sensations which compose them.

The judgment of existence does find its chief significance in connection with the experience and exercise of force, since here, united with that of causation, it leads to the telling affirmation of the noumenon, the one permanent, underlying the phenomenal, external, material world ; and also of the spirit, the abiding source of changed and changing mental states. To affirm phenomenal existence seems a merely formal act, beside this doubly pregnant one by which we go deeper than consciousness inward, farther than consciousness outward, and fill supersensual regions with supersensual forms of being. Phenomena are known directly, and thus directly yielded in consciousness; but now the conditions of a judgment are found which penetrates beyond appearances, and affirms permanent and unphenomenal existence, a fact incapable of experimental verification, and thus of appearing directly in consciousness. We are conscious of judgments, not of their truth.

We refer then this idea of existence to an independent faculty, the reason; because it is not in the sensation as a sensation, nor to be secured by a passive flow from sensation to sensation, each equally destitute of it; but is found first and fully in the incipient action of mind, when it begins to deal with and handle its hitherto unobserved experiences.

§ 3. The second regulative idea is that of number. This, like that of existence, is so simple and direct, so constantly merged in the very perception to which it is attached, as to have called forth little discussion, and made but slight claims for explanation on sensualistic schools of philosophy. Language also favors this oversight. I see one apple, I hear several sounds, I feel three distinct points, are examples of familiar expressions. We cover directly by verbs of sensation, their objects, and the numerical relations of those objects. Yet it is evident, that we do not see an object to be one. The numerical notion is brought to the mass of colors before us as one of the ways in which the mind may regard it. Indeed, the same object differently contemplated, yields a great variety of numerical relations, the sensations remaining exactly the same. It may present several colors, and while, therefore, we call it one in cohesive connection, we may separate it into a multiplicity of parts by diversity of shades, or by outstanding members, or by relative position. An object of regular outline and uniform color may still yield a plurality of parts through the unit of measurement we apply to its lines, angles, surfaces. The mind plays upon it with standards of its own, divides it with various linear and solid measurements, finds with each a diverse numerical expression, and terms it now one, now many, as suits the purposes of thought. All this is not a simple action of the senses ; nor any more is it when the incipient step of the process is taken by roughly calling the whole one thing. The color is seen, the hardness is felt. the odor is smelt, and the sources of each are regarded as one object, or more than one, as the mind chances to contemplate it, bringing to it one or another of various combining ideas. There is no object of sense which is not in some relation one, as a tree, a grove, a forest, a world, a universe ; and none which may not be divided and thus yield plurality. Now this action of the judgment and attention must all go on under the notion of number, and, till this is furnished, all objects must remain undistinguished either as single or manifold. Objects of sense may reach the mind without drawing from it a numerical estimate. One may gather berries without regarding the number taken or left, though both be clearly seen. Distinction in the senses is not distinction in the intellect, and does not necessitate it ; any more than distinction in existence is distinction in thought. A dozen calls may bring a dog, though he has taken no note of them as a dozen. Articulate sounds may convey the designed thought to the mind, a thought dependent on the exact number of elements, without attention directed to them as twenty, less or more.

This separable character of number from the objects perceived, is seen in the fact, that two impressions on the senses, as on the eyes of men, or a thousand, as on the eye of an insect—become one object in the intellect ; and still more strongly in the fact, that numbers are treated independently in arithmetic and algebra, are accumulated in amounts entirely beyond experience, and are divided and compounded by processes not founded on observation, or proved by it; but which belong to the nècessary character of numerical conceptions. Our powerful algebraic solvents are general formulæ, are wrought out wholly independently of things, and are brought to explain outside facts otherwise numerically unintelligible. Thus most evident is it, that in the more abtruse application of numbers, as to curves and to complex motion, phenomena receive their solution from numerical conceptions, and do not, through the senses, yield it. Moreover, these estimates are reached by an arbitrary supposition of an equality of units never found in experience. One pound is regarded as absolutely equivalent to every other pound of the same denomination; one foot, one mile, to the like measurements elsewhere. To fix on standard units, in which the approximation to equality is sufficiently close to enable us safely to neglect errors, is a large share of the difficulty in mixed mathematics, and only when we deal with pure conceptions, as with that of space in geometry, do our numerical processes show their full power, stretching an unimpeded wing in realms as airy as themselves. Existence and number are among the most general of our notions, finding inherent, and to a rational mind, necessary, application everywhere.

§ 4. A third intuitive idea is that of space. This has drawn much attention and been one of the centres of discussion between the different schools of philosophy. Space, as immaterial and exterior to the object of perception, cannot be directly referred to the senses, or lost sight of in that which is furnished by them. It is not, like existence, so the very thing itself, or like number, the inseparable form of it; but stands an antecedent and independent condition of the objects it contains. The derivation of this idea has therefore been assiduously labored over by philosophers who accept no intuitive faculties beyond those of perception, Herbert Spencer has given this subject a statement considered highly satisfactory and conclusive by those who share his general view. We will take from his *Principles of Psychology* sufficient fairly to present his conclusions. Those who wish the entire argument by which they are supported we refer to the above work. It is impossible for us to do more than present its initial features.

"Imagine that an immense number of fingers could be packed side by side, so that their ends made a flat surface; and that each of them had a separate nervous connection with the same sensorium. If anything were laid upon the flat surface formed by those finger-ends, an impression of touch could be given to a certain number of them—a number great in proportion to the size of the thing. And if two things successively laid upon them, differed not only in size but in shape, there would be a difference not only in the *number* of the finger-ends affected, but also in the kind of *combination*. But now, what would be the interpretation of any impression thus produced, while, as yet, no experiences had been accumulated? Would there be any idea of extension? I think not. To simplify the question, let the first object laid on these finger-ends, be a straight stick; and let us name the two finger-ends on which its extremes lie, A and Z. If now it be said that the length of the stick will be perceived, it is implied that the distance between A and Z is already known, or, in other words, that there is a pre-existent idea of a special extension, which is absurd. If it be said that the extension is implied by the simultaneous excitation of B, C, D, E, F, and all the fingers between A and Z, the difficulty is not escaped; for no idea can arise from the simultaneous excitement of these, unless there is a knowledge of their relative positions; which is itself a knowledge of extension. By what process then can the length of the stick become known? It can become known only after the accumulation of certain experiences, by which the series and fingers between A and Z becomes known. If the whole mass of fingers admits of being moved bodily, as the retina does; and if by virtue of its movements, something now touched by finger A is next touched by finger B, next by C, and so on; and if these experiences are so multiplied by motions in all directions, that between the touching by finger A and by any other finger, the number of intermediate touches that will be felt is known; then the distance between A and Z can be known —known, that is, as a series of states of consciousness produced by the successive touching of the intermediate fingers—a series of states comparable with any other such series, and capable of being estimated as greater or less. And when by numberless repetitions the relation between any one finger and each of the others is established, and can be represented to the mind as a series of a given length, then we may understand how a stick laid upon the surface, so as to touch all the fingers from A to Z inclusive, will be taken as equivalent to the series A to Z—how the *simultaneous* excitation of the entire range of fingers, will come to stand for its *serial* excitation—how thus, objects laid upon the surface will come to be distinguished from each other by the relative length of the series they cover, or when broad as well as long, by the groups of series which they cover—and how by habit these simultaneous excitations, from being at first known indirectly by translation into the serial ones, will come to be known directly, and the serial ones will be forgotten, just as in childhood the the words of a new language, at first understood by means of their equivalents in the mother tongue, are presently understood by themselves; and if used to the exclusion of the mother tongue, lead to the ultimate loss of it. The greatly magnified apparatus here described, being reduced to its original shape—the surface of the finger-ends being diminished to the size of the retina, the things laid upon that surface being understood as the image cast upon the retina, and its movements in contact with these things, as the movements of the retina relatively to the images—some conception will be formed of one part of the process by which our ideas of visual extension are gained."—*Pages* 221-2-3.

The difference between the view we wish to enforce, and that presented in this passage, lies here : Do we interpret the experience here detailed by a notion of space, of extension—for the one involves the other—*at some instant* evoked by it, or do we, *at its conclusion*, as *its result*, finally eliminate such a notion? This may seem a slight difference, yet it is a fundamental one. We give a further quotation in completion of the above. "How, through experiences of occupied extension or body, can we ever gain the notion of unoccupied extension or space? How from the perception of a relation between resistant positions, do we progress to a perception of a relation between non-resistant positions? If all the space attributes of body are resolvable into relations of position between subject and object, disclosed in the act of touch—if originally, relative position is only thus knowable—if therefore position is, to the nascent intelligence, incognizable except as the position of something that produces an impression on the organism, how is it possible for the idea of position ever to be dissociated from that of body? How can the germinal notion of empty extension ever be gained?

This problem, though apparently difficult of solution, is really a very easy one. If, after some particular motion of a limb, there invariably came a sensation of softness, after some other one of roughness, after some other one of hardness—or if, after those movements of the eye needed for some special act of vision, there always came a sensation of redness, after some other a sensation of blueness; and so on—it is manifest that, in conformity with the known laws of association, there would be established a constant relation between such notions and such sensations. It positions were conceived at all, they would be conceived as invariably occupied by things producing special impressions; and it would be impossible to disassociate the positions from the things. But as, in our experience, we find that a certain movement of the hand which once brought the finger in contact with something hot, now brings it in contact with something sharp, and now with nothing at all; and that a certain movement of the eye, which once was followed by the sight of a black object, is now followed by the sight of a white objeet, and now by the sight of no object; it results that the idea of the particular position accompanying each one of these movements, is, by accumulated experiences, dissociated from objects and impressions, and comes to be conceived by itself; it results that as here are endless such movements, there come to be endless such positions conceived as existing apart from body, and it results that, as in the first, and in every subsequent act of perception, each position is known as co-existent with the subject, there arises a consciousness of endless such co-existent positions; that is, of space."—*Pages* 233-4.

We hold that these experiences must call forth at some point the idea of space, as the light under which comprehension must commence and proceed, and that they cannot close with a gleam of generalization waiting farther experience to grow into knowledge. Till this idea is evoked every movement will, in its spacial relations, be utterly unintelligible, provoking indeed no attention; after it is evoked, these movements will but make it the more definite and precise in its application. Take the illustration offered by Spencer. Let a stick rest on imaginary finger-ends, by its two extremities, designated A and Z. Can that fact alone call forth the idea of space? We think it may, provided it be known as a fact, and two mutually excluding positions are recognized in sensation. It would evidently be thus interpreted at once by the adult mind, and a farther movement of the fingers would only be sought after as giving confirmation to the fact of two mutually exclusive sensations, and as furnishing a distinct estimate of the distance between the two points. The objection expressed by Spencer, in the words, "If now it be said that the length of the stick will be perceived, it is implied that the distance between A and Z is already known; or in other words, that there is a pre-existent idea of special extension which is absurd," has no particular force; for it only holds against the assertion, that the space A Z is not merely recognized as a space, but accurately known in its dimensions. This knowledge, our latest adult experience fails to give us, and certainly a general notion of some space must go before this, its careful estimate. The precisc and exact do not precede in knowledge the vague and general. If the points A and Z are recognized as distinct, according to the comparison on distinct finger-ends, or in the sense of sight, which these multiplied points of touch are intended to illustrate, at different parts of the retina—then this simple experience of sensations, at diverse positions excluding each other, can only find apprehension, can only be an initial step of knowledge, by and through the comprehending idea of space. Only under this fact of space, can the phenomena occur; only by it can they be understood for what they are, and there are no possible steps toward their solution, till this first idea is present, as an apprehension of the conditions of the problem. If the sensations are not known as in position, and in distinct position, then there is not yet the germ of suggestion, the rudiments of inquiry; if they are so known, there is already present the initiatory knowledge of space.

Let us suppose, with Spencer, this notion to be wanting, that we have sensations at A and Z, and at such other intervening points as we choose, and yet have not any suggestion therein of position or extension. The mind remains perfectly quiet.

The sensations as sensations merely lie in consciousness, but in their space-relations no attention is directed to them, or evoked by them. Exactly the same mental state might remain when the sensations should change by becoming serial, by alternating backward and forward on successive finger-points, by furnishing in any way farther data of that exact knowledge which the first data had done nothing to call forth. The images in a mirror may lie still, or move among themselves, and in neither case is any apprehension, comprehension of them made necessary to the mirror. No more would there be if the mirror were simply and permanently conscious of them as mere sensations. Suppose, however, the attention of the mind is awakened and directed to this movement. How alone can it *begin* to understand and explain the facts before it, except by applying the notion of space, now so strongly plucked at among its comprehensive solvents? If "numberless repetitions," are requisite, that is, if an entire series of movements can be closed and the mind still remain without the idea—remain quiescent, dead, mirror-like, holding distinct sensations in distinct spacial relations without knowing them as distinct, reaching no judgment—then a second, a third, a fiftieth repetition, as mere repetition, having the light of no new idea cast upon it, may leave the mind, nay, must, unless at some point it be awakened to a new method, as quiescent and dark as at the outset.

The only ground on which any other conclusion is possible is, that space is not an idea, but literally a series of sensations; or at least a sensational fact or quality generalized from a series of experiences, as sweetness is a quality separated clearly by repetition from other qualities, red, a color distinguished by repeated observation from other colors. In these cases the reiterated sensation enables us to distinguish and abstract its peculiar quality.

Absurd and impossible as this view of space, that it is a quality of sensation, seems to us to be, we believe that it lurks in the arguments and statements of the sensational school. Thus, in the passage given above, it is "the serial excitations," which are identified with the notion of space, and are made by association to underlie and explain "the simultaneous excitations." In fact, however, the one set of phenomena no more requires the explanation of the idea than the other, no more contains it than the other. It is merely because there is in the first a movement, a variation of the sensations, that they give, or rather seem to give, a foothold to explanation not found in the second. Yet this change must be observed in the very quality of the sensations and not in the relation of the sensations, or no ground of exposition is afforded by Spencer. Relations are intellectually seen, the qualities alone are a matter of perception. Elsewhere Spencer speaks of the "sense of *ability to move*," "the sense of *freedom for motions*," as a constituent in our idea of space. Observe that this ability, freedom, is not spoken of as something explained *under* the idea, but as a *constituent* of the idea.

Bain says yet more explicitly: "Extension or space as a quality has *no other* origin and no other meaning than the association of these different sensitive and motor effects," Mark the words *quality* and *no other meaning*. Again, "the mental conception that we have of empty space is scope for movement, the possibility or potentiality of movement; and this conception we derive from our experience of movements."—*The Senses and the Intellect, p.* 378. How is it as to the interstellar, or the intermolecular spaces? What has experience to say concerning these? Do we in them derive our belief of space from the changed sensations of motion? Bain proceeds still farther. "By such steps as I have endeavored to describe, we derive our notion of extended things, of extension in the concrete. And from this we can obtain an abstract notion of the extended in the same manner as we gain any other abstract notion, as color, heat or justice." This can only be true if our knowledge of space, like our knowledge of heat and color, is a sensation; and this belief, not explicitly stated, underlies logically the sensualistic philosophy. The doctrine that space is a sensation or "quality" of sensations, or a series or concatenation of sensations, or in any way an immediate product of sensation, we are willing to leave without argument to the refutation of simple statement. It would thus sink wholly from the intellectual field, and, if allowed to drag other kindred ideas with it, would leave neither occasion nor opportunity for any other faculty than that of perception. Sensations lie together, and need no conjunction by the judgment; and as for any notions wherewith the mind is to comprehend and classify them, there are none; those thought to be such, are themselves sensations. Feel your way, feel on and feel ever, would be the comprehensive direction to a being—we can scarcely say mind, for the mind is now resolved into one form of activity—so formed. Feel space, feel time, feel number, and look to your finger-ends for liberty and right or eternally lose them.

Let us carefully guard against one point of misapprehension. We say nothing as to any definite time in the progress of the infant in which the idea of space will arise. Sensations as sensations may come and go. We know not how long, without evoking the idea; but when it does come, it will come at once from within; not in an abstract, discriminated, but in a concrete, obscure form, and prepare the way for a new series of intellectual actions. All precise estimates and measurements are, of course, the sole fruit of experience, and give the infant mind abundant occupation under this regulative idea.

One may study Geometry with little or no abstract consideration of space as space, yet the idea is tacitly present everywhere. The child may come to a knowledge of the position and dimension of its own members, with no abstract direction of the mind to the notion of space as such, though that idea quickly informs the whole process.

In the second of the longer quotations above given from Spencer, we have the notion of space, empty space, derived from a vacant organ of sense. Direct the mind steadily to this point. An organ, as the finger-end, or the eye, with no content of sensation in it, a simple blank, is one thing; and this fact accounted for and explained to the mind by the idea of empty space is quite another. If the first, generalized in any way he pleases, is Spencer's idea of space, then that idea consists in the mere absence of sensation, and should exist in the highest degree in connection with paralyzed organs. A recognition of blindness, or even deafness, should be one of space. If, however, the fact of a vacant organ becomes significant only in connection with a process of mind, we wish to know under what guiding clue that process proceeds. What is brought to the explanation of the fact? It seems to us that but one answer can be given—space.

Spencer, with the marked approval of Bain, makes, in another phase of the argument, the notion of space dependent on co-existence, and co-existence the fruit of experience.

"Not only is it that the idea of space involves the idea of co-existence, but it is that the idea of co-existence, involves the idea of space. Fundamentally space and co-existence are two sides of the same cognition."

"On the one hand space cannot be thought of without co-existent positions being thought of; on the other hand co-existence cannot be thought of, without at least two points in space being thought of. A relation of co-existence implies two somethings that co-exist. Two somethings cannot occupy absolutely the same point in space. And hence co-existence implies space. Space can be known only as presenting relations of co-existence; relations of co-existence can be known only as presented in space."

"If now it should turn out under an ultimate analysis—that a relation of co-existence is not directly cognizable, but is cognizable only by a duplex act of thought—only by a comparison of experiences; the question between the transcendentalists, and their opponents, will be set finally at rest. When after it has been shown as above, that our cognition of space in its totality is explicable upon the experience hypothesis, and that all the peculiarities of the cognition correspond to that hypothesis, it comes to be shown that the ultimate elements into which that cognition is decomposable—the relation of co-existence—can itself be gained only by experience—the utter untenableness of the Kantian doctrine will become manifest."—*Pages* 243-4.

Herein our author hardly agrees with himself, having insisted that the co-existent points, A, B, Z, cannot give the idea of extension, though it now turns out that a knowledge of their co-existence would have been essentially a knowledge of space. We believe that the notion of any simple position involves that of space, is explained under it, and therefore that a single sensation of touch, complex indeed, yet regarded as simple, might, abstractly considered, call forth the idea. This we do not care to dwell on, as it is doubtless in connection with many simultaneous and serial phenomena, presented in several senses, that the notion actually does arise. We cannot accept the statement that the ultimate element into which the cognition, space, is decomposable, is co-existence. On the other hand, the notion of external, material co-existence is subsequent in the order of thought to that of space. Nor are the two by any means the same. I may have the idea of empty space. I may put one object in it, or two or three objects in it, but the idea of space has preceded each and all before they became to me external objects, or the images of such objects. Indeed, simple co-existence, as of an act of memory and a thought, of a thought and a feeling, does not bring or involve the idea of space; single existence, that is contemplated by the mind, localized in an organ of sense, does, or at least may bring this idea, since this is pertinent to its explanation. The contrast of the inner and the outer, of the ego and non-ego, may, or may not go forward; but the *first* step in such a contrast, the initial stroke of light in handling a local sensation, is the localizing idea of space. How often, and how long I may have one, two, three sensations, and not contemplate, understand, expound them, is simply the question, How long do the senses ante-date in development the other intellectual powers? When these come, they come thus, not otherwise. The fact of co-existence is a mere blind data of sensations, until contemplated under the idea of space. The *actual* co-existence of two *things* is not involved in space, but only its possibility. The extension of space, the possibility of such a co-existence, is the notion of space, is in and of the very idea. Actual co-existence alone rests on sensation, the possibility of it on the intuition. Mr. Spencer is not to think and speak of the co-existence of two positions as if it were identical with the co-existence of things. The first is in no way lodged in, or a data of sensation. If he tries to make it so, he is thrown immediately back onto his former proof, and loses his present foothold.

We have made no distinction between extension and space. We regard the first only as a specification under the second. The extension of particular objects, and the duration of particular events, are forms under which the mind applies the intuitive ideas of space and of time. A knowledge of actual spaces, extension, a measurement of material objects, are the fruits of experience; but these estimates proceed always under the prior notion of space, which makes them intelligible.

Space, in its analytical contemplation, furnishes a variety of intuitive conceptions which are the basis of the demonstrative reasonings of Geometry and Trigonometry. Such a notion is position, a line, a surface, perfect curves, figures, solids. A circle in its accurate form, a ground of demonstrative truth, is an intuitive conception, as are the propositions which flow from the immutable relation of its parts, and of the lines which define, and are defined by them. A surface without thickness, a line without breadth, a point without dimensions, are all intuitive conceptions under the primitive idea, and are the elements of a purely intuitive science. The most marked of those secondary conceptions is that of position. It is to be entirely distinguished from an infinitesimal body; as the infinite of the metaphysician wholly transcends the infinite of the mathematician. Position is not arrived at by the futile sub-divisions of the fancy, is not the result of the dogma of divisibility. There is here absolutely no length nor breadth, and the idea is reached directly by the grasp of the reason. The imagination may falter in struggling by additions to reach the infinite, and by subtractions to arrive at pure position; but the reason easily and at once accepts both notions, and rids them of those measurable parts by which the imagination baffles itself in the pursuit. Position is absolutely without measurements, and hence without parts; the infinite is absolutely beyond measurement, and hence also without parts. There is no whole, therefore no division of that whole.

§ 5. We now pass to time, a regulative idea, like that of space, which has attracted much attention as obviously open to a super-sensual reference. We need not, however, dwell upon it, as the line of discussion is quite similar to that pursued under space. The sensations occasioned by phenomena into which the idea of time most obviously enters, are indeed diverse in their relations from those chiefly suggestive of space. Or rather, things are viewed in distinct bearings in the application of the one or the other notion. In each case, nevertheless, the diversity is only understood by an *a priori* recognition of the controlling idea of the relation under which it arises. Some objects can be contemplated indifferently in one order of succession, or in a reverse order. We may move from A to Z, or return from Z to A. Others, transpiring in time, confine the attention to one direction. We pass from A to Z, but cannot retrace our steps. The cars enter the field of vision at the left, and pass out at the right. In these facts there is an occasion, though not an explanation, of the notion of time. The mind cannot, under the influence of a mere series of sensations, discover this relation; since it is not in and of the sensations, but that which expounds them. Nor can it institute a comparison between the two relations of objects which shall issue in any comprehension of them, without itself supplying the essential conditions of that explanation —the notions of space and time. We must either hold that time is an order of sensations—and this supposition even would not relieve us of our difficulty, as we shall show under the notion of resemblance—or we must admit it to be that transcendent idea which expounds that order, and is therefore supplied by the mind.

Says Spencer, "As the ideas of space and co-existence are inseparable, so also are the ideas of time and sequence. It is impossible to think of time, without thinking of some succession; and it is equally impossible to think of any succession without thinking of time. Time, like space, cannot be conceived except by the establishment of a relation beween at least two elements of consciousness, the difference being, that while in the case of space, those two elements are, or seem to be, present together, in the case of time they are not present together."—*Principles of Psychology, page* 247.

This statement, so far as it is admissible at all, is so as a statement of the circumstances under which the idea of time arises, and not of the nature of that idea itself. Used for the latter purpose, the author legitimately reaches the conclusion that time *is* "relativity of position among the states of consciousness." The process of arriving at this result, is farther explained thus: "Gradually, as by the accumulation of experiences, there are found to be like and unlike sounds, tastes, smells, sizes, forms, textures; the relationship which we signify by these words, like and unlike, will be more and more dissociated from particular impressions; and the abstract ideas of *likeness* and *unlikeness* will come into existence. Manifestly, then, the ideas of likeness and unlikeness are impossible until multitudes of things have been thought of as like and unlike. Similarly in the case before us. After various relations of position among the states of consciousness, have been contemplated, have been compared, have become familiar; and after experiences of different relations of position have been so accumulated as to dissociate the idea of the relation from all particular positions; then, and not till then, can there arise the abstract notion of *relativity of position* among the states of consciousness—the notion of time.

"Thus so far is it from being true that time, as conceived by us, is a form of thought; it turns out contrariwise, not only that there *can* be thoughts while yet time has not been conceived, but that there *must* be thoughts, before it can become conceivable"—*Page* 252.

Our objection to the above conclusion is double. The comparison itself cannot go on, as we trust later to show, without a regulative idea, that of resemblance, under which it can be instituted; and that in which it is said to issue is not the notion of time. That which is explained by time is very different from time itself. If the first were the second we should have no need of an independent, explanatory notion, the phenomena would be complete, intelligible in themselves. The sequence of events provokes the notion, but is not that notion. Sequence and time do not mutually contain each other—but time is that *idea* without which the *fact* of sequence is unintelligible. That time is not identical with succession, is seen in our measurement of it. A succession of events may be completed in a shorter or longer period, and if time to us were their mere relation in sequence, we should insist on its identity in the two cases. We distinguish time from any given sequence, indeed from all sequences, longer or shorter according to the forces at work. We do not identify it with that series of events even by which we measure it. The conditions for its exact estimate and general apprehension are different. The notion of time, with no actual events transpiring in it, is quite consonant with thought. Moreover, many sequences are simultaneous. The relativity of which one of these is it that constitutes time? It cannot be one to the exclusion of the remainder, for no one has such a pre-eminence over every other. Neither can it be all, since they are constantly varying among themselves. What effect has it on time, that one drives faster than he has been driving, that a railroad train has stopped at a station, that the thoughts have been quickened by danger? The quality of sweetness may exist in many things, and have shades of diversity in each; is this also our conception of time?

The prior notion of time, moreover, imposes sequence, when there is no sequence in the states of consciousness, but rather alternation. The mind may pass from A to B in contemplation, and back again; it may vibrate between the two in alternate thought: yet it does this as certainly under the idea of time as if it had simply passed on to Z. Motion in a circle is felt to be motion as much as movement in a straight line. Bare contemplation without conscious progress is felt to occupy time; it is for the measure, not for the fact of time, that we revert to external events at the expiration or change of a single absorbing feeling. There is doubtless some succession in every phase of mind, but it is not necessary for us to contemplate these minor and obscure transitions to be aware that every act, the very act of attention, occupies time. We might as well endure an intense, absorbing pain for an hour as for an instant, if we are not able to distinguish between the two cases. That which we urge is, that the notion of time imposes the sense of sequence where there is no proper sequence in the sensations as sensations, and the alternate consideration of A, B, like the beat of a clock, marks distinctly the flow of time. Indeed all consciousness is made sequential, no matter what the order of its states, by the very notion of time in which they transpire. We cannot escape the inner succession of impressions, because we cannot elude the interpreting idea, that of time. The position of "states of consciousness," must, and can be only that of succession, whatever their character or the number of times they are repeated. The inner law overrules the outward appearance, and imposes the notion of sequence.

Suppose, on the other hand, with Spencer, that we could pass from A to Z, without the idea of time. In that case we should not only be destitute of it, but have made no progress towards it. We should simply have experienced sensations without explanation, or interpretation. No repetition of this process, however frequent, could make it fruitful of a new notion. The simple idea must be present to open the inquiry. Time must be a sensation, like that of green and red, or its distinct separation, abstraction cannot follow from repetition. The sensation green is given in each particular instance, and then, by distinguishing attention, by generalization, is made to assume the abstract form. This process is possible only to sensations,—and even then involves more than sensation—not to relations; since a relation is addressed to the intellect, and not to the sense, and can only be understood in connection with an idea under which it arises and is defined as a relation of place, time, dependence. On no supposition is the closing statement of Spencer admissible. "So far is it from being true that Time, as conceived by us, is a form of thought, it turns out contrariwise, not only that there *can* be thoughts while yet time has not been conceived, but that there must be thoughts before it can become conceivable."

As a sensation, time must be experienced in each sensation from which it is to be abstracted, as a relation also it must be discoverable in each series or it cannot be generalized from all; and as an idea disclosing a relation it must come at once. Time, must be a sensation, or it must be a specific relation under some general idea, or it must itself be a primary idea, the condition of actual, individual connections. The first supposition is plainly false, while the second is as unacceptable to the empirical school as the third, since it also implies original, intuitive action of the mind. Yet I see no escape except in the assertion that a relation can be discovered, by the senses discovered, of no specific orders or kind, and this is not an escape, since such a relation could not be generalized into one of a specific order or kind, to wit, that of time.

§ 6. The next regulative idea we offer is that of resemblance. This has been constantly overlooked, and with great injury to the arguments sustaining the Intuitive Philosophy. It has been quietly assumed, that resemblance is a matter of sensation only, that in it exclusively are given the data of this category; that one color is seen to be like or unlike another: one taste tested as like or unlike a succeeding one. We might as well claim the judgment in which this relation is expressed to be an act of sense. Green, red, sweet, sour, are known as qualities by sensation, and here the sense pauses. The eye sees a green color once, twice, thrice ; but it makes no comparison, institutes no judgment, recalls no impressions. These, the labors of other intellectual powers, must commence and go on in the light, and this light is that of an interpreting idea. What is resemblance? It is not the red in the apple; no more is it the red on the leaf; no more is it these two sensations united in time and place. It is a specific relation between the two, intelligible as a given case of a general notion. Can the specific relation be first reached, and the general idea be deduced from it? No! As a relation it is an intellectual product, a judgment, two sensations explained in their bearings on each other under an idea. The sensations alone do not contain in their sensational matter the relation, and cannot furnish it, nor can the intellectual movement proceed without the forecasting apprehension, the head light. Moreover, the specific relation must hold, must express, in one form of it, the general relation, or that relation cannot be deduced from it. Resemblance is intellectually involved in the first instance of it: and, as it is not a sensation, it must be involved for the direct, intuitive apprehensien of the mind there present for its interpretation. It is not the result of the judgment which expresses it, but an element and ground of that judgment. There are sensible and supersensual data for the declaration, The leaf is like the apple.

The frequent oversight of this fact has, we say, greatly embarrassed the discussion between the two schools of philosophy. The idea of resemblance has been quietly appropriated. The observation of agreements and disagreements has been allowed to proceed as if it were purely a matter of perception, and thus a play of mind has been secured, a germ of judgment, a nucleus of thinking, with no recognized *a priori* material. From the elements of intellectual action thus secured, it has been comparatively easy, by patient composition and slight oversight, similar to that which characterized the first step, to broaden the grounds of thought, and to surreptitiously include one after another of its essential conditions. This process is arrested at the outset, if we reclaim, as we should, the idea of resemblance. No generalization can go forward without it, and the fictitious growth of regulative ideas is checked at once. We cannot, for instance, compare sensations as co-existent or as successive, and under the one agreement smuggle in the idea of space, and under the other that of time. We are left, as we should be, standing on sensations alone; knowing color, odor, taste, but with no opportunity for comparison, classification, generalization, as we have no luminous idea under which a movement of thought is made visible.

There must be a little play given to thinking somewhere. in some direction, under some notion, before it can work out anything whatever; before it can acquire momentum, institute a process, and, in the superficial movement established, give apparent ground for the true connections of thought. The sensations are indeed present as the material of thought, the judgment is waiting as the agent of thought; but there is no plan of thought, no direction of thought, no space or orderly way wherein thought can find exercise, till some notion, most frequently this of resemblance, is furnished. The axe cannot cut while it is pressed close against the timber; tools are of no avail packed tightly in a chest. Give the hatchet the play of an inch, and with patience and an increasing sweep, it will at length hew for itself a broad path. Scope must be granted for wielding a weapon. One after another the implements must be loosened from their lodgment, and to initiate this movement, *room*, the ground and condition of effort, must be granted. So must room, an *idea* under which to move, be given to the very first judgment, before generalization is possible, and the one stolen for this purpose, is that of resemblance.

§ 7. The sixth regulative idea is that of cause and effect. This is one of the most undeniable of them all, and is either greatly restricted in its statement, or entirely rejected by those who refuse to accept the reason as a source of knowledge. Indeed, a correct, adequate presentation of the notion as it lies in the general mind, shows it at once to be beyond sensation, generalization, or any action that these processes can verify. The convenience of expression has led to the extension of the term cause, not merely to remote agents, but even to the condition of their action. Any one of all the circumstances necessary to an effect, is spoken of as its cause, though no direct efficiency proceeds from it. In a stricter sense, the word cause includes only those antecedents which are active in the effect, and in a yet closer sense, the sense which belongs to it in the present discussion, the forces *immediately* operative in the fact before us. *The* cause is strictly contemporaneous with the effect, underlies it, momentarily occasions it. The antecedent effect had its antecedent cause, and though this cause may have been identical with the cause now operating, it remains a cause by virtue of its present activity. The effect is the immediate evidence of the cause ; and though the last is prior in thought to the first, neither can exist an instant without the other. The sound of the steam-whistle is remotely attributable to the distant locomotive, is more immediately to be referred to the movement of the air and the tympanum, but finds its causes exactly in the forces which sustain the movement, and the living powers which receive and interpret it. In this sense the cause is always and necessarily transcendental, out of the range of the senses, incapable of verification by any other than the very faculty, which in the first instance yields the idea.

The statements of Empirical Philosophy are quite different from those now made. Says Bain, "The successions designated as *Cause and Effect*, are fixed in the mind by contiguity. Belief in external reality is anticipation of a given effect of a given antecedent; and the effects and causes are our own various sensations and movements." More clearly still does Mill speak of the notion as one of simple antecedence; while Spencer treats of it under the caption, "The Relation of Sequence." If these and other kindred statements are correct, then there is no veritable idea of cause and effect in the precise, intuitive sense, since a fixed sequence finds explanation under the notion of time, and requires for its statement no other form of thought. That there is any sufficient knowledge or idea of the ground of such a sequence is simply denied by this class of philosophers. There is in this attitude an abandonment of the idea of causation as irresolvable into experience, insolvable in empirical acids, and a substitution for it of a certain application of the notion of time. The ground of debate, therefore, is narrowed down to the correctness with which the phenomena under discussion are stated by the respective parties. If it be shown, that simple sequence does not, in the common mind, cover the entire ground of causation, there is in the empirical philosophy an abandonment of one actual, universal, regulative idea as inexplicable; a superficial substitution for it, of the fragment of another, and this for no other reason than that its own theory can find no place for this fixed conviction. It is the facts of the mind's action that philosophy inquires into, and the above proof being given, there will here be left a form of action as universal and persistent, and hence as ultimate and authoritative as any, uncovered by materialism.

The universal conviction, if it can be arrived at, is not

to be pushed aside, to be left unexplained, to be regarded as a fanciful, accidental, invalid movement of mind, without a reason rendered, distinguishing this from kindred affirmation of our faculties. We may not impeach the action of the mind at one point, without at least separating this point broadly and decisively from every other. To deny any of its explicit data, is an *a priori* and groundless attack on the good faith of our faculties, and that by these very faculties themselves—is to decide that there cannot be intuitive ideas, because, forsooth, they are intuitive ideas, and thus not explicable under other powers. If they were so explicable, they would not be intuitive. Is a persistent notion found which is not referable to sensation; in this fact is furnished the desired proof of original, independent matter. Certainly this proof cannot be met in way of argument by a denial which precludes all proof, and forestalls discussion; which assumes an antecedent impossibility so great as to make proof impossible. These universal convictions are not to be obnoxious, merely because, as otherwise inexplicable, they demand the intuitive insight claimed for them. There is here really *a priori* conviction brought to disprove *a priori* truths; for what but an *a priori* bias of mind, is this antecedent reluctance to admit the possibility of regulative ideas?

What then is the fact? Which statement best conforms to the popular, the universal conviction, that of fixed antedence, or of present, underlying power. There can be no doubt on this point. The case is a plain, almost an admitted one against Empirical Philosophy. Language is full of this notion of an inherent, sub-phenomenal connection between events. The word *force* distinctly expresses this causal link, and few words are more familiar, or play a more important part in speech. Of the same kind, are the words *power*, *influence*, *energy*, *strength*, and more or less markedly most of the words which express physical action. *Pull*, *push*, *press*, *pry*, *lift*, *lug*, *labor*, the entire vocabulary of effort are saturated with this causal notion of an invisible efficiency, which expends itself in all forms of activity. Behold any striking display of force, the blasting of rocks, and every mind is impressed with the power of the invisible agent. To look upon the lifting of detached masses, the seaming of the solid bed, as a mere sequence of disconnected events, is impossible to any mind, in its first, spontaneous action. No descriptive language was ever applied to such events, that regarded them simply as a sequence. The popular, the universal conviction is unmistakable, that here is force, invisible power.

Equally present is the idea to all science. Gravitation, cohesion, chemical affinity, the correlation of forces, the various theories of physical facts, like Darwin's theory of gemmules, or Spencer's of physiological units, involve the notion of inherent power, working the results under consideration. Science could not carry forward its investigations without this recognition of force. To discover the traces of its presence, and the lines of its action, is the constant triumph of knowledge. To confound fixed antecedents with efficient force is impossible to successful inquiry. The shadow of an object approaching us from the light, would thus be its cause; the effervescence of lime and water, the cause of the heat; the dissolving of salt in the water, the cause of the cold. The first fact, in each series of associated effects, would be the source of the remainder. No sequences are more fixed than those of day and night, summer and winter, yet there is no direct, causal connection between them, and no one ever so conceives the dependence.

Philosophy likewise reverts constantly to insensible, unapproachable causes. A large share of philosophers admit their existence and the grounds of it; and those who through their denial of the latter are content to sacrifice the former, do not, and cannot, use language, except in a few guarded passages, consistent with their own statements. They must, with Bain, in each inadvertent moment, speak of "active energy," of "mechanical powers," of "rousing the dormant energy," and to deny themselves these and kindred expressions, to forego the ideas back of them, would be to take away the opportunity of composition, or to make language most cumbersome, and untrue to our convictions. The generally accepted dogma, that the mind cannot know anything beyond its own modifications; a dogma insisted on by many of the empirical school, finds its ultimate support in this notion of cause and effect. The existence of the object perceived outside of the perceptive organs, independent of it, removed from it—at least by insensible distances—has determined the large majority of philosophers to deny the possibility of direct perception. If, however, the connection of cause and effect, is one of antecedence merely, then this separation of the object perceived, from the organ perceiving it, should oppose no obstacle whatever to direct perception. A fixed sequence can be established between things remote and wholly unlike, as easily as between things like; and occupying common ground. If therefore, this connection of sequence is the deepest, nay the only connection between things thought to act on each other, it would seem to suffice for knowledge, or if not, to make knowledge impossible. How shall even successive states of mind lie fruitfully together in simple sequence, if sequence after all is a barren connection. If it fails to unite remote, how can it unite proximate objects? If one set falls apart, all must.

The general point is too plain for farther statement. Evidently the doctrine of simple antecedence does not express the universal conviction, does not cover the phenomena under explanation, does not accept and expound the affirmation of knowledge, which every mind is constantly making.

Quite a different explanation of cause and effect has come from another quarter. Sir William Hamilton applies to it what he terms the law of the conditioned. The notion of causality is thought by him to arise from the weakness of the mind, its inability to conceive a beginning. The mind, he affirms is unable to conceive events without a beginning, nor yet with a beginning. "We can conceive neither the absolute commencement, nor the absolute termination of anything that is once thought to exist; nor any more the opposite alternative of infinite non-commencement, of infinite non-termination." Herein is given the principle of causality: "When an object is presented phenomenally as commencing, we cannot but suppose that the compliment of existence, which it now contains, has previously been; in other words, that all that we at present come to know in it as an effect, must previously have existed in its cause." This is a most inadequate explanation for several reasons. In the first place, it inverts the order of dependence in our mental action. We cannot conceive of anything as absolutely commencing, because of this notion of cause and effect. The existence of the notion is the ground of our embarrassment, not the embarrassment the occasion of the notion. What would be simpler, were it not for causality crowding us backward, than merely to conceive any landscape, any personage, any event, with no thought of what has preceded it? The present act of the imagination is not conditioned on the past, neither should we be compelled to evoke the present from the past, any more than to carry it forward into the future, were it not for causation. Any cross-section of the events of time would be as complete as a single pebble on the shore.

Thus, often in dreams, when the imagination finds unrestrained phenomenal play, the judgment not being sufficiently active to impose the check of this purely sub-phenomenal idea of causation, we in a great measure disregard it, and, with no other sense of jar, suffer the sudden, unexplained presence of unexpected persons, and an incongruous order and issue of events. The ideas regulative of space and time relations are present, while cause and effect, regulative of consecutive thought, is in whole or in part overlooked. A city makes its appearance suddenly, the ship moves unobstructedly across the land, the facts and figures of fancy come and go freely, bound to no ordinary sequence.

A second objection is found in the fact that the theory affords no explanation of the alternative adopted by it. We can neither conceive, it is said, the commencement, nor the non-commencement of anything. Very well, but how is this dilemma to be escaped by the present notion of causation. The conclusion accepted under it of "infinite non-commencement" remains as inconceivable as ever, and therefore, as far as the conception is concerned, presents as many difficulties as would the opposed alternative of an immediate, independent beginning of events. If the mind is as open to one of these conclusions as to the other, and can properly be satisfied with neither, what reason has it for preferring one to the other? The difficulty is met only when causation is made a positive notion, compelling us in the one direction. Accompany this acceptance with a denial of our right to direct the imagination in explanation to that which, according to our very notion of it, is sub-phenomenal, and we have at once the ability and the inability of the mind explained. We have a reason for its convictions, and also for their inconceivable character.

Again, this theory is a concealed theory of antecedence, and fails to cover the strict idea of causation. The real, efficient cause is present with the effect, immediately underlies it, and sustains it. Thus the substance and force, which constitutes matter, each instant gives occasion to its qualities. The power, the personal being, which is in mind, is the groundwork and source of its thoughts, feelings and volitions. The stream of causation flows under the stream of events, and momentarily floats them, as the surface of the ocean is supported by its invisible depths. Simply to insist on an antecedent event to every event, is to throw up the phenomenal path along which the imagination travels, but is not a recognition of the true force and nature of causation. The imagination exploring the past, does indeed require that distinct, tangible foot-stones should, in due order, link its steps ; but that which impels the mind in thus sending it to search its way backward, is a sense of an unbroken series of causes, and that which the mind finds everywhere beneath the phenomenal supports of the imagination is the permanent power and flow of causes. This theory of the weakness of the human mind signally fails to account for so positive and pervasive a notion as this of cause and effect.

If we accept this notion in its full, universal application, leading us to those invisible forces which thread together the phenomena of the universe ; if we do not deny or limit the facts presented to us in our own spontaneous beliefs, in universal action and universal language, it is at once evident, that this idea must have a direct, intuitive origin. Admittedly it transcends all experience, is wholly unapproachable by the senses. The presence of such a notion, evinced by language, by science, by philosophy, by our spontaneous and inevitable interpretation of events, is undeniable ; to discard it as a gratuitous assumption of the mind, as a purely fanciful notion superinduced on the facts, is to deny and not to explain, the phenomena of the mind ; is to construct our theories in neglect of the facts too broad for them ; is to invalidate an action of mind, as universal as strong in the confidence and spontaneous trust of the mind itself, as any of its processes. This is to make our several forms of activity intuitive and rationative, contradictory and self-destructive; is to bring one form of knowing from its own field into that of another faculty, and, because it fails, as it must necessarily fail, to understand the diverse action of a power, given on purpose to do a work different from its own, to expel as fictitious and fanciful, conclusions wrought out by a special, native power of mind. Daily life pursues its hourly labors; natural science accomplishes its great achievements, ollowing the clue of causation; and yet a speculation termed philosophy steps in to declare the light under which these processes proceed, wholly false and deceptive. We do *see* by it, and we do, indeed, *walk* by it, and reach most valuable conclusions. Extinguish it, and we *grope* in darkness, yet it is no light, says philosophy, because, forsooth, not kindled by the match-friction of experience, and there are no lights but these dipped candles called generalizations, boxed and labeled by us. It seems to be light, and does marvelously well the work of light, and all men insist on using it as light; yet evidently it is not the tallow taper we are after; we cannot handle it as we wish, trace its making, or discover the mould in which it was run. This, then, cannot be our predetermined light, and as there is no other, it follows plainly that this is not light, b[illegible] darkness rather. Correct ideas must come from experience, and be capable of its verification; this is not so reached, and cannot be so explained; therefore it is no valid notion. In all this there is a flagrant begging of the question. We thus put the grounds and tests of validity in the faculties that directly concern experience, and then deny validity to ideas that must confessedly, if they exist at all, transcend experience and the judgments which unfold it.

The doctrine of intuitive ideas is often damaged by its advocates. It is asserted that consciousness testifies to much not referable to this source. The direct matter of consciousness, sensations, thoughts, feelings, volitions, are undeniable. There is no ground for dispute, when any fact is a direct product of consciousness, that is, belongs to mental states. It is quite a different question, What is involved in the data of consciousness? The accuracy, the validity of our judgments, the ideas under which they proceed are to be arrived at by analysis, by reasoning, and are not directly vouched for by consciousness.

It is sometimes said we are conscious of force, and therefore of a cause in putting forth voluntary effort. The true statement would rather seem to be, we are conscious of volition, and of the subsequent sensations which accompany action, but not at all of the hidden link of power which unites them. Indeed, it is not always possible for us to tell whether the intended muscular result will follow the volition. Some paralysis may have intervened, arresting the flow of power, and the interior connection lies so wholly beyond consciousness, that we can only determine the presence or absence of suitable muscular conditions by a tentative effort at movement. If we were conscious of force, force itself would be phenomenal, and lose its subphenomenal character. It would cease to be a causal idea, and would become a sensible fact or effect.

The simplest statement of causation is, Every effect must have a cause. In this is involved the expectation of the perpetuity of nature, since every change in the effect, as itself an effect, would demand a new, specific cause. With no apparent change in causes, we anticipate previous results, since this must follow from the unchanged forms and conditions of action. A prolonged duration of the present physical system is expected by us, unless we see, or think we see, reasons for change in the government of God, or grounds of change in the system itself—an introduction at some point of new forces.

§ 8. The six ideas now presented all pertain to matter, though most of them are also applicable to mental phenomena. The five that remain belong exclusively to the conceptions, the facts of mind. None of these pertain directly to matter, as matter. They all involve the existence, or previous action of thought. The first of them is consciousness. There has been no debate concerning this idea, because it has not been presented as belonging to this department of our intellectual furniture. If, however, it shall appear that consciousness exists in idea rather than in substance or quality, that it is therefore directly arrived at by the mind, and also that it furnishes the distinctive feature or style or form of a class of phenomena, the transcendent predicate of a series of judgments, it will be plain that it belongs properly to the class of regulative notions. Consciousness is often spoken of as if it were a faculty, a form of knowing; yet a little thought at once shows that it is not. I see a ball. I say in farther enforcement, I know that I see it. This language has divided the first simple act into two, an act of perceiving, and one of knowing directed toward that of perception. Yet this is merely a convenience of expression. The one single act of seeing the ball is all that is present. If there were a second act of knowing, this also would require sub-division in order to reach the element of consciousness in it. Thus analysis must go on indefinitely, unless we finally accept an act of knowing which is simple and indivisible. There is no double faculty, or double movement of one faculty, in thinking, feeling, willing. A thought is a thought, only as it is known; a feeling is a feeling, only as it is felt. They do not first find existence, and then an added quality or element of consciousness; but consciousness is the condition and form of their existence. Consciousness, then, is not, like judgment, a power; nor like pain or pleasure, a quality of certain states; it is not a feature or a relation of a sensation, but involved in the very notion of a sensation. This idea, therefore, as neither a faculty to be known by its exercise, nor a quality of mental states to be learned by observation—indeed every act of observation, must itself contain it—must be evolved by the mind as an explanatory idea, or conditional notion in considering the phenomena to which it is applicable.

It is not only unphenomenal itself, it is introduced as the antecedent condition, the regulative idea of a large class of facts, to wit: those of mind. What space is to material facts, consciousness is to intellectual facts, the interpreting light under which they occur. The words we constantly apply to it, recognize this relation. We say, "the field of consciousness," "transpiring in consciousness," "coming up into the light of consciousness," "the flow of consciousness"—that is of thought, feeling, in consciousness. These and like expressions are shaped under an image in which consciousness is presented as an arena of mental movements, as is space of physical events. The peculiar nature of knowing, feeling, willing, is not understood till the idea of consciousness is present: yet these facts remain in their integrity possessed of all the elements that analysis discloses in them, without accrediting to it any distinct, additive form or quality of being. Consciousness thus shows itself to be to the inner, invisible world, what space is to the outer, visible one; the condition of its existence, the only canvas on which its colors can appear. To occupy space, is to have physical existence, to occupy consciousness is to have an intellectual existence, to occupy neither is not to exist, is to present no one of the known forms of existence. This idea is seen to be regulative in the large class of propositions which arise under it. I know; I see the book; I feel the pain, are of this sort. Each of them is comprehended by virtue of the notion of consciousness, which expounds their several predicates.

This view also finds support in the difficulties which attend on the ordinary explanations of consciousness. What is it? is a question that has greatly perplexed philosophy and has seldom received a very definite answer. Some have striven to conceive it as a faculty, yet this faculty must be present in the action of every other faculty, and that other faculty would be absolutely null and void without this. To divide an act of knowing into one of knowing, and one of consciousness, each taking a distinct moiety, is impossible. Others have said, "Consciousness is the genus under which our several faculties of knowing are contained as species." But our faculties of knowing, no more require it than those of feeling and willing; and what exactly is a genus in distinction from the species it contains? Nothing, but a word. Certainly an effort to make definite this view, prepares the way for regarding consciousness as a general idea, under which all specific acts of mind, in themselves complete, find recognition. Others figure consciousness under the image of an internal light. This is virtually to decline the inquiry, What is it? since the illustration can reflect no explanation on this point.

§ 9. The second idea regulative of our intellectual life is that of beauty. Concerning the existence at this point of peculiar phenomena that require explanation, there is no discussion. Yet results of analysis are quite different; some reaching a simple, original idea; others resolving beauty into utility, or unity and variety, or making it the product of association. That beauty is intimately connected with utility, that it is always accompanied by unity and variety, that taste is strongly influenced by association, and, in some cases overshadowed by it, are undeniable; yet that these explanations, in conflict among themselves, fail each of them to cover the entire facts, seems equally plain. Beauty is not proportioned to utility, is not always attendant upon it, exists sometimes with little or no utility, save that which the gratification of taste itself affords. Unity and variety are frequently present with no corresponding beauty, belong to structures which do not pertain to the fine arts, and thus show an independent existence and range. Association explains many of the judgments of those who give little attention to intrinsic beauty, who under the influence of others yield their opinions to be swayed by the prevalent sentiment ; yet just in proportion as the presence of taste is manifest, as the perception of beauty is developed, as the phenomena to be accounted for are obvious and declared, this explanation fails. The leaders in fine art have no higher association from which to derive their estimates of excellence, while the different, external, accidental pleasures, that may for them incidentally find connection with works of art, are no sufficient ground for their high, common, uniform estimates, singling these forth in all generations as objects of peculiar power and value.

But this theory of association, of character transferred to objects of beauty from the relations in which we find them, is met by the fact, that we have a pertinent example of what association can do in affecting our estimates of things ; and that it wholly fails to sustain the explanation here offered of the facts of taste. The admiration the general public express for a new fashion is almost wholly due to association, and what are its characteristics ? This esteem is fickle, contradictory, and wholly destitute of standards of judgment. Though in the present, unanimity may be complete, successive periods differ greatly in the forms rejected and accepted. Fortuity and the most extravagant fancies reign, and are equally imperious in their contradictory commands. The whole realm of fashion is one of unreasoning association, and it stands in conspicuous contrast with that of taste, refuting the explanation offered of its stable phenomena. The uniform admiration bestowed by different nations and generations on objects of beauty; the first high estimates which give direction to public opinion; the word beauty, accepting in careful speech no synonym; the fine arts, a distinctly bounded territory, eliciting the most skillful and prolonged attention; and the well-established principles of this department, show that the fickle, fanciful connections of association furnish no sufficient theory of taste.

That the quality, beauty, accepted as unresolvable into any other, is of intuitive origin is seen in the fact, that it is not directly a quality of things, but of intellections. An intellection is the product of the mind. The qualities, forms, and relations of an object, its expression are by studious observation brought before the mind. This estimate which the intellect makes of all that unfolds the character, the emotional power of an object, is an intellection, and in the object thus conceived, thus unfolded in the thoughts, beauty is seen to inhere. As beauty thus does not belong to a flower, a tree, a landscape, a bird, a man, merely as a sensible object, but to them as products of an arranging, vitalizing, perfecting power; as it is seen not in the thing simply, but in it as conceived by the mind, it must be the object of an interior, intuitive faculty, which can take into its contemplation the appropriate intellection. There has followed perception, an act of exposition more or less complete, and thus the object has been taken from the senses into the mind, and has there awaited the insight of the reason. The qualities one and all which make up the expression pronounced beautiful are not the very beauty which we attribute to the cathedral, the painting, or the statue. The skill, proportion, height of the towering edifice may be discerned separately from that final effect, that joint and supersensual power, that more than analytic pleasure, which we term beauty. This is not the craft of the workman, the single nor the combined excellences of the work, but an overshadowing quality, through which these have their chief value, by which the seal of a fine art is put upon them. The intellectual relations, qualities, powers of an object, capable only of an inner presentation, are that in which, as substance, the reason sees beauty to inhere. Beauty is not these simply, though it comes and goes with their varying combinations.

§ 10. We have now reached an idea, whose nature and origin have been the occasion of much diversity of opinion. The conclusion we arrive at as to the nature of right, will profoundly affect our intellectual and practical life. The phenomena that call forth the discussion, though often narrowed by the theory adopted for their explanation, are, in a general way, accepted and agreed upon. They are these. Certain forms of action are known by us as right, others are wrong; a sense of obligation accompanies the former when urged upon us, and of satisfaction and approval when performed by us. The latter, on the other hand, when distinctly contemplated as wrong, deter the mind from acceptance by a minatory sense of duty, and punish the commission by a clear feeling of guilt. Of the presence and operation of these facts, history and language are full. Neither the speech nor the actions, the laws, nor the religion of men, are intelligible without them. The testimony of individual experience is repeated in that of communities and nations. From the beginning men have been dealing with virtuous and vicious acts, with right and wrong courses of conduct, with innocence and guilt, responsibility and irresponsibility, honor and shame, praise and censure, rewards and punishments. These ethical ideas grow in the race as it advances. Our legislation, our social institutions, our daily actions, our religious beliefs are full of them; and new labors of reform are constantly putting them into more pithy and pungent shape. Ethical science commands a large share of attention, and takes under its survey more and more broadly the actions of men. The shades of feeling involved vary from remorse and despair to the slightest uneasiness, from the triumphant self-justification of the martyr to a transient thrill of delight. Sin, wickedness, guilt, duty, right, righteousness, integrity, justice, holiness, are a few of the weighty words under which these grave thoughts take their way.

The facts involved being thus comparatively bold and salient, in a measure admitted by all, what is that theory of intellectual powers which best covers and expounds them? The perception of right, and the feeling of obligation, are inseparable; they are the intellectual and emotional sides of one mental state. An obligation cannot be felt without some direction or line of action to which it attaches. An obligation must be of a specific, definite character. An obligation without attachment to any act, is unintelligible, is no obligation. The quality right, seen in an act, is that which at once calls forth the feeling of duty, and directs it into a particular channel. No more can the perception be separated from the feeling than the feeling from the perception. Indeed, it is chiefly through the strong sentiment that accompanies it, that we discover the distinct character of the intuitive act. Language abundantly recognizes this double bearing of ethical insight. We have the word right, primarily expressive of the intellectual quality of the action; and the words, ought, obligation, duty, presenting chiefly the emotional element.

The theories which do not accept the original, simple, inseparable character of the idea right, explain the intellectual element by the generalized notion of utility. This is done with very different degrees of success by earlier and later writers: but nearly all of the empirical school agree in making utility the intellectual ground of ethics. We have appetites, sensibilities, tastes, affections to be gratified. Any thing or action which affords pleasure to any one of these is useful. The common power which belongs to so many objects and relations of furnishing some form of enjoyment, or some condition of it, is abstracted under the word *utility*. The inquiry which guides the conscience, which furnishes light to moral action, it is said, is this inquiry into pleasure, into good, into immediate and future enjoyment; and that if fairly and thoroughly pushed and made to cover all gratifications higher and lower, it is an exhaustive statement of all that takes place in ethical research. While this is an inadequate theory of the intellectual grounds of duty, it is difficult to disprove it. What is affirmed by it does take place, and is a most apparent and a most necessary part of the process by which we arrive at a practical conclusion as to a line of action, whether it be right or wrong. The usefulness of an action, in a broad and deep sense of the word, is a correct criterion of its moral character; it becomes, therefore, very difficult to show, that it does not cover the entire ethical element.

The truth is, the quality right, like the quality beauty, is seen in an intellection, that is in an act whose relations and bearings backward and forward have been inquired into and settled. What are the results which flow from it? What are the feelings it expresses? How will it work forward in the world of facts? How does it work backward on the emotions? These are the inquiries which disclose to us the intellectual bearings of the action, and prepare us to pronounce wisely on its character; they are also those which determine its utility. So far the ground is common to the two theories, sensualistic and intuitive. At this point they diverge. Says the one philosopher, these facts exhaust in the case the grounds of intellectual action; says the other, they prepare the conditions of a final, intuitive act overlooked by you, pronouncing the action not useful or otherwise, but right or wrong. The last words are not, and cannot be measured by the first. In the intellection which we have reached in part at least as you have reached it, we discover a farther, a transcendent quality, which we term right, and from which springs all our ethical action. In this we affirm we have the testimony of language with us, which by no means confounds, or allows us to confound, these two notions of the right and the useful. Nay, it separates them in clean and clear division from each other, reserving an emphasis for the one which it never thinks of bestowing on the other.

It is, however, when the emotional element is considered, that the utilitarian theory is seen to be most obviously inadmissible. It does not satisfactorily meet the question, Whence arises the sense of obligation which is the salient feature of the right? It strives to make answer by affirming that the feeling of duty is conventionally imposed by the community in satisfaction of its own sentiments, and in view of what is advantageous to itself. The obligation of ethical action is thus referred wholly to education, to social and civil institutions, in their own behalf laying the pressure of duty on their subjects. Says Bain, "Authority or punishment is the commencement of the state of mind recognized under the various names—Conscience, the Moral Sense, the Sentiment of Obligation. The major part of every community adopt certain rules of conduct necessary for the common preservation or ministering to the common well-being. * * * * Every one, not of himself disposed to follow the rules prescribed by the community, is subjected to some infliction of pain to supply the absence of other motives : the infliction increasing in severity until obedience is attained. It is the familiarity with this *régime* of compulsion, and of suffering, constantly increasing until resistance is overborne, that plants in the infant and youthful mind the first germ of the sense of obligation."—*The Emotions and the Will, p.* 481. His definition of Conscience is, " An ideal resemblance of public authority, growing up in the individual mind, and working to the same end."

The community grounds the law of action partly on utility, and partly on the transient sentiments which possess it, and thus, with a variety of sanctions, trains the child to obedience. "A certain dread and awful impression is thus connected with forbidden actions, which is the conscience in its earliest germ or manifestation."

This theory derives a force which does not belong to it, from the very fact that social law, appealing, as it often does, to our moral nature, acquires thereby a prescriptive power which would not otherwise be attainable. If there were no foundation for custom and law in our moral constitution, the results of social instruction and discipline would be much less than they now are. With this grave advantage afforded by the frequent coincidence of our moral constitution and social customs, the theory still plainly fails to cover the facts. It should be observed, moreover, that man's protracted and habitual disobedience to moral law has weakened its authority, obscured its phenomena, and thus greatly aids the effort to confound it with conventional rule. Notwithstanding these causes of obscuration, we believe a better theory still remains visible in the facts.

We have repeated examples of what general agreement and enforcement can accomplish, and the results are of another kind or power from those arising under true moral force. Take again, from another point of view, the illustration afforded by fashion. A kind of censure to which the masses of men are exceedingly sensitive, is constantly and unsparingly inflicted on those who disregard fashion. Yet the most infatuated devotee of the fickle goddess, would hardly venture to regard scrupulous obedience as a virtue. Such an one is quite content if she escapes positive censure in her fashionable follies. How very different, also, the feeling arising from a violated fashion, from wearing a proscribed coat or hat, from that which affects the sensitive soul under the sense of wrong action. Allow each violator to be equally appreciative to the law whose precepts have been infringed, and we have, in the one case, mortification, and in the other guilt. The most scrupulous observance of the details of fashion, of fashion enforced by two thirds of the community, cannot, does not, bestow the sense of virtue; nor disobedience the feeling of vice.

Take again the standard of honor enforced among certain classes, as among soldiers, or gamblers, or on the Stock Exchange. The penalties here inflicted on disobedience, are as unsparing as the parties can make them. Yet such a custom as dueling is broken down by a purely moral sentiment based on the individual conscience, struggling with and at length conquering, the general consent of the community. It may be answered: Yes, but the sense of utility is with those who favor reform. Granted, but it is not, under the theory as presented in its present form, the notion of utility that imposes obligation, but the concurrent, educational force of the community, and this is fully pledged to a custom which nevertheless calls forth on the part of a few a staunch condemnation, finding at length such response in the consciences of all, as to lead to the abandonment of the censured act. Now, if the question were one merely of wisdom, there would be no mystery in the formation of a new opinion, and hence in a change of action. The difficulty under the theory lies in explaining how moral obligation, which rests on an educational basis, which arises from the enforced sentiment of the many, which is the volume of sound made by a multitude of voices, can be brought to bear against an overwhelming majority, to the breaking down of those very beliefs from whence it springs. How can one, two, three, outscream the crowd? How can there arise a counter-sense of duty, when this sense is the concurrent opinions of men now sustaining as sacred, the censured institution. Duty would thus be like respectability, popularity. They do go, and must go with the dominant party, and cannot be used as an incipient force against themselves.

The thief, the gambler, the speculator, rest their laws on an educated sense of honor peculiar to themselves, and while they do secure obedience, sometimes more self-sacrificing and implicit than much of that which arises under moral law, it is notoriously with little or no reference to such a law. They do not mistake their precepts for morality; they are scrupulous, not conscientious, in their obedience to them. Occasionally, to throw a slight coloring of morality, of self-justification, over their actions, is the most they aim at. In a community in which slavery for many generations has been the law of the land, we find, nevertheless, an independent moral element getting a foothold. Conscience is appealed to, and a vigorous moral warfare springs up in the teeth of uniform custom. Nor do those who justify slavery, do it on the ground of uniform practice, except so far as this is regarded as an expression of opinion on the part of those who have thus held their fellows in bondage. Other grounds than the mere fact of custom are sought, grounds which, so far as they exist, have a true justificatory element in them. The good condition of the slave; his inferiority; the general social order; the exigencies of the case. I may almost say, that never is the appeal directly made between intelligent parties in an ethical discussion to naked custom and its penalties, for the justification of a line of conduct. Yet the theory insists, that this common sentiment is the source of obligation, and ought therefore to be the constant reference. This is a fact very damaging to the explanations offered. Men are never reverting to the bare fact of enforced law, as the ground and justification of law; yet this after all is made the source of the sense of law. Moreover in the very face of such enforcement, there does spring up in single minds, a moral sentiment, which, with pure moral power, breaks down institutions hitherto unanimously sustained. We thus see what proscriptive force can do; that it is by no means identical with morality, and that it frequently comes in contact with the power this manifests, and yields to it.

Again this theory fails most signally in cases in which the moral phenomena are most distinct, most declared. In the explanation of mixed conduct, of actions assuming an ethical form, disguising themselves under moral sentiments, it prospers somewhat; but when the moral element is prominent and pure, it comes short. A conscientious man becomes a martyr to his convictions of duty. He stands against the community, and confronts its authority, its alleged line of duty, with his own independent convictions, his own sense of what is right. All the explanations of these most startling and pregnant facts in the world's moral history, facts that above all others catch the rational eye, and disclose the new force that is flaming up in them, is that of the "Self-originating or Idiosyncratic Conscience." It is an instance of "the transfer of the sentiment of prohibition from a recognized case, to one not recognized." That is to say, with no notion of obligation but the enforced one of education; the individual may, nevertheless, transfer it so strictly to his own independent, unsustained speculations as to oppose these serenely and unhesitatingly to the utmost stretch of the authority of the community over him. This is a transfer indeed, a transfer that is a transformation, that discloses a sentiment in kind and quality, totally unlike that with which it commenced. It went into the cocoon a worm, it comes out a butterfly. This is no explanation; it is a confession of defeat. Better would it have been to have left the phenomena unexplained.

Kindred expositions, insufficient to cover the facts to which they are applied, are found everywhere in the works of philosophers who advocate this theory of morals. "By remorse, we understand the strongest form of self-reproach arising from a deep downfall of self-respect and esteem." *The Emotions and the Will, page* 106.

This definition applies to a conspicuous act of misjudgment, and most plainly does not reach the fact of remorse. Again, love is said to be "as purely self-seeking as any other pleasure, and to make no inquiry as to the feelings of the beloved personality." This assertion leaves out the entire moral element which belongs to love as an affection, and is true of it only as a passion. The peculiar effect of "signal generosity" is referred to the "shock," given to the "mind totally unprepared," to see kind offices rendered to an enemy. Mill makes our sympathies with others in their injuries the basis of our sentiments of justice, a condition of feeling, certainly, which as often perverts justice as secures it. These and kindred solutions, show the weakness of utilitarianism in handling striking moral fac s, and how greatly it abridges and mars the facts themselves by a forced, belittling estimate of them.

Nor is the sense of obligation any more satisfactorily accounted for under this theory by referring it directly to the idea of utility. At times, Mr. Mill seems ready to do this. As the useful in the concrete is but the pleasurable, this reference would involve the assertion, that pleasure, as pleasure, is felt in human experience to be obligatory. This would farther include the statement, the stronger the pleasu re, the greater the sense of duty; and, as our own enjoyments are more distinctly conceived than those of others, that these are pre-eminently enforced in practical morals; and farther, as present gratification yields more intense feeling than anticipated indulgence, that the pleasures of the hour are especially watched over by conscience. Each and all of these conclusions are in exact contradiction of the facts. If there is anything in reference to which we feel ourselves left to our own unrestrained choices, it is our pleasures. The moral nature has not laid upon it the superfluous task of enforcing these; but rather that of restraining them. By playing cunningly between the two, public sentiment on the one hand, and utility on the other, some embarrassments may be evaded by the theorist, yet neither nor both can be successfully made the source of the sense of duty.

While these failures of explanation rob utilitarianism of all claims to acceptance, is there not in it a yet deeper difficulty in supposing that a simple notion, like that of obligation, can be other than primitive and independent of the action of society? What would be thought of a philosophy that should refer compassion, love, hope, as induced feelings, to the influence of others over the mind. Evidently all extraneous action is of no avail to awaken a feeling not given in the emotional constitution itself. A sense of duty, of obligation, is as simple as any emotion can be, and if we acknowledge its presence, we must look on it as primitive in our constitution. But a sense of obligation has no significance, is not intelligible as a general unattached feeling, indicating no definite line of conduct, haunting the mind as a vague, premonitory fear, ready to be seized on by the first foreign force, to be applied as an alien impulse, having no necessary existence in the individual, or office for him. The imposed opinion of others cannot create a feeling; the feeling of duty, like every feeling, must have a deeper basis than this. A general notion of obligation, with no intellectual element, no specific direction given to it by the mind whose it is, is as unintelligible as would be a general impression of truth, or delight in truth, with nothing presenting itself as truth; or a vague satisfaction in beauty, with no object regarded by us as beautiful. What can be found in our constitution, allied to such an unattached, unelicited emotion? The vague feelings of fear sometimes present to the mind, nevertheless disclose to more careful inquiry some occasion and ground of attachment in past experience and existing circumstances.

Further, we do not day by day impose these duties on others in the manner that would be indicated by the above theory. Scarcely anything could be more adverse to the methods of those who are constantly using moral force, who are addressing and stimulating the conscience, than an appeal to the common sentiments, that is popular sentiments, of those approached. Indeed, to such persons it would seem unworthy, sometimes even absolutely immoral, to urge action on others, primarily on the ground of the customs and censures of general society. Nor could these censures often be made to subserve the purposes of morality. The apostle of moral truth expects more frequently than otherwise to confront this public sentiment, and his appeal is not, to what has been or is, but to the individual idea of what ought to be. The practice therefore which would flow logically from this theory of enforced morals, is not at all the practice of the actual, ethical world ; it is rather that of those classes who are feared and warred against, as always careless of the law of right, and often disobedient to it.

There are but two open, plausible theories of our moral constitution : the one which recognizes it as an original, independent part of our constitution ; and the one which, through generalization, explains its manifestations by the facts of our physical and social position, making utility and public sentiment the germs of its intellectual and emotional elements. The last, in its pure, naked form, produces a far off semblance of the facts, replacing love and duty with fear and interest, and mistaking the forces at work in a selfish, immoral world, for the true constitutional links of a higher, an holier, state.

There are, however, theories which strive to combine

these two, and while in the last analysis, they are utilitarian in their principles, they keep aloof from the avowal, and surreptitiously include elements which only logically belong to an intuitive philosophy. Utilitarianism relies on the happiness afforded by correct action as the sole motive to it, and falls short of ethics in not being able to impose any line of action with authority, or to enforce one form of enjoyment in preference to another. Indeed, it has no sufficient standard by which to decide between pleasures, and to prefer one class above another. The question of the actual satisfaction experienced by different persons in different lines of action, must, like that of physical tastes, be left with the individual, and if he prefer physical, to intellectual and social enjoyments, one cannot, under a mere law of highest gratification, impose on him the opinions of others, though he may deem them wiser. I do not need to inquire of a philosopher as to which apple is sweet, and which sour, which agreeable, and which disagreeable; nor shall I much respect his view if it differs from my own. Thus, in all questions of pure pleasure, each man has his bias, and is not likely to yield it to a speculation that runs counter to his own experience, the final interpreter to him of the nature and quality of enjoyments.

An effort to obviate this difficulty has been made by affirming the superior, the ineffable character of moral pleasures, the "blessedness" of obedience, and from this supreme satisfaction, this supreme quality of ethical pleasure, to reflect back on the actions which secure it a sense of obligation. Herein is found the stolen element of a better theory. If we rely on the good which diverse lines of conduct and indulgence produce to define and enforce our action, then we are entitled to these several kinds and degrees of satisfaction to direct and establish conduct, and to no more. Let all the sources of pleasure, making the catalogue as discriminating and exhaustive as you please, be represented by the letters A, B, C, D, E. Let each one choose between them as he, under the guidance of his own tastes and capabilities, is able, in kind, degree, duration, difficulty of attainment; and thus mark out for himself the path of prudence. He cannot now go farther, and add to the motives urging any one proposed line of conduct a peculiar blessedness which is to crown it as right above all others. This is to establish again in our constitution a moral law, to restore to it intrinsic obligation, and thus secure the unspeakable satisfaction of obedience. All that our quiet, careful reasoner, overlooking the various sources of pleasure, and choosing between them, is entitled to, is, if he select wisely, the satisfaction of sagacity. He is always right when he is prudent, and the rewards of right sink to those of prudence. The self-congratulation of shrewdness, of quiet forethought, takes the place of an approving conscience, of the blessedness of a law implicitly obeyed, clung to in darkness and in light. No peculiar happiness can follow obedience to right, till we have recognized it as an antecedent, supreme, self-enforced law. As long as it remains a line of conduct resting for support on its pleasurable results, it must look to these exclusively, adding nothing to them, save the satisfaction of sagacity, and the delight of prudence following the mind in any line of conduct whatsoever that has drawn forth a shrewd play of powers. We are not, under the name of blessedness, to steal away the fruits of obedience to an independent law, and by means of this reflect authority on a simple precept of wisdom. The right must come before the satisfaction which springs from obeying it.

Herein is revealed a difficulty which more or less embarrasses every presentation of the utilitarian theory. We do indeed grant, that what is right is always ultimately in a broad sense useful, but the moral nature, itself an independent means of gratification, a pre-eminent source of good, is often the necessary condition of its being so.

The martyr sets this one pleasure over against all other pleasures, and wisely; yet he never would have done this, if he had started with the idea that the right action is only the sagacious choice between enjoyments other than those which belong to the moral constitution. We are not in our theories to have, and not to have, at the same time, the law and the rewards of conscience, of the moral intuition. We are not to make ethical pleasures to arise simply from the successful pursuit of other pleasures, and yet allow them themselves to be furtively included among these pleasures between which we are deciding. Many lines of action are obviously useful when accompanied with the gratification of our moral sensibilities, which are not so, when these, as independent sources of good, are left out of the calculation, as they must be in any honest evolution of a utilitarian theory.

A philosopher may assign to pleasures an order of precedence satisfactory to himself, may give sufficient ground on which to choose between them, yet he therein bestows no sense of obligation upon any of them, nor can he enforce his view of their respective rank, except as it conforms to the experience of others. Enjoyments are not so much dependent on judgments as on sensibilities.

Nor is the intuitive philosophy, rightly presented, at all open to the repeated taunts of Bentham, that each individual by a blind irrational power may thus pretend to decide what is right, and capriciously lay down a law absolute for himself and for others. All the investigation that Bentham or any other philosopher may bring to the practical effects of action, to its immediate and ultimate results, finds a place in our moral judgments. It is in the full intellections made up by exhaustive inquiry, that the reason sees the right and affirms its obligation. We might as well say, because the judge authoritatively decides a case, it is of no avail for the lawyers thoroughly to present it, as to say, that because conscience adjudicates between right and wrong, it is of no moment that the action to which the discussion pertains should be fully understood. It is the intellectual conception of this action which is declared right, and if this conception is incomplete, then a verdict intrinsically correct is practically false, as pronounced on a hypothetical case, and not a real one. The last decision, that of conscience, we believe to be correct; the presentation of the case, that on which this decision is made, to be, as often as otherwise, incorrect. Here enter the full fruits of investigation and protracted experience, an opportunity for a broad, honest, faithful survey of the facts of the exact case to be made and presented at the judgment-seat of the ethical sense. This merely gives new authority the weight and the character of law, to what the other faculties have pronounced upon as prudent and wise. There is no more opportunity for caprice, and individual assumption here, than in any debate concerning the qualities and bearings of actions—for instance their usefulness.

We designate in common language as conscience that action of the reason which discovers the right, and this is the ground or centre of our entire moral nature. Any theory which regards obligation as simple and ultimate, therein accepts the intuitive and independent nature of the right, in the meaning in which we have employed it. Obligation must arise in *view* of something, and in view of it in a *moral relation.* This perceptive element is inseparable from the emotional element, and, together, they constitute the idea, right; as a certain form of perception and the pleasure therefrom, constitute the intuition of beauty. The two are as indivisible as the flavor and savor of a peach, the perception of the one and the enjoyment of the other. We can no more talk of the ultimate nature of obligation and the derived, secondary nature of the right, than of a simple, final sense-pleasure, deduced inferentially from certain premises. The pleasure is no more ultimate, than the perception which gives rise to it, as they are inseparable. Moral feelings that are peculiar necessitate intuitions as peculiar, which may be their basis. Otherwise we have intellectual feelings with no ground or occasion for them. Nor can it be rightly said, that "virtue is not the choice or love of virtue, or of right; it is the love of God and of our neighbor as ourselves—the willing of good—the good will." Love has a moral quality only as it contemplates moral actions or moral relations, and these are suffused through and through with obligation. Any other love than this is either constitutional, or calculating; either instinctive, or selfish. The moral law is in and under spontaneous moral obedience, as truly as under constrained obedience.

The system of ethics to be evolved from the above view is briefly this. All moral emotions, the entire moral nature is conditioned on a moral intuition, which we term that of right. This quality or relation of rational acts, arrived at by a simple, ultimate stroke of the eye of reason, in grounds or premises previously unfolded, and which uniformly relate to the actions of free, intelligent, sensitive beings, involves as an inseparable element the feeling of obligation. Here is the final authority of morals in the moral intuition. A reason can be given for the decisions of conscience in this sense, that the character and bearings of the acts pronounced right can be given; not in this sense, that the intellectually discerned relations of these actions are, aside from a distinct action of the moral faculty upon them, a ground of obligation. No "supreme end" can of itself inspire a feeling of obligation, since there can be no such end till the moral intuition has given it its authority, its *supreme* position. No "good," as a good, can give a law, can give a moral basis of action, since to do this it must go beyond its own appetitive range, and reach into the moral field of authority. It is to account for *authority* that we invoke the moral nature. No "worthiness" of the individual can explain the authority of the right action, for it is this very authority which makes it so infinitely worthy of him. In a dozen cunning ways the consequences of right action may be made to reflect an explanation back on the right itself. They all fail, for the simple reason that effects are found in causes, not causes in effects. In this discussion we have used the word *right* as expressive of the moral law itself, or that intuition which gives such a law, not of the conformity of action to that law.

§ 11. The regulative idea we have now arrived at, that of liberty, presents many difficulties. A more convenient opportunity for the discussion of these will be presented under volition. We shall now strive merely to show, that it belongs with intuitive ideas. Proof of the actual possession of liberty by man as a voluntary agent, and a precise statement of what is involved therein, will be presented later. Liberty is to be distinguished on the one side from those necessary connections which are causal in character, and on the other, from chance, fortuity, the denial of all dependence on antecedents. Indeed, strictly construed there can be no chance events. The positive notions of causation and liberty, which cover the entire phenomenal field, do not permit them. It is only under the qualified form, as events with unknown or incalculable causes, that chance ever appears in the field of facts. Liberty allows the influence of motives, but not the measured, definite, irresistible influence. We admit and deny in the same instant the application of the word influence, admit the word in its substance, deny it in the form which its connection with causal events has given it. Herein is the peculiar and primitive character of the conception, that of a connection which is not necessary, of persuasion which is not imperative in either branch of the alternative, of influence which does not push with a fixed, determinative force towards a given volition. The will is neither wholly capricious, nor mathematically calculable in its action. It is free, and submits freely, so far as it *submits* to the motives before it. There is no great difficulty in this conception so long as we let it alone. It is when we begin to compare it, to classify it with other conceptions, that its obstinacy appears, and this we are liable to mistake for intrinsic absurdity, falsity.

This idea of liberty, connection without necessity—the motives lying before the will, not back of it; persuading, not impelling it—is primitive, and brought by the mind to the explanation of a class of facts that require it, those of choice and responsibility. The sense of obligation, of responsibility, with the subsequent feelings of virtue and guilt, of approval and condemnation ; the facts of government, of reward and punishment, the mind cannot understand, or fully accept without the interpretation of the idea of liberty; without making the connection between choice and motives, between personal action and the circumstances under which it takes place, one of freedom. Hence springs the notion of liberty, and the obstinate defense and maintenance of it by so many, in spite of faulty definitions, in spite of this inability to render any explanation of it satisfactory to the purely scientific mind.

We are not conscious of liberty. If we were, there would be no room for discussion. We no more know the exact nature of the connection between the motives and the will from experience simply, than we do the connection between the volition and subsequent muscular action. In view of the accepted fact of accountability, and the absence of all sensible constraint in motives, the mind predicates of the connection liberty—itself supplying the idea, and applying it to the phenomena ; exactly as to another class of facts, it, in the same independent way, brings the idea of causal interdependence. The last process is not more valid than the first, and is of the same nature and authority with it. In each case the mind proceeds to meet, search and expound the facts with its own independent notion, seen by itself to be applicable to the conditions of the problem. The movement is exactly that which takes place in the explanation of other experiences under the notion of space; and of still others, under that of time. The super-sensual nature of the idea of liberty must be admitted by all, certainly not less by those who deny its intelligibility, and ridicule the assertion of its existence, than by those who accept both. As the facts which establish its actual presence, as the significant feature of volitions, are so closely connected with the will, we defer its farther consideration. It seems quite evident, that if freedom does exist, it is the expository, the intuitive, regulative idea presiding over the facts of choice; the form under which the connection of the will with the causal forces about it, is to be conceived, courting it as motives, not pressing upon it as powers. Indeed, philosophers of the empirical school usually deny the existence and notion of liberty, at least under the form insisted on by Intuitive Philosophy. No one can reach, or has striven to reach, the notion of liberty through outside experience. It has, when accepted, been referred directly to consciousness, or to an intuitive power.

§ 12. It only remains to speak of the infinite, the last of the intuitive ideas, and one that has recently given rise to much discussion. It finds application in several directions, and perhaps, in the development of the mind, as early to space as to any other form of thought. The notion of space cannot be dwelt on without soon suggesting this idea of the infinite. The mind soon sees the inapplicability of any measures, limits, finite relations to space, and that, in the very moment of establishment, they are swept away by the on-going movement. Space lies without as much as within any line we choose to run, and the nearer has no advantage over the farther side. The mind under this new necessity laid upon it, with this new occasion given to it, grasps the idea of the infinite, of unmeasured and immeasurable extension. This conception, as we regard it, is not the result of mere weariness, is not the affirmation of an inability to proceed farther, does not spring from repeated and reiterated failure; it is rather the force and insight of the mind that discloses it. It is seen, inherently seen, that there is, there can be, no advantage in pressing the imagination to its utmost flight, that the conditions which are now present at this point of space, must recur everywhere, no matter what the position attained by us; that one point and one position here or there, that each bound longer or shorter, are *fac-similes* of every other, and therefore contain the solution of the problem as perfectly as if it had been raced after with the most wearisome efforts. The mind does not then distress itself in search of a limit, and fail; it discovers that there *can* be no limit; it penetrates the conditions of the problem, and brings forward the notion of a true infinite, which it sets over against the finite, which it applies to space, and is at rest, as it knows that nothing other or more is to be found elsewhere.

Thus the mind hits upon the true infinite, not by experience, not by exhaustive effort, but by its own penetration of relations; and through this idea it understands another of the conditions of its experience, and declines exertion which it sees to be necessarily futile. Standing, not moving; by insight, not by baffled effort, it grasps and henceforth uses this notion, so super-sensual in character, so necessary for the exposition of the being we possess, the universe we inhabit. Space, as infinite, admits of no division. No plane can cleave it, no line pierce it. In strict language, it is without parts, at least so far as these imply remainders. Nothing can be taken from it, nothing added to it. The true infinite is subject to no addition, subtraction, multiplication or division. These are processes which find play in the finite alone.

A second point at which this notion would arise early, is the contemplation of time. Here, too, the mind discovers that the conditions of conception are not in the least varied by movement, and that the years which beheld the laying of the foundations of the world were no less central than those which now are, or those which shall behold its overthrow. Geologic æons lie lapped in eternity, with no more power of measurement than the point which defines pure position on the board before me. Here again there is no opportunity to take aught from, or add aught to the infinite, to eternity. Indeed we may not strike it into two infinite halves by this fleeting moment the present, as if it were a node jointing the past to the future. A hemisphere is not a sphere, because it meets on one side the conditions of the definition. A true infinite must be immeasurable in all the directions in which measurement can be applied. A forward or a backward stretch, leaving a definite, finite period in the opposite direction, constitutes no true infinite; the lines which pass out from any given point are not infinite, they lack an essential feature of the infinite, interminableness. They are limited in one direction. We are always to distinguish between the indefinitely great and the infinite. Mathematics deals with the one, and not with the other. A series of figures increased as you please, can never *express* an infinite amount, and therefore no infinite can be twice or thrice as great as another infinite. This borne constantly in mind, and we shall easily dispose of a portion of the perplexities Sir William Hamilton has thrown around the subject.

"A quantity, say a foot, has an infinity of parts. Any part of this quantity, say an inch, has also an infinity. But one infinity is not larger than another. Therefore an inch is equal to a foot." Neither an inch, nor a foot, nor any other definite quantity, has an infinity of parts—parts, that are parts, that have any size, will exhaust any dimensions short of the infinite, and the quotient still remain finite. "A wheel turned with quickest motion; if a spoke be prolonged, it will therefore be moved with a motion quicker than the quickest."

This example and similar examples, are mere riddles arising under a play of words. There is no absolutely quickest motion, and no motion that is infinitely rapid. The perplexity in these cases does not at all spring from the notion of the infinite, but from the effort of the imagination to transcend its own conditions in a false search by a false method after the infinite, or the infinitesimal. The imagination must have finite, phenomenal quantities to deal with. These, therefore, are always capable both of multiplication and division. The fancy may carry on the process till it gets weary; confounded with the results, it may mistake its own embarrassments for those of the entire mind. It does this only by overlooking and denying the true nature of the infinite, and the source whence alone it can be rationally looked for. It should not distress the mind, because the end of a circle cannot be found by chasing round and round it. No more should it, because that which has not dimensions cannot be reached by cutting down, and at the same time saving, that which has. This is striving in the same instant and act to hold on to the finite, and to take it away, to keep it and to get beyond it. It is no more a startling and discouraging fact, that the imagination can make nothing out of nothing, nor give limits to that which is without limits, than it is that the body cannot be suspended by a spider's thread. Remove the support beyond a certain amount in either case, and there must be a downfall.

A third direction in which this notion is applicable, is to the attributes of God. God is infinite in power, in wisdom, in goodness; that is there are no limits to these attributes within their own nature. All that power can do, the power of God is able to do. The infinite in space presents itself under other forms from the infinite in time, and both of these in a way yet different from the infinite in power. The nature of power is not altered by the affirmation of its infinite extent. This merely removes its limits. It can no more do now than before what is not pertinent to its nature, what must be the product of wisdom or of grace. The notion, in its application to God, comes to assume those personal relations, that independent perfection of existence which we designate by the Infinite, the Absolute. God is thus lifted above the reflex action of causes, as well as above their antecedent action. Not only is nothing back of Him, there is nothing before Him, giving condition and law *ab extra* to His nature. The infinite in this form, in these its various applications, we must defend as a positive, intuitive idea—indeed, if it be an idea at all, it must be an intuitive idea.

The first objections against the positive, valid character of this notion which we shall consider, are those of Sir William Hamilton, presented under what he terms, *The Law of the Conditioned.* It is there claimed, that this impression, like that of causality, arises from the powerlessness of the mind, not from its insight. The line of argument is much the same as in the case of causation above treated. The following, with omissions, is his presentation of the subject. It is found in the *Lectures on Metaphysics, p.* 527.

"We are altogether unable to conceive space as bounded, as finite; that is as a whole beyond which there is no farther space. * * * On the other hand, we are equally powerless to realize in thought the possibility of the opposite contradictory; we cannot conceive space as infinite, as without limits. You may launch out in thought beyond the solar walk, you may transcend in fancy even the universe of matter, and rise from sphere to sphere in the region of empty space until imagination sinks exhausted; with all this, what have you done? You have never gone beyond the finite. * * Now then, both contradictions are equally inconceivable, both are equally incomprehensible; and yet, though unable to view either as possible, we are forced by a higher law—that of excluded middle—to admit that one and but one only is necessary." He then treats in the same way, the minimum of space, the maximum and minimum of time, and proceeds, "The sum therefore of what I have now stated, is: that the conditioned is that which is alone conceivable, or cogitable. the unconditioned that which is inconceivable or incogitable. The conditioned or the thinkable lies between two extremes or poles." Later he says, "These poles are the absolute and the infinite; the term absolute expressing that which is finished or complete; the term infinite that which cannot be terminated or concluded."

The doctrine of the law of the conditioned is the most characteristic feature of the philosophy of Hamilton, and is open to obvious and fatal objections. It does not explain why the mind is thus embarrassed in its conception of the maximum and minimum of space and time, nor why it is ever led to vex and torment itself with these impossibilities, forsaking the conditioned where traveling is practicable, comfortable and profitable, to scale cloud heights which never give foothold to the foolhardy assailant; nor yet, most strange omission! why of two impossible conceptions equally perplexing, we are called on to accept the one, that of infinite space, infinite time, in place of the other, that of bounded space and time. A better theory is able to offer an explanation of these difficulties. The mind is baffled in a conception of a maximum and minimum of space, because a faculty is set to the task which deals exclusively with the phenomenal, and it is no more curious or surprising that the imagination cannot attain to the infinite, than that these limbs of ours cannot mount a sunbeam, and so reach the heavens; or more aptly, than that we cannot see, hear, smell the infinite; since the senses are the analogues of the fancy, both covering in a different way the same field. We have given the imagination a work to it impossible and preposterous. Why is there these excursions of fancy into impracticable regions? Because, overlooking the direct, intuitive grasp of the mind, and still haunted by the notion of the infinite, we put spurs to the steeds of the imagination to see if we may not in this way overtake it. The sober, plodding judgment turns aside from the thinkable to the unthinkable, in hunt of a ghostly conception which is real enough to bewilder the eye with strange appearances, but too unsubstantial to be grasped and handled in physical fashion. To pursue spirits or flee from spirits on horseback is of little avail, though with man's belief in the spiritual world, the nature of the pursuit and its philosophy are sufficiently plain to the quiet looker-on.

A third, most fatal failure of this theory, is to explain why we uniformly and certainly accept infinite space which has no advantage to the mind over the supposition of finite space. This embarrassment at once disappears, if we suppose the notion a positive one, provided by the mind to be placed in explanation and comprehension over against the finite. The theory of Hamilton succeeds in eliciting the perplexities of the subject, but brings to them no solution.

But it will be said, the intuitive theory has its own and yet more fatal difficulties. How can the infinite be a positive idea? Very easily if we assign it to the right faculty, and make it simple and ultimate; as easily and intelligibly as red is red, or sweet, sweet. In neither case can we go beyond the ultimate fact, and we have fortunately learned in the more familiar instance to give up the effort. This objection may come in the form of a second theory of the infinite, to wit that the notion is a negative not a positive one, involving a denial merely and not an affirmation. That the word is negative in form is a fact of no significance ; so are inhuman and indecent. If the word infinite simply set forth the fact of non-existence, we should at once lay aside the article, and no longer speak of *the* infinite, any more than of the nothing. It is because it stands over against the finite, embracing the sum of possibilities and powers not expressed or measured therein, that we call it *the* infinite. If its negative form contained the true secret of the word, it would occasion no more perplexity, would contain no more profound depths, than does the finite. Nothing is as intelligible as something, the termination as the extension of physical objects, and if the mind did accept the word as a mere denial of anything more, it would accept it contentedly, without this endless bother and perplexity, this groping on for something not yet reached.

It is said, in proof of this negative character of the notion, that it is inconceivable. This we grant, and have given the reason why it is inconceivable. It is not an object for the imagination. No more is the notion of causation, nor of liberty, nor of right, nor of beauty. Nothing which is not phenomenal, nor under the immediate form which phenomena are assuming, is a subject for the imagination. It is further said, The infinite is not thinkable. "To think is to condition" is to throw into finite relations, is to destroy the notion of the infinite. The same answer as that already made is still open. The list of our faculties is not exhausted when we have marked off the imagination and the judgment. It is possible that the reason was given to us for this very end, to reach ideas *not otherwise present* to the mind. We hardly see why it should be present, or thought to be present, to furnish thinkable and conceivable objects, that is, objects arrived at by other faculties.

In what sense, however, is it true that the infinite is not

thinkable? It is true in this sense only, that it cannot be approached by explanations grounded on resemblances, that it cannot be made the subject of judgments, at least, of those which limit it under finite analogies, and this is an important restriction so far as the statements are regarded as precise and exhaustive. And why should we expect it to be? Do we not antecedently see and say, that this process must be destructive to the very nature of the notion? Why then proceed to allege the fact against it? We can do this rationally only by involving the assertion, that the judgment and imagination are our sole final, conclusive faculties of knowledge; and this begs the question at issue. To reject the reason because it does not do the very superfluous work of giving an idea capable, by likeness and relation, of falling into the list of previous ideas, is to misunderstand the object of the faculty, or to assume that its existence is impossible. We might as well object to the validity of our knowledge of an odor, because it is not thinkable, or, forsooth, conceivable under color or sound. In this sense, then, we admit the infinite is not thinkable; but all thinking is not under limitations and conditions. Sometimes it is quite the reverse. To say that God is infinite is to deny conditions of Him. To say that The Infinite is, that He is free, that He is holy, is not to condition, to limit God, rather the reverse. The fact that we cannot go farther, and conceive the acts in and by which His liberty and holiness express themselves except under a measured, a finite form, does not destroy the meaning or significance of the antecedent assertion. It merely presents another case of a familiar difficulty, that of getting from one province of knowledge to another. Different tracts of cognition do not lie together, like the provinces of one empire, the transition one of movement only.

Here springs up another modification of this theory, that of Herbert Spencer. He regards the notion of the infinite as of an illusory character, shown by the very fact that every effort to give proportion and definiteness to it, baffles us, and results in driving it into more remote regions. We admit the perplexity which a portion of our faculties, whose action we are most familiar with, and from which we are accustomed to receive most of our conclusions, experience in handling, or rather in striving to handle, the infinite. This fact presents to us no difficulty; we see the reason why these faculties are not adequate to the labor laid upon them. Indeed, our belief in the infinite would be overthrown by a successful presentation of it, either by the imagination, or by the judgment under its own forms, and is established by this very failure on their part. The objection of our adversary is proof with us.

On the other hand, the opposite view, that the action is wholly illusory, is involved in difficulties that it cannot evade. How can Spencer insist that any presentation of the infinite is not adequate, when he has no notion of what the infinite is? How can a notion be shown to be illusory, except by a growing intuition? How can Hamilton require us to accept by faith that which is unintelligible, absolutely and completely so. Here are real contradictions. There can be no general denial of the applicability of any and all conceptions of the infinite, without postulating thereby some notions of the infinite with which these are compared, and, as falling short, are pronounced wanting. One notion of an utterly unknown thing, is as good and as adequate as another. Neither can faith make that an object of belief, which is utterly unknown to the mind. The faith of Hamilton, and the vanishing conception of Spencer, are both self-contradictory, as being alone able to arise under the furtive, but real light of an idea present and ruling in the mind. No false conception of the Deity can be set aside, except by one which is better, or is deemed better; no faith can be expressed except toward a Being thought to be. These perplexities find no removal. To escape, therefore, difficulties whose reason is forthcoming by difficulties that find no solution, is to forsake the light for darkness, is to employ exposition with a loss of expository power.

Nor are formulæ of thought which are inadequate, in a limited sense false, unservicable, if their deficiencies are clearly seen by the mind that uses them. The expressions infinite power, infinite wisdom, infinite goodness, contain as statements two things : the qualities indicated by the nouns, *power*, *wisdom*, *goodness ;* and their unlimited degree, pointed out by the adjective *infinite.* Our ideas of the first may gain in precision and clearness without affecting the applicability of the adjective which sweeps away their limits. We may inquire experimentally into the nature and forms of power, and yet well understand that these precise manifestations are swallowed up in, included under, infinite power. We thus use in mathematics the first term of an infinite series to define and represent the remainder ; or we make the rule for the area of an inscribed polygon, that of the enclosing circle, on the ground of the constant approximation of the one surface to the other, with each increase of the number of sides. Yet the one never absolutely conforms to the other. The moral formula for the infinite is, This and more. The noun gives that which is to be expanded, the adjective, the law of its expansion. The *this* of the formula gives room for inquiry and growth, the *more* cuts us off from regarding a part as the whole. This is a movement of thought practically simple and safe ; no more inexplicable, no more dangerous than the use of suppositions in mathematics which reach toward the exact truth without finally covering it, which put one thing for another on the ground of constant approximation. Conceptions are habitually employed in mathematics which are inconceivable. We regard circles as perfect, yet the description of a perfect circle is to the imagination an impossible task, for the same reason that it is to the senses. Start with a describing point. If it move for the least interval in a straight line, so far the line is not curved? if it begins to bend before it has traced the least portion of a line, it has nothing from which to bend or curve. It must bend and curve at once, and an image of this the fancy cannot form. Even a point, in order that progress may be made by passing through it, must have some breadth, and this breadth, if it is to give an initiatory direction from which the curve is to depart, must be straight. In analytic conception we resolve the descriptive process into motion and departure, or bending from that motion; we cannot conceive these two to be absolutely and constantly synchronous, yet without this the circle is imperfect. The imagination follows after the hand and eye, and as these are not exact, neither is it.

§ 13. Having presented the eleven intuitive ideas which constitute the mind's intellectual furniture, and also the grounds of proof in each case, we propose further to draw attention to some considerations which belong to all of them, establishing their character, and separating them from generalizations. Necessity and universality have been fixed on as the criteria of these notions. The two tests are liable to be mistaken for one, and are so under a certain rendering of them. To distinguish these from each other, we should understand by necessity, that immediateness and certainty of conviction which attaches in all minds to truths purely dependent on intuitive ideas. Thus there are in the definitions and axioms of Geometry, many secondary intuitions, referable to the primary intuition, space. From these there spring convictions and proofs, in the quickness and certainty with which the mind receives them, wholly unlike those dependent on experience. That two straight lines, lying in the same plane, and for a space equally distant, will remain so through their entire length, is an assertion which the mind accepts at once, as a necessary truth. Nothing, probably, but the exigencies of a theory, would ever lead one, with Mill, to strive to trace a conviction like this to experience. Certain it is, that no mathematician ever thought of establishing it by induction. Experimental truth never imparts such immediate and perfect belief. Of a like nature is the instant and unavoidable assurance that the changes taking place before us have a cause. Whenever a statement is solely dependent on a regulative idea, it becomes a necessary or demonstrative truth.

Universality, remaining a separate criterion, may now refer to the constant presence of one or other of these ideas in every judgment; to the fact of the impossibility of thought, distinct, declared thought, in any mind without them. These universal antecedents of thought cannot be furnished by thought itself. Thought cannot supply its own conditions. The universality of their presence in each act of mind and in all minds becomes thus a proof of their supersensual nature. It seems to us, however, that it is a careful analysis of the processes and growth of thought, that is to establish each idea by itself; to lay open its transcendental character, as in the case of the infinite and liberty, or its necessary, antecedent presence to a certain class of judgments, as right to ethical judgments, consciousness to the apprehension of mental facts. The three criteria, the necessity of the involved truths, the universal presence of one or more of those notions in all judgments, the transcendental nature of the conceptions themselves, are not applicable all of them with equal clearness to each of the eleven ideas, and must be applied and sustained by a distinct analysis of the mental phenomena involved.

§ 14. There is another very vital point in this discussion; whether these ideas are to be regarded as purely subjective as mere mental forms brought to the object-matter of thought or whether they pertain as external, necessary forms to that matter itself, thus possessing a complete independent being. The first belief is that of certain phases of idealism, and is as contradictory to the universal opinions of men as any philosophy well can be. We do not say, that it is contradictory to consciousness, for it is not, but that it sets aside as wholly invalid, and without foundation, the universal convictions of men, thereby casting great improbability on its own conclusions.

Cause and effect seem to be the notion by which we more especially establish the existence of the external world. Not to accept as just and safe the inferences to which this notion of the mind lead us, is to deny the integrity of our faculties, and to introduce a fatal scepticism to which no after limits can be set. It is a fundamental principle of sound philosophy, that the integrity of no faculty can be denied, nor its guarded, normal action be set aside. If, therefore, we recognize the universal presence of the notion of cause and effect, we have no more right to treat it as illusory, than we have thus to regard vision or memory. Spencer justly says, "That Space and Time are 'forms of sensibilities,' or 'subjective conditions of thought,' that have no objective basis, is a belief as repugnant to common sense as any proposition that can be found." This conclusion is reached in philosophy by rejecting without reason an action of mind, a faculty universally present. We do not, indeed, know the objective world in perception, since consciousness discloses—is a condition of—mental phenomena only, and these are not identical with the physical phenomena which they represent or accompany ; but we do know it inferentially under causation. The action of the mind herein, as clear and constant and universal as any, implies a power or faculty whose office it is to make these disclosures.

It may be said, that this view is as open as the opposite

to the criticism of disregarding the general conviction, since this is not merely that we know, but that we actually see and feel, the outside world. The cases presented by the two theories are very diverse. The one rejects entirely conclusions universally accepted ; the other, in careful analysis of a complex operation, refers them to an obscure element, easily and more frequently overlooked. The popular mind regards sight, touch, as simple operations, and so ascribes to them our knowledge of the external world. It is deficient in analysis, not erroneous in its reference. Philosophy resolves sensation into distinct operations, and assigns to one of these, that of causal inference, the immediate proof of outside existence. It is to be claimed that the general action of the common mind should be regarded as normal ; it is not to be claimed, that analysis may not go farther than ordinary concrete judgments.

Let us trace a little the entrance and ground of this conviction of the independent existence of things about us. The mind soon learns to distinguish between sensations and thoughts, between phenomena which come and go at its own bidding, and those which are entirely independent of its will. It necessarily assigns the one a different source or cause from the other. As sensations in different organs are found to be connected with the same object, this fact, in an additional and confirmatory way, establishes, for the mind, its external and independent existence. Touch and sight aid each other in fixing and locating the source of the impressions in each sense. The sensations and perceptions are found to come and go together, and are therefore inferred to spring from a common cause, external alike to each organ. The location of the senses themselves, the gradual apprehension of the objects, distances, and relations of the external world, are processes of which we shall have occasion to speak more fully. It is sufficient for our present purpose to observe, that under the notion of cause and effect, sensations and perceptions are distinguished from other facts of mind as having an independent origin; that these external causes are slowly fixed on by repeated experiences, entering through a variety of organs, and that as a result of this normal movement of mind, men do everywhere arrive at, and believe in an external world, the same to them all. The cause is as real as the effect, and to accept a sensation as actual, is virtually to accept for it an independent cause, and under the instruction of protracted experience, an external cause, external not merely to the mind, but usually to the body also. This movement is spontaneous and universal, and cannot be invalidated without an overthrow of the credibility of a portion of our faculties.

Observe also that the result is the same for all; men move in *one* external world. One set of objects, one relation of objects belong to them all, and they harmonize their action by the validity of this their common experience. Make the world subjective to each individual, and you virtually deny for each the existence of all others. The preposterous conclusions of pure idealism could only be made to rest on the most undeniable proof; nor on that, for the effect even then would be rather of general confusion, of speculations wholly at war with practical conclusions; of the discord of knowledge, than of sound, settled, consistent belief.

A similar line of proof has been carefully applied by Dr. Hickok to the notions of time and space. The reality of space has been shown to be the only condition in which the phenomena of the physical world can be the same for us all, included in "one whole of all space," open to common knowledge and common use. Moreover we distinguish imaginary space—space which the fancy furnishes as a setting for its pictures, from real space. The space of the senses and that of the imagination are entirely different, showing that space as a form of thought is at once distinguishable by us from space, an external form for real being.

§ 15. The eleven ideas now presented are capable of being grouped in various ways. Space and consciousness may be regarded as expressing the two diverse and complementary fields in which respectively all phenomena, phenomena of matter and mind, occur. The higher plane has ideas peculiar to itself, beauty, liberty, right. The lower plane shares its ideas with the higher. The only ideas peculiar to physical events are space, and cause and effect. The infinite, on the other hand, is an idea that keeps aloof from the phenomenal, comes in only to explain and comprehend the finite, and, in its personal form, to give the investigations of the mind a final goal,—one from which they may start, and to which they may return.

The six ideas that pertain to matter, fall into couplets, existence and resemblance, space and number, time and cause. Existence finds its chief significance in its resemblances ; space, in its numerical relations ; time, in the causal sequence of events. The first couplet gives us the facts of being, and their character ; the second, the most abstract relations of things in co-existence ; the third, their relations in sequence. By them collectively we are able to determine that a thing is, what it is, where and when it is, and its relations to the objects about it, thus completing the circle of inquiry. Cause expresses the law of evolution in the physical world ; liberty, that of the spiritual world. Forces are installed in distinct measure and form in space, their initiation is an act of mind. Mind antedates matter, matter is the product of mind. Liberty in actual choice forecloses liberty, and henceforward realized power moves with an imparted, necessary impulse to its goal.

CHAPTER V.

The Dynamics of the Intellect.

§ 1. We are to speak in this chapter of the growth and interaction of the intellectual powers, of the dynamic or active states of the mind. The Intuitive Philosophy has been censured, not without reason, by the Sensualistic School for contemplating the mind only in its maturity, with no sufficient allowance for the results of previous conditions upon it,—for the effects of growth. This criticism we so far respect as to find a conspicuous place for truths which have been chiefly urged by such men as Spencer and Bain, always shaping them, however, to a new position and purpose. We are not prepared to admit any hereditary influences which vary the fundamental conditions of the problem of our intellectual nature. The varieties of character, the growth of national and race distinctions, find explanation here; but no sufficient proof has yet been given to establish, or even to render probable, the transformation of species by the accumulated changes of descent, especially in those cases of decided difference to which the human family belongs. We must still regard each normal individual as a full type of the race in its essential features, nor are we ready to look upon any one of these faculties as the product of external conditions, the sum of growing, hereditary tendencies.

When, on the other hand, we contrast the infant with the mature man, it must, we think, be admitted, that the complete activity of the latter, is very different from the tentative, experimental, partial movement of the former. It is to this development of intellectual power that we first direct attention. The first distinct, mental phenomena are doubtless those of sensation, are physical feelings. These should be conceived as perfectly pure, that is as simple states or activities of mind—for our present purposes there is no difference between a state and an activity of mind: both are activities. These first sensations may be of one kind or of another, but are more likely to enter through the general, sensational system than through a specific sense, to be sensations of pain, local or pervasive, demanding relief, and rising with acute, jagged certainty into the light of consciousness. It matters not what are the first sensations, since it is a changing series of sensations that invites attention. These are each simple, single, mental states known in the very fact of their existence as sensibilities. Separately, they are capable of no analysis, no division whatever. A pain, a taste are as individual as any objects of contemplation can be. To suppose these, in the case of special sensations, to reveal directly an external object, would be to suppose that the phenomena of matter become the phenomena of mind, and are known directly as such. We can only be conscious of a mental state, and if we are not conscious of external objects or events, then we do not directly know them. Than such a supposition nothing can be more destructive of the fundamental distinction between the two fields, the physical and the mental. By means of it we shall logically travel back to that pure idealism which forced us, in defence, to make it. If, in reaching the external world, we break down the division between the two, we are, with our captured facts, thrown back at once on the enlarged domain of mind. We have seen matter not as matter, but as productive of events, perceptions within the circle of consciousness, that is within the mind itself. Thus the mind knows matter immediately, and that too in its own acts. Then the same phenomena are at once phenomena of matter and of mind.

We can only allow, then, that sensations directly in consciousness disclose themselves ; all beyond this is inferential. At this stage of growth, possessed of sensations merely, the infant is as ignorant of his own physical organs, as of the world about him. He absolutely knows nothing save the fleeting, varying pains and pleasures that flit through that unlocated region called consciousness, itself more often hidden under the cloud of dreams than open to the new light of waking perceptions. A tongue, a hand, an eye, a foot, are wholly beyond the scope of his knowledge ; nothing physical, external to consciousness, is as yet recognized. In adult years we so instantly locate each sensation, that it seems to us that it itself declares its position. We are doubtless to conceive of the mind as using the entire body, as making it directly and immediately instrumental in reaching and influencing the external world. The brain is the chief seat or centre of power, but is no more the mind, is no more a condition of its activity than the nervous system generally, spreading through and through the body, and perfectly possessing it. But this instrument of the mind is not directly known to it. It uses it, and controls it unconsciously, in the dark, not in the light. Its shape, form, and members even, are all to be learned by experience. We may hesitate at first to admit this, but a little thought will compel the concession.

If the mind in sensation itself knows and locates the instruments of those sensations, then ought the mind to know its internal organs as well as its external ones. These are often independent sources of pain, and in the nervous system are as indispensable means to perception as the special senses ; yet the existence of the stomach, the brain, the liver, the interior formation of the eye, the ear, the nervous fibres and their ramifications, have all to be learned, must all be made objects of examination, and declare nothing to us directly of their own existence. These do not differ as regards our original knowledge of them, from the tongue, the finger-ends, except in the fact that we necessarily learn the existence and form of the one set of organs much earlier than we do of the other.

That the special senses do not directly declare locality and form, is further seen in an analysis of their action. The ear, and the eye, though more frequently indicating instantly the directions and relations of objects, merging, obscuring the judgments of the mind by their rapidity in the sensations which they accompany, are often so slow and uncertain in their decisions as to make the presence of their reflective processes conspicuous. We frequently have occasion to listen attentively in order to judge of the character and distance and nature of an unfamiliar sound. An object seen across the water deceives us, is farther off than we think it to be. Our estimates of the height of a cloud are very uncertain ; or of the size of unfamiliar objects, especially when our ordinary standards of measurement are taken from us, and the proportions, as of a cathedral, are grander than those to which we are accustomed. The incomplete state in which the work still remains, here reveals the fact, that size, form, direction, are to the eye solely matters of judgment. That the eye and the ear do not directly disclose themselves is evident. One whose eyes were couched late in life, was at first under the impression that visible objects were directly in contact with the eye, interpreting the action of this sense by that of touch with which he was familiar. He was utterly unable to dispense in vision with the training of experience, and, by constantly comparing the results of the two senses of sight and touch, was at length enabled to use the first independently.

Touch is the sense whose localizing power is regarded as the most immediate, while its acquisition of this facility is most concealed from us by remoteness of time. This sense can, by special cultivation, when other senses are wanting, be made so much more perfect than it now is, be so filled and rounded out with instantaneous judgments, as to have but a slight resemblance to its former self. The raised letters of the blind are distinguished by most persons slowly, and with the utmost difficulty, while the trained touch glides rapidly along them, almost as the visual nerve moves over the printed page. The blind in some instances acquire a power and precision of touch inexplicable to us, and are enabled to carry on employments, like engineering and warfare, from which we should regard them as entirely excluded. Ziska was among the most distinguished of generals. When the entire mind is directed to this avenue of communication with the external world, it brings it by included judgments to an unthought-of perfection, and widens it into a wonderful inlet of information.

The dependence of this sense, in common with others, on experience for its localizing power, is also seen in the fact, that on the finger-ends, where it exists most perfectly and in most constant use, we distinguish much more completely and accurately than on other parts of the body. A considerable space must intervene between two points applied simultaneously to the person elsewhere, before we can discern them as two; they may approach very closely, and yet be separated in sensation by the fingers.

The eye is sometimes deceived. The fans of a windmill seem to revolve in a direction opposite to the real one. We explain this, as an error of the accompanying judgments, induced by an unfavorable position. The same form of error occasionally occurs in touch. The fingers being crossed, and the hand placed behind its possessor, he is often not able to decide which one has been touched. The ordinary accuracy or judgment is lost on account of the unusual conditions under which it is exercised. The vast majority, then, of our localizing power being manifestly of an acquired and experimental character, we are inductively led to the conclusion, that all of it is of this nature ; and the more so when we find, that the most steadfast and stubborn conclusions are occasionally at fault, when formed under changed conditions of judgment. The patient whose limb was to be removed, returning to a state of consciousness, can only determine by observation, whether it has been amputated. Indeed his sensations may often lead him, through the accustomed reference of pain to the accustomed quarters, to suppose the limb in its place, and this though weeks may have elapsed since it was lopped from the body.

We return to the consideration of our first intellectual state, the flow of simple, subjective, unlocalized sensations.

Be it at once observed, that this is the form in which they present themselves to us, not at all that in which they are contemplated by the nascent spirit. Quite the reverse is its method of contemplation, so far as contemplation can be predicated of a state so controllingly sensational. The limited number of sensations are at first distinguished as pleasurable and painful, and each class is accompanied by more or less of spontaneous, automatic, muscular effort, gradually changing into voluntary effort, fitted to retain the enjoyment or escape the pain. The pleasures of touch and taste are especially concentrated on the tongue, and the infant spontaneously seeks the breast in gratification of its sensibilities. Later, the feeling awakens in the hands, and the child is not at ease till these are laid on the mother. In these earliest, tangible sources of pleasure, secured and maintained by muscular effort, the infant rests ; wanting these it worries, and moves inquiringly till they are regained. Later, other forms of sensation succeed ; the hand grasps more definitely, and seeks a greater variety of objects ; the ear is cheered by the voice of the parent ; the eye is delighted with the brightness of the lamp-light, or with the sun-light. In these last cases, it is evidently more as sensations than as perceptions, more as organic impressions, than as distinct cognitions, that the new objects find admission and confer pleasure. Slowly the eye learns to separate objects just at hand, and distinctly discern them, though possessed of no peculiar brilliancy. It recognizes the face of the mother, and at length follows, even into the distance, her retreating form. Still, its range, for a considerable period, seems limited, scarcely passing the verge of the cradle. Later, the ear learns to direct the eye, and the distant voice wins the attention of both organs. The process of acquisition goes on till a definite mastery of each member is secured; its peculiar impressions discriminated, and the visible world unfolded and rolled out in its marvellous complexity of forms and relations. Most busy and fruitful are these early years of childhood. Scarcely again do we learn so many and so perfect lessons in so brief a period. What the painter by slow analysis is able to reverse, presenting spaces, directions, distances, forms, on a plain surface of varying colors; rendering the landscape, with an area of many square miles, on a canvas of scarcely more square inches; the child of a few years has learned to do with far more perfection, opening up and out the simple vignette of the retina, till it fills in every part the magnificent stretches before and about us.

This movement, from the beginning, takes place under an objective form. The sensation is not enjoyed subjectively, dreamily; but objectively, really. The pleasures are attached at once to an object and a state; thus also the pains. The spontaneous, muscular effort with which they are connected, facilitate this external form of experience, by attaching enjoyment to objects independent of the senses themselves, to things momentarily lost and momentarily regained. Distinct, muscular exertion aids in distinguishing different states, in marking their attainment, maintenance, and loss.

The objective character of early experience is also heightened by the degree in which it is composed of sensations as opposed to perceptions, and later, of external, as contrasted with reflective pleasures. Language presents the mind as especially passive, receptive in feeling; and attributes the efficiency, the activity to the exterior occasion of the emotions. This we observe also in uncultivated, immature persons. Their attention is particularly directed to the objects and sources of pleasure. Their appetites and passions lead them inevitably to this objective life, to this hanging upon the external conditions of pleasure, this clinging to the bosom of nature. The notion of cause and effect—its own momentary enjoyments the effect—attaches the mind, as yet little more than a bundle of sensations, strongly and at once to the external world. Slowly it unfolds the facts of this world, the avenues and dependencies of its own pleasures, its senses and the things which minister to them. The internal rather than the external is overlooked. The senses are separated from the objects which affect them, but the attention of the mind is much later referred to itself, as truly subjective to them all.

If we were to neglect the objective character of experience from the outset; if we should suppose the mind for a time floating from sensation to sensation on the inner, tidal movement of its own phenomena, we should find increasing difficulty in making the transition, and in justifying it when we had made it. We are rather to regard the mind as at once borne outward toward the sources of its enjoyments, and as realizing these in and by their causes. We should likewise observe the great aid which muscular effort gives in interpreting and locating sensations. By this means the child at first automatically, later voluntarily, renews and discontinues its physical impressions, till the mind has matured its knowledge of them, their diversities and conditions. The relations of space are especially dependent on movement for their determination. The eye and the hand work with each other in exploring surrounding bodies and intervening spaces, while a series of sensations record the motions of the arms and fingers. By movement we repeat at pleasure the problems offered by extension, and secure ever varying conditions for their solution.

In this growth of the mind into the possession and handling of its instruments, into the rudiments of experimental knowledge, the appropriate, regulative ideas are present doing their work, though of course they are unrecognized by the mind, as is the fact of sensation itself in the first feelings, or the fact of judgment in the early perceptions of likeness. It is the substance of experience, not its forms, the facts of experience, not its conditions, that occupy the attention. Experience is not for this reason destitute of form, or without conditions. The first when and where, though as yet unanalyzed, involve time and space, as certainly as the last.

Regulative ideas are not first present as objects of attention, of distinct recognition, but as unthought-of principles which guide our consideration and apprehension of the phenomena before us. They may sooner or later, or not at all, be analyzed out as distinct elements of thought, though as unconscious ingredients they are, in some one or other of their forms, present from the very beginning. It is not till the class of phenomena to which it pertains are brought forward, enter into the experience, and call forth the attention and judgment, that any one of these ideas, as that of beauty, of liberty, or of right, will find development and application. That the notion of beauty remains so obscure, so confounded with other qualities to the mass of men, is no reflection on the Intuitive Philosophy. It is not asserted, that regulative ideas are from the beginning present in complete power, but when a fitting experience is here to evoke them.

§ 2. The mind, once in possession and use of its faculties; its perceptions and sensations made complete and instant in their action by the absorption of the needed judgments; the intuitive notions, all present aiding to expand, locate, relate, and expound the several objects and events of experience, and give form and rational coherence to thought, is ready for the acquisition of what is more commonly known as knowledge. This mastery of the conditions is so early, so spontaneous, so inevitable, that we more frequently overlook it altogether, and regard the entire complex result as immediate and direct. For the same reason we hardly expend a thought on the ways in which spoken language is secured by the child, and look upon education as commencing with the learning of the letters—the written alphabet. Yet the first acquisition, though imitative and spontaneous, involves a more fundamental training, penetrates deeper into the physical powers than the second.

The intellect once in possession of itself, finds chief occasion to expand its knowledge under the notion of resemblance. It is through this that it traces and interprets the lines of force, the streams of causation; and by these that it gains power, the means of gratification. Yet we cannot accept the statement, that all judgments can be analyzed into resemblance, into agreement and disagreement; and yet more do we not assent to the assertion, that these resemblances are sought for their own sake. Each regulative idea furnishes the ground of a distinct predication, not to be resolved in its very essence by the most subtle analysis into any other. Moreover, resemblances are of value, and only of value, as they are the indices of agreeing forces, as they are the surface marks which disclose the concealed lines of connection between objects and events.

Power is the fundamental element of knowledge, that which makes its search pleasant, and its acquisition profitable. The desire for knowledge which gives no power, which stands in no connections, is, like avarice, the morbid play of a just impulse. To know the exact number of leaves on a tree, their position and form, the precise way in which some ancient but insignificant event happened, the very words in which some second-rate poet expressed himself, is to know to no good purpose, is to have the semblance, not the substance of wisdom, the shell, not the kernel of truth. Resemblances which are accidental, which betray no relationship, as the size and form of a boy's marble, when compared with the pebbles on the beach, or the agreement of sounds and signs in unrelated languages, have no interest, and subserve none of the purposes of knowledge. A resemblance which is a mere resemblance, which casts no light on the past, and gives no clue to the future, which discloses none of the forces at work in the world, is unfruitful, and the knowledge of it of no value. That which makes the search after agreements so unremitting are the axioms of causation: That like causes are followed by like effects, and That like effects indicate like causes. These transform a knowledge of real, central agreements into power, put us in connection with the plan of the world, enable us to bring new forces into it, and take new and coveted effects from it.

Uncultivated minds, so far as they pursue knowledge at all, do it under this form; an observation of resemblances with reference to an ulterior possession and control of causes. The savage distinguishes between the different kinds of timber, because he expects the same external indications to remain the accompaniments and marks of certain interior qualities of strength, weight, elasticity. A bow of the same material he believes will exhibit the same good points with which he is familiar; a spear of like wood possesses like pliancy and toughness. Language comes in to mark and hold together for the mind these agreeing things, by which the implements of man, and his successive wants are to be supplied.

Science, the advanced and complete movement of thought, is but a more rigid separation of like from like, a more careful selection of central qualities, a complete and interdependent classification of objects, both that the resources of the globe, in all its ministration to human life, may be laid open, and also, that the concealed chart of laws, according to which the events of the present come pouring down from the past, and go forth to occupy the future, may be disclosed. While our experience, then, finds its first efforts directed to resemblances, these lead to profounder inquiries into causes, those links of force which lengthwise and laterally bind together the physical events of the world.

At length the purely objective character of knowledge passes somewhat away. The mind gives heed to the agent as well as to the instrument. Having acquired power, it learns to value itself, the possessor of that power. With more pure reflection and subjective attention, it inquires into its own faculties, and the laws of their control. Now come forward new intuitive ideas, beauty, liberty, right, disjoining philosophy from science, and setting the first over against the second as independent of it, and complementary to it. This change and jar of transition constitute the great danger attendant on the acquisition of this form of knowledge. The forces and notions of the one field are intruded into the other, and those who suppose themselves the most patient of inductive philosophers are really visionary theorists, adopting a disguised, *a priori* method ; since they bring to a new department methods and conceptions alien to it, and refuse, vacating the mind of prejudice, to examine and classify these fresh phenomena according to their inherent characteristics, directly observed. There is thus more or less of vibration between the two fields. Now the philosophical, now the scientific, conceptions rule the inquiring mind, and the present, passionate, physical researches and methods of thought are sure to be followed by a recoil against forms of inquiry so partial, so one-sideed, so unscrupulous in their application. The deductive method was never more arbitrarily applied to science, with less correction from experience, than is the inductive method now to philosophy, bringing with it the forms and forces of physics. Induction transferred from one field to another, without fresh starting points and new limitations, is really disguised and unsafe deduction. Knowledge stalks on with alternate strides, and, in the rhythm of progress, the swing of one limb makes way for that of the other.

The mind measures all things by the scope of its own powers too much to rest on the naked facts of the world. The forces which they disclose, the plan which they reveal, the wisdom of its conception, and the kindness of its execution, push the thoughts farther back to the source of these truly intellectual and moral elements. The progress, also, which is discovered, together with that irresistible claim, which the mind institutes for completion, for ends reached, for fruits achieved; push it forward in thought, and lead it willingly to gather up the issues of existence into the hand of Him who gave it. That this movement may be final, that a true compass and circuit, source and conclusion of the actual, the finite, the necessary, may be found; that the mind may rest in one last stroke of comprehension, it brings forward the highest of its intellectual solvents—the Infinite, the Absolute. A free and holy personality is to be made to the mind and heart, the cause and compass of the universe. This movement becomes complete and assured in connection with revelation, an outer voice, which takes hold on inner powers, and gives steadfastness and certainty to their conclusions. The mind is not left alone to travel these outlying highways of thought.

In this growth of knowledge, through science, philosophy and theology, deduction and induction play intermingled and inseparable parts. Deduction from necessary ideas, from definitions and axioms intuitively conceived under them, gives us that everywhere present instrument of mathematics. Induction is nothing without a theory, a conception of some sort, running side by side with its classifications, guiding and interpreting them, and ready deductively to furnish shining strokes of exposition. The theory with its derived conclusions is most impotent and misleading, save as induction presides at the birth and growth of it. The wise mind is always laying up the facts of nature, like stones in a building; but laying them up under a plan, a conception, which it has caught by penetrating beneath the surface, by interpreting signs and relations unintelligible to the merely physical eye. Here, then, in the growth of general knowledge, we have the counterpart of that which we find in the individual mind. The elaborative faculty, the understanding, is ever playing between the sensations and the intuitions, weaving them into a rational experience. In like manner, the philosophy and the science of the world are bringing downward, deductively, the conceptions, the theories of the mind; are bringing upward, inductively, the phenomena of nature and mind, and slowly uniting them into one compact web of knowledge; the exposition running as light through the facts, and the facts embodying and presenting the exposition. The one process is as necessary as the other, the woof as the warp.

§ 3. We wish to mark briefly the means by which the mind advances in acquisition, the instruments of intellectual growth at its service. Sensations, perceptions, enlarge for it the material of thought, and are themselves a simple, ultimate form of knowing. Nothing can replace them. Colors, sounds, odors, flavors, are apprehended exclusively in the organs by which they enter. Further, they give us inexhaustible material for inquiry, facts to which the mind may bring its explanatory processes, and which it may work up into knowledge. Intuitions without these, as mere intuitions, would remain empty formulæ, intellectual solvents with no mysteries to resolve.

Next come judgments. These are the steps in the rationalizing, comprehending process. To be able to form a judgment, is to be able to put forth true intellectual effort; is to turn the key in locks that guard all knowledge. It implies completeness of mental furniture, the entire material of growth. Simple judgments are the staples of knowledge; while they may be formed under any idea, that of resemblance assumes chief significance. All classification proceeds through this, and is a first and last step in progress. It is by a comparison of qualities, that our knowledge of the objects about us becomes servicable. Much, perhaps the larger share of our progress, is made by simple judgments, related indeed to one another, but not interlocked in reasoning. By a series of inquiries, we place objects in their appropriate classes, and furnish them ready both for our intellectual and physical uses.

Reasoning, or interlocked judgments, follows simple judgments as a means of progress. There is considerable disagreement as to the forms and character of reasoning, arising largely, we think, from a different use of words. One form of procedure is covered by the words *reasoning* and *logic* as used by Hamilton, and another as used by Mill; while others combine, with more or less confusion, the two uses. Hamilton, by a definition, confines the province of logic to the necessary laws of thought, or practically to the demonstrative evolution of conclusions from premises that are given. He does not inquire into the manner of obtaining the premises, but only into the forms, the certainty and safety of that purely intellectual process by which, as verbal propositions, they are found to hold those other verbal propositions known as conclusions. The whole movement is thus detached from facts as facts, and, according to the general use of words, is, when reasoning at all, deductive reasoning. That is, the conclusions are wholly contained in, and demonstratively taken from, the premises. Hamilton gives a technical and peculiar application to the words inductive and deductive, regards both forms of reasoning as equally demonstrative, and leaves wholly out of his logic that true induction, usually so-called, to the elucidation of which Mill has given his entire strength. Induction in its commonly accepted meaning, the establishment of a general principle through a limited number of specific examples, is all the reasoning which the sensualistic school can consistently recognize. What others regard as deductive reasoning, they are compelled to look upon in ultimate analysis as inductive. Deduction can be nothing more with them than the re-statement of a specific case already included in the establishment of the general principle, or *major premise* from which it is now taken. No conclusion is strictly demonstrative, since it is in advance of the premises on which it rests. The degrees of evidence for new statements, statements not confirmed by direct observation, vary with the amount and character of experience on which they rest.

The entire system of logic, therefore, as presented by Hamilton, has for them comparatively little interest or value. It is a cunning play upon words, rather than an estimate of facts. They are interested in the growth of laws, principles, out of those separate instances which are only to be gathered and interpreted by patient, careful, and often doubtful induction. Each party thus neglects a valuable field which the other exclusively cultivates. All that Mill regards as reasoning, Hamilton scornfully rejects from the province of logic as invalid, as not presenting with certainty the conclusions in the premises from which they are taken. Mill, on the other hand, can only look on the complicated syllogisms of Hamilton, as a cumbersome statement of work already done, of knowledge already gained.

Much is undoubtedly included by Hamiltion, in the formal expansion of his terminology, as reasoning, which would generally be regarded as simple statement, as the fruit of single judgments, as the results of classification. This desk contains this drawer : This drawer contains this paper : Therefore this desk contains this paper. These propositions form a syllogism under one of the forms into which he divides deductive reasoning. Most would regard them as in no proper sense reasoning, but rather as a formal, unserviceable statement of a fact, learned by observation. So also his inductive reasoning is made up of cumbersome formulæ of classification. "Gold is a metal, yellow, ductile, fusible, and so on : These qualities constitute this body (are all of its parts) : Therefore this body is gold." Here is no argument properly so called, but the rendering of the results of the experimental test of a bit of metal, with the accompanying act of classification. There would seem to be room in a logic, covering all the forms of reasoning, and those of reasoning only, both for deduction and induction, using the words in their more general and generally accepted meanings. An important branch of logic finds representation in Hamilton and Mill respectively.

What is reasoning? It is the reaching of new conclusions, certain or probable, by means of two or more interlocked judgments. We would lay stress on the word *new*, and on the words *certain* or *probable*. Our necessary ideas and our theories suffer expansion by a purely deductive process. Geometry is a deductive science, derived from intuitions, definitions, and axioms. Astronomy and mechanics are full of pure deductions, resting on conceptions of force confirmed by experience. How much is involved in certain, simple statements, we often only learn by a series of related judgments,—by various applications of the included principle. This is one of the earliest forms of scientific reasoning, and presents in mathematics, pure and mixed, its most extended and servicable forms. The certainty, and, when fitting data are found, the celerity of its conclusions, abundantly explain its fascination, and the position it has held in investigation. The introduction of a mathematical unit, and application of the force of numbers to a subject, have usually been the signal for a rapid advance.

This deductive reasoning rests on intuitive steps, and will readily fall into the syllogistic form. The syllogism is perfect ; for the premises as premises, in their very statement, are seen, as intuitively unfolded, to contain the conclusion. No outside circumstances affect their relation.

Inductive reasoning, on the other hand, deals only with probabilities, because it pertains to things imperfectly known, and to facts whose conditions are ever changing. It rests at bottom on the intuition of causation, the simplest statement of which is, Every event must have a cause. Its corollaries are, that every effect measures its cause, that the two are exactly commensurate, and, that sameness in one is proof of sameness in the other. These spring from the original, independent conception of causation. Proof, under this notion, would be as certain as under the ideas of space and time, were we always dealing with perfectly fixed, and perfectly known, premises. We do not by observation so penetrate the nature of objects, and the character of complex phenomena, as to be sure of the elements present, and sure, therefore, of the effects that may be expected. We do not know exactly how far one wood differs from another, one metal from another, one element, so called, from itself at a former period. Much less do we know all the circumstances which affect the complex problems of life, which influence the growth of a tree, which are concerned in the health of a man, in the welfare of a community. We here, therefore, advance from one case to another along uncertain links of likeness, not knowing positively, whether the agreement covers the essential points of the two cases or not. The various degrees of likeness are identity, sameness, resemblance, analogy. So far as we are sure of the first, are we certain of the results, as compared with those of a previous experiment.

In induction, by which from several examples we infer a general principle, we are proceeding on a resemblance more or less obscure, hence more or less uncertain. Different cases stand on their own independent merits, and the probability in each is in proportion to the certainty with which the agreement in the example covers the force or forces involved in the causation under consideration. That all magnets attract iron, is a conclusion on which we rest with entire conviction, having by such uniform observation traced this result to this cause. Yet it is not an impossibility, that some new substance or combination of substances should exhibit the other properties of a magnet with the omission of this. We cannot say, how new conditions of action may modify the force termed magnetism, or indeed, what conditions, aside from magnetism, are influential over it. Now, by far the larger part of the reasoning of natural science and of every-day-life is of this character, creeping from resemblance to resemblance, and unable to affirm of its best conclusions, that they are demonstrative. To this reasoning, the syllogism is not applicable, since the premises as premises are partial, and do not contain the law in its full breadth which is to be evolved from them. The philosophy of experience, therefore, can lay no great stress on the syllogism. The only service it can assign it, is that of a convenient re-statement of conclusions already arrived at, and this, not in the exact line in which the first, the real argument lay. This was on the road upward to the principle, whereas the syllogism lies in the way downward to a specific example included under it. When inductive matter receives syllogistic statement, either the statement is defective, or the general principle is assumed, and then the case in hand taken from it. The argument by which we mount to a general law, does not suffer a syllogism ; the seeming argument by which we descend to a particular fact is but a re-statement of previous knowledge, and yields a syllogism deductive in form. Of the defective, intuitive syllogism, the following is an example : The metals A, B, C, represent (not are) all metals ; A, B, C, expand under heat ; therefore all metals expand under heat. This result is proximately not absolutely true. If the law had been established by sufficient observation, that all metals expand when heated, the following would be the deductive syllogistic statement of a single fact covered by it. All metals expand by heat : A is a metal ; therefore A expands under heat.

The two kinds of argument, deductive and inductive, are fundamentally distinct, and stand in very different relations to the syllogism. The one is demonstrative, the other probable ; the one turns on intuitive, the other on observed relations ; the one on necessary connections, the other on imperfect resemblances. The confusion which has arisen in the various estimates of the value of the syllogism seems to find its sources in the language employed, in two restricted definitions, and, more than all, in failing to estimate the influence of different philosophical systems on the respective methods of logic.

As a last step in the growth of knowledge, beyond those achieved by observation and reasoning, we should place a recognition of the nature and limits of intuitive truth, and a quiet resting of the mind on the ultimate action of its own faculties. To accept the conditions of explanation of comprehension, to repose on the simple, single basis of insolvable ideas, standing in their own light, seems to be the most difficult, not practically, but philosophically the most difficult thing for the mind to do, and the most needful.

§ 4. The intellect being thus furnished with faculties, and stored with their fruits, we inquire into its control over them, its directing influence. We speak first of the government of the thoughts. The mind can direct the eye, the ear, to any object it chooses, and command their prolonged attention. It can also make any object the subject of protracted contemplation, and confine the analytic and reasoning processes to it. It can intensify and guide its mental activities in degrees varying with the power which previous practice has given it. This voluntary direction and handling of faculties is attention, and is referable to that personal force from which all the faculties as separate forces or directions of action spring.

The number of objects which can at once be made the subjects of attention has been a question vigorously debated. The mind seems to be single in what may be termed its line of movement, its chain of connections; but to be able to unite in this movement many diverse things. Our thoughts braid into one experience, link in one argument, diverse subjects: they proceed by junction and inclusion, evening and strengthening the thread with material drawn from the right hand and the left.

The reason why it has been doubted whether the mind can attend to more than one object is in part found in the fact, that the very effort of the mind to decide the question serves to occasion that fixed, full, complete attention which is concentrated on a single object, and leads to the partial exclusion of other objects. Of course we cannot give the entire attention to two objects as two, struggling in the same instant to contemplate them with distinctness separately. Failing in this, we have hastily concluded that the mind can attend to but one thing at a time. Let the thoughts move freely, and it seems obvious that we do consider several objects at once, some of us more, some less. The shepherd counts his flock as they pass before him or stand around him. He will more likely do it by threes or fives, grouping the numbers by a stroke of the eye. One practiced in dividing paper into quarter quires will instantaneously, on the ruffled edge, select the number six, and with astonishing rapidity run through the pile. This tendency in enumeration to divide objects into greater and smaller groups, according to the degree of skill, plainly reveals the power of the mind to contemplate at once several objects. Indeed, were the mind limited to absolute singleness of attention and direction, its states would succeed each other in a disconnected and independent form.

A more important question arises, as to the power which the mind possesses in introducing to itself the objects which it may afterward consider. So far as these are external objects it may open for them the avenues of perception, and then select among them those which it will more carefully observe. It may also seek the locality of remembered or described objects, and thus prolong its consideration. In this direction, the mind is limited, first to things that are; second to those among these known to it, and accessible to it. A large share of the government we have over our thoughts is found in our mastery of the external conditions of life, of situations and circumstances. A deeper inquiry lies in the questions, How far does the mind control the order of ideas that are passing through it? How far is the flow established and maintained by independent connections?

The doctrine of association, used as a universal solvent of mental phenomena, has been the occasion of ascribing a dependence and passivity to intellecutal connections, which we deem wholly false. The association of ideas has been accepted as an ultimate fact, and itself without explanation, been proffered as an explanation of every other. This solution has proceeded under physical analogies, especially those of habit in the body. A form of activity, often returning to the muscles, so interlocks the nerves and muscles, so passes over their connection from the voluntary to the automatic region, that the mere fact of repetition becomes a reason for many movements not directly intended. Under the suggestion, perhaps, of this fact, ideas are spoken of as associated, and this association seems to be often thought of as involving some direct, almost mechanical or vital connection of one idea with another; as if the first evoked and drew on the second by an immediate force. Thus we have such expressions as the "cohesiveness of ideas," "the principle of cohesiveness," "the property of plastic adhesiveness," "the tenacity of association." These physical ideas should find no place in philosophy. Neither should the mere fact of sequence, though dignified with the title of the law of association, be regarded as any final explanation, except by those who resolve all our knowledge of events into that of naked succession. Those who thus use the law of association, refer the order of ideas in the mind to it, and give the mind itself but little control over them, beyond that of hastening or checking their movement.

The real link between associated ideas would seem to be chiefly that established by memory. It is the living power of the mind, rather than an intrinsic coherence of ideas, that combines them into thought, and locates them in revery. Memory underlies association, rather than association memory. The memory proceeds along the connections of place, time, resemblance and causation, because these are the forms under which objects are principally presented to it; and the groups of memory principally determine the connections and dependence of conceptions, when they return to the mind. One object tends to restore in memory, more or less distinctly, the entire group of which it forms a part, and its earlier and later relationships are renewed, because the memory is by it directed to that portion of experience in which it has played a part. Ideas are thus interlocked in memory and by memory, and return to the mind surrounded more or less completely with their adjuncts, their companions in previous knowledge. The mind does grasp objects collectively, as time and place present them ; it is natural, therefore, that it should restore them in the same way in memory. A second ground of association is that of the deductive dependence of ideas. The logical power of the mind on the presence of a part expounds it by a reference to the whole ; or on the presence of a whole unfolds it in its parts.

These two forms of association correspond to the two methods of acquiring knowledge. Observation, induction present objects as physical wholes, and the memory so retains them ; analysis, deduction unfolds ideas, and the memmory and the logical faculties combine to repeat, on fit occasions, this process. The cement of ideas is the living forces that use them, not a dead adhesiveness belonging to them as ideas, or dependent on the nervous conditions of their presence. It is not a reverberation of tissues, but of thoughts to which attention should be directed.

We see at once, then, that the power of the mind over its trains of ideas is greater than many are willing to admit. Take any one moment, with the tendencies and memories of the past fixed, the circumstances of the present established ; the current of the desires strong and declared, and thoughts and conceptions may seem rather to sweep independently through the mind, a deep, uncontrollable current, than to be called forth and used by it. Take, however, a longer period, let the mind desire to assume control, and this appearance of helplessness will pass away, and our impressions will be reversed. Times are set apart to definite inquiries. The passing hours bring each its suggestion of its part of the plan. The memory is more and more stored with material suitable to the investigation and effort in hand. External circumstances favorable to the inquiry, are secured. The desires, quickened by exercise, lend their aid in constraining and spurring on the thoughts. The purpose, kept in view, evokes from the memory on each new exigency, every fitting idea in the increasing circle of its information, while the logical connection of ideas, guides the pursuit along the right trail. Under these conditions, we shortly behold an intellectual power which works as intensely, as directly, as uninterruptedly toward its end, as the engine whose valves and pistons and wheels are driven by a mechanical agency. A wayward pleasure of vagrant connections may turn the thoughts for a moment aside, but not more frequently nor more unfortunately than the flower or the fruit, the wayside traveller steadily pursuing his journey. States and powers of mind are not indeed instantly determined, immediately gained ; but tendencies are established, and control acquired as certainly here, as in any form of effort. The chain of thought does not drag itself along, the mind being left a spectator, to observe its links, or by a spasmodic effort to arrest them. The person himself may determine within the limits which the surrounding world presents him, what shall be his resources of thought, and what the motives calling them "into act and use."

The selecting power of the mind is found in the purposes it is pursuing ; aided by memory, they restore at the suggestion of the present thought, all the pertinent material which its store-houses can furnish. The whole movement is a living one, under a living intelligent power, and is no more to be expounded as a dead process, an adhesion of one thought to another, than is the life of the plant, or of the animal to be traced to simply chemical forces. The very secret of life is to combine material into living organs ; the very knack of mind is consecutive, coherent, self-supporting thought.

§ 5. The last point on which we have occasion to speak under the dynamics of the intellect is the difference in mental endowments between the brute and man. We are necessarily somewhat theoretical in handling a subject so much beyond direct knowledge ; but trust our theory will commend itself as the simplest explanation of the facts, with the least assumption, and the fewest forces. There seems to be no proof, that any animal, the most sagacious, possesses any intuitive ideas, and consequently that it forms any judgments properly so-called. There is no conscious estimate of the value and bearings of sensations, no classification of them inductively, no conclusion deductively drawn from the premises as such. Sensation, perception, memory and imagination, evidently belong to the higher animals, and by these faculties, we believe, all the intellectual phenomena they present can be readily explained, while the ascription of fuller powers than these to them, brings difficulties which cannot be easily met. To those who doubt the possibility of presenting the appearance of reasoning processes, of complete intellectual action, with these limited and elementary powers, we would commend the works of Bain, and kindred philosophers, who, with patient and adroit analysis, think themselves successful in resolving the phenomena of mind, in their most exalted forms, into the automatic play of sensations and perceptions, on the nervous, the intellectual constitution. They at least render this service to true philosophy, of enabling us to explain brute life, without elevating it in gifts to a rational platform. Those who do not believe that the races of men could have sprung from one pair, may be referred to Darwin ; those who cannot explain the sagacity of the dog, his apparent sense of shame and approval, without endowing him with the entire circle of human powers, moral and intellectual, may well find profit and conviction in the works of the sensualistic school.

The truth is, memory and perception can, by conscious yet direct action, present, with close agreement through quite a wide range of conduct, an image of rational and moral behavior. Memory can unite impressions and their appropriate accompanying actions in permanent associations, exhibiting results as safe and sagacious, as if the union had taken place by judgment. We constantly interpret the conduct of animals under the analogies of our own experience; an act more unphilosophical even, than for the accomplished and sensitive man to infer the exact counterpart of his own feelings in the clown from an agreement of external actions. The aspen trembles without fear: the dog skulks and crouches in apparent shame without a sense of guilt. The severe tones of voice, the sharp eye, punishment associated in experience with like action, are a sufficient explanation of conduct which we often hastily regard as showing the germs of a moral nature.

Indeed, this inferring the same sweep of thought and feeling from coincident actions in man and in the animal, leads constantly to the most insecure and unfortunate conclusions: unfortunate when they are made the grounds of cruel exactions, and the tyrannous handling of domestic animals. Says Professor Whitney, in his treatise on *Language and the Study of Language:* "A dog, for instance, as surely apprehends the general idea of a tree, a man, a piece of meat, cold and heat, light and darkness, pleasure and pain, kindness, threatening, barking, running, and so on, through the whole range, limited as compared with ours, of matter within his ken, as if he had a word for each. He can as clearly form the intention, 'I mean to steal that bone, if its owner turns his back and gives me a fair chance," as if he said it to himself in good English. He can draw a complex syllogism, when applying to exigencies the results of past experience, and can determine 'that smoking water must be hot, and I shall take good care not to put my foot into it,' that is to say, 'water that smokes is hot: hot water hurts: this water is hot: ergo it will hurt my foot.'"—*page* 414.

While making no objection to the spirit of the passage, we regard its philosophical implications as all wrong. Keen perception and quick association by an active, retentive memory offer a complete explanation of the facts involved, and of kindred ones, without supposing the presence of a single act of judgment, of one thoughtful junction of premises and conclusions: nor the recognition of any general idea or general principle. The fear of the master is present, and the desire of the bone; withdraw the first, and the last comes into unobstructed operation. The sight of steam, and a delicate, distinct sense of heat, associated with pain under exposure, apply as direct a restraint to action as the shutting of a valve to the ingress of water. The difference between the two cases lies in the fact, that in one instance, the restraining power appears in, and works through consciousness, and in the other it does not.

That association is sufficient to explain the apparently thoughtful, deliberate action of brutes, is seen, in the first place, in the way in which their sagacious tricks are acquired. A cow learns to open a gate; but how? First, by accidentally or impatiently rubbing her head and horns against it, and thus loosening the latch. This process, repeated once or twice, establishes a connection between the act and its results, and later, when she wishes to be free, she worries the gate open. A change of fastening relieves the difficulty, not because the new method of reaching the latch is necessarily impossible to her, but because it is not accomplished by the same blind movement which removed from the catch the previous one. The horse learns to untie himself; vary the knot, and his skill disappears. That the protracted experience of the brute must yield to it not very unfrequently a repeated concurrence of the same cause and effect, and thus enable it to reach the one through the other, in those cases in which appetite impresses on the memory the connection, is obvious. Indeed, that this happens so rarely, is quite as much a matter of surprise, as are the few cases of apparent skill. We know the cunning, vicious tricks which a street animal acquires ; but we also know that in a keen appetite on the one side, and much persecution on the other, it has under the law of association the most unwearying and vigilant instructors. The restive horse, scorning the restraint of fences, has compounded his education of short and easy attainments. The spiteful nag, grazing on a city common, has learned the ins and outs of advantage, the safeties and dangers of provender, by many a sharp thrust and sturdy thwack, and it is not surprising that it has quite a store of ideas pricked into its tough, retentive hide.

The same truth is seen in the method of training the dog and the horse. The first effort is to establish a definite, pleasant association of reward with the action to be done, and one of suffering with the action to be avoided. Says a skillful handler of horses, "The difficult point is to secure the right action in the first instance. Every approach to it should be at once recognized and encouraged. The animal should be petted and rewarded at each repetition, till the thing required becomes habitual"—that is, till the right association is established. On the other hand, the wrong action is painfully and peremptorily checked, till the tendency to it is corrected. In the meantime, the fitting words of command uniformly accompany the discipline, and it requires no intelligent apprehension of language to lead the horse to stop at the word *whoa*, when it has been repeatedly accompanied with a severe jerk of the bit.

A change of masters always interferes with the training of animals, as for instance of a yoke of oxen, because there is a breaking up of associations, a diversity, and hence a confusion, of methods. Passion and hasty punishment, likewise retard the education of a horse. The reason is obvious under the principle of association. If the brute were in a measure rational, he might interpret aright the flogging, and profit by it; but, acting under association, his consciousness is simply flooded with suffering and fears, and henceforth, on the like provocation, he becomes restive and excited in anticipation of a similar, painful experience. So too, punishment that is not proportionate to the wrong, or does not immediately follow it,—and spring as it were out of it, is of no avail. The association is lost, and no reasoning process is present to take its place. All the facts of skillful and successful discipline in animals come in to corroborate the assertion, that action, with them, follows the appropriate perception under fixed associations.

But it may be asked, what is the negative proof? Why is not the opposite supposition of reasoning an admissible one? We answer, it involves at once the entire circle of regulative ideas, postulates more powers than are needed to explain the phenomena, and is not consistent with the fact, that brutes exhibit no such growth as should, in some instances at least, follow the rudimentary possession of such high endowments. If the animal reflects, there is no reason why he should not occasionally express by language, at least by signs, the results of that reflection. One rational thought is not possible without the possibility of two, of three, of many thoughts. One syllogism carries with it the entire logic, and such powers would quickly command expression. This utterance of judgments we should the more anticipate, as the most sagacious brutes are in constant company with man, and might learn from him, in some instances, vocal language, in others, sign language.

The only way, however, in which a brute does show intelligence is in action, and this may as well spring from association as from reflection. The utmost efforts of instruction expended by man on animals, even when it has reached to the mechanical repetition of words, has only secured results in conduct readily referable to slow, established, and patiently confirmed associations, the varying perceptions of the animal putting it, in connection with accompanying pains and pleasures, on the clue of the behavior designed for it.

Moreover, if rational ideas are conceded to the brute, they must be granted in a more powerful and perfect form, rather than in a less perfect form than to man. The chicken, the young of animals, almost immediately begin to successfully estimate all the relations of objects in space. They evince more mastery over them at the end of a few hours or days, than does the child at the close of as many years. If, therefore, any judgments intervene in this process; if the perceptions do not directly, by an immediate transfer of stimulus, secure and guide the motion; if there is not the same spontaneous completeness in the action of the mind that there is in that of the body, what a marvelous, unaccountable rapidity of development should we have here. We must exalt in accuracy, ease and celerity, the reflective processes of the animal far above those of man. This seems, to us at least, a *reductio ad absurdum*. But, if the sport of the lamb, its leaping and running; if the flight of the bird, and the ease with which it hits and rests on the spray, indicate no conscious recognition of space, the presumption is that other less astonishing powers have no basis in reasoning or in intuition.

We object, also—though this consideration may have little weight with some minds—to the character which this idea of reflection ascribes to the consciousness of the brute. A thoughtful animal would be one of the most unfortunate of beings, the incubus of its physical structure weighing down its destiny. Hope and fear to a being like this would be an unnecessary and cruel source of suffering; nor do animals often show apprehension and alarm except in the immediate presence of danger.

But it will be said, there are examples of sagacity on the part of animals which candor forbids us to refer to association, to anything short of reflection. To this we answer, these examples require more searching inquiry as to their exact form and value than they have received, as the shades of action that distinguish association and reflection are unobtrusive and delicate; and few are aware of the extent of results easily within the scope of association alone. Farther, we are not considering what would be referred in man to reflection; but how much is possible to quick perceptions, strong appetites, and a ready memory, when they are left to act alone, and are not therefore superseded or embarrassed by reasoning. Says the writer last quoted, "It has often been remarked, that the crow has a capacity to count, up to a certain number. If two hunters enter a hut, and only one comes out, he will not be allured near the place by any bait, however tempting; the same will be the case, if three enter and two come out, or if four enter and three come out, and so on till a number is reached which is beyond his arithmetic." How far we are to give credit to these current statements is very uncertain, but granting their accuracy, they do not require for their explanation a distinct recognition on the part of the crow of numbers, a conscious subtraction and the acceptance of a definite remainder. Concede these, and the sagacious bird would quickly find in the objective teaching of the rowed corn-fields before him, an express provision for a grander arithmetical procedure. Within narrow limits, groups of two, or three, or four, or five objects are directly and readily distinguishable in perception aside from numeration; beyond these they do not so vary the impression as to make the difference easily observable. Groups of twenty—and of twenty-one persons will hardly be distinguished by a stroke of the eye. Certain separable sensations, therefore, may be associated in the experience of the crow with danger, while others inseparable have made no such impression. Let, however, one of the twenty men always remain, and doubtless the crow would soon attach danger to this number also, and the philosophers find in the new fact proof of a growing power of calculation. The crow learns by experience to fear man, that is to connect danger with certain perceptions. In rare cases, under protracted experience and varied discipline, he might carry this association two steps farther, to three definite, closely united impressions; a hut, the entrance of three, the departure of two. This experience, provoking alarm in him, would extend by admonition to others, and would at once receive the interpretation above given. We find it very difficult not to attribute to actions the same degree of thought and intelligence which would be indicated by them in us. Yet this tendency should be easily overcome, when we remember that we are compelled to cover up by the word instinct, actions which in man would show the most wonderful knowledge and skill. It is certainly no very strange thing, that three perceptions should, in the ready memory of a crow, alert and watchful, by life-long instinct and habit directing its attention to like facts, find at length a fixed association with danger.

It is narrated, that a raven hit upon this method of defrauding a dog of a portion of his dinner. The raven would approach so near and so annoyingly as to provoke pursuit.

This pursuit would draw the dog from the dish, and the raven, quick of wing, would immediately rise and pounce down on the unguarded meal. Observe how easily such a series of associations would be formed, the acts constituting it finding union and undesigned repetition in experience, till they became a habit apparently shaped on a rational purpose. Impelled by hunger, the raven would naturally approach the dog as near as he dare venture ; the dog as naturally would resent the intrusion. The raven, pressed by pursuit, and rising on the wing, would see the unprotected dish, and at once pluck a portion of the coveted food. This process would repeat itself a second and a third time, till, connected with the desired result, it would become direct and constant. What shall be said of the reasoning of the dog who repeatedly suffered from such a form of depredation ? It matters little whether the above instances are true ; others like them are true, and admit of similar explanation. The fear and caution of a dog when he has committed an offense, the cunning and skill of a fox, the pliancy of a horse, are not surprising, when we consider their quick senses, retentive memories, and protracted, varied, and severely enforced experience. Knowledge, moreover, is communicable between animals by inheritance and by transfer. The obedience, docility and training of the horse are readily imparted to his yokefellow, and the fear and sagacity of a fox help to awaken like qualties in his companion.

The practical value of the above conclusions is very great, in teaching us how to handle, and how to estimate, brute life ; and still more in establishing an impassable barrier between it and rational life. If this difference exists between them, then is man unapproachable by the animal. He stands on another platform of being. It is not an accident of physical structure, the absence of language, less fortunate or less protracted development, that divide the two; but entirely new endowments, bringing with them a new and exalted sphere of being. Man shares consciousness, a perception and retention of external events, with the animal; but not an intuition of the invisible, not the rational apprehension and government of action, not his moral and spiritual endowments. Whatever may be the fortunes of the body under physical classification, philosophy sets up a sufficient defense against the invasion of the lower world. The spiritual, the truly spiritual realm cannot be grappled with hooks of steel, nor boarded and defiled by a harpy throng of unclean things, of merely sensual beings.

BOOK II.

§ 1. We have now reached the second class of mental phenomena, that of the feelings. These have received less attention than the intellectual faculties. They are far more numerous and complicated, and have been more recently regarded as a distinct division. The three classes recognized by Kant, have since his day been generally accepted. Knowing, feeling, and willing, are each forms of action so simple, that it is easier to perceive, than to state their differences. Indeed, expository definition of each is impossible in other than synonymous terms. Each is known and only fully known by experience. There are, however, certain diverse relations of these several acts, or states of mind that may be pointed out.

Though the feelings were late in being recognized as a distinct portion of our mental endowments, popular language has so far severed them from our thoughts, as to refer them to a separate part of our nature. It is a method of expression still somewhat unusual to common speech, to talk of the emotions of the mind; we more frequently hear the words, the sentiments, the emotions, the feelings of the heart.

A first distinction to be marked between knowing and feeling is, that the one proceeds under a double, the other under a single form. The thought, and the object of the thought, lie distinguishable in the mind, while the feeling is a simple mental state. This has been expressed by saying, that the processes of thought are more objective, those of feeling more subjective. This language, however, seems not quite explicit. In one point of view, the feeling is more objective than the thought. To be sure, the thought attaches itself necessarily and distinctly to an object, but that object is itself usually a subjective one, something grasped and held by the mind as an object of contemplation, so that the entire movement maintains a subjective character. On the other hand, a feeling is usually occasioned by an action or an object external to the mind, under whose influence the emotion is suffered. This object, in connection with our stronger and more well-defined feelings, evokes especial consideration, is sedulously sought after or avoided, and thus imparts a peculiarly objective turn or tendency to emotion. Take such passions as love or hatred, such sentiments as admiration and contempt; consider the appetites and the desires, how objective are they in the frame of mind and cast of action they produce. Indeed, the first condition of contemplation, a quiet, subjective handling of a topic, is, that the feelings be hushed, that these restless children of the household be put to sleep, and the thoughts be left to move uninterrupted within their own circle. On account of this ambiguity of the word subjective, and the marked external tendency given by feeling to action, we prefer to speak of thought as *bi-partite* and feeling as simple.

Neither method of presentation holds equally well in all forms of the phenomena concerned. Perception is distinguishable from sensation by its more objective bearing only on condition, that we regard a feeling within the body as subjective in reference to the contemplation of the mind, which, strictly speaking, it is not. Sensation most distinctly separates itself from perception by its more definite and local action in the organ involved. In speaking of a feeling as subjective, reference is had of course to the emotion itself, and not to the contemplation of the object which may accompany it.

A second diversity in thinking and feeling is found in their dependence on volition; the former is more, the latter less immediately the result of voluntary effort. The thoughts are more directly reached and guided by the will than are the feelings. Indeed, the most of these are so occasioned by the immediate and unavoidable presence of external conditions, that it is only indirectly and with considerable delay, that volition can reach and change them. Our thoughts, our subjects of reflection are the primary objects of volition, while the feelings are slowly changed with a change in their intellectual conditions.

While the thoughts are more directly subject to will than the emotions, the emotions more immediately influence the will than do the thoughts. Here is found a third difference of relation. The state of feeling is the direct ground and occasion of choice, while our opinions govern the will only as they first govern the heart.

The only opportunity of confounding knowing and feeling, seems to arise from their common relation to consciousness. We express the fact that our feelings, as our own, are present to the mind, by the language, I know that I feel, I know that I am angry, I know that I have sympathy with the suffering. We thus seem to underlay feeling with knowing as if the one were but a peculiar form of the other. The same reasoning, however, would apply to volition, and the difficulty springs only from the defect of language. We express the simple and single fact of a feeling under the form of a double act, one branch of which is an emotion, and the other is a cognition. A better analysis has enabled us to see that the expression, I know that I feel, no more implies a double act than the kindred assertion, I know that I know. Divide the act of knowing into two, and we must still farther part it into three, into four, and be left finally without any simple basis for it.

§ 2. The feelings may be divided by their intrinsic character, or by the objects or conditions which draw them forth. The first would seem the more just ground of distinction, yet the second finds easier application, and closely allies itself to the first, since different grounds or occasions give different emotions. Our first division into physical, intellectual and spiritual feelings proceeds on the conditions or occasions on which they are respectively called forth. The physical feelings are located in the body, have a physical source, and pertain to the state of physical organs. The intellectual feelings arise in connection with the estimates, the judgments of the mind. It is the perceived relations in which we stand to objects about us, and especially to other men, which call forth these emotions. Their ground then is an intellectual one; since, if we were destitute of thought, forethought, if we could form no conclusions concerning the effect of things, their approach or their possession, the effect of the actions and character of others upon ourselves, we should be left destitute of these feelings, and only subject to the immediate play of physical forces upon us.

The third class of feelings is the spiritual. The word spiritual is not so definite as the other two. We employ it to designate the highest portion of our nature, that by which we have a spiritual, a rational, and responsible life as opposed to a merely intellectual one. Now it is our intuitions, more particularly a limited portion of them, which confer these higher powers, and put us in these higher relations The sentiments elicited by these more profound revelations, this deeper insight into the rational world, the truly spiritual world, are the spiritual feelings. More concisely, the spiritual feelings are those immediately conditioned on the intuitions.

Of those several classes, the first may belong in feeble form to the lowest animal life, and in full form to the highest. The second belongs chiefly to man, though in a few of the nobler animals, it finds partial presentation in connection with the tacit anticipations, the informal conclusions of association. The dog does, through the education of a retentive memory, permanently interlock what, for want of another word, we must call conceptions, and is, therefore, ready for the feeling of joy or fear in view of anticipated results. Yet, in fullness and variety, these emotions do not compare in the most sagacious brute with the corresponding class of feelings in man. Indeed, much that we regard of this character in the animals below us, is but the false, the flattering interpretation which we bring from consciousness for the explanation of acts, in their external form alone, like ours. The dog licks the hand of his master, and that master conceives it, not as the act of a blind, instinctive fellowship, worth intellectually no more than the good will of the cow that cards with her rough tongue the hide of her gratified companion, but as a distinct expression of a clearly defined attachment. The third class, from the nature of the case, belongs exclusively to man, and, in its full forms, to the cultivated, the developed man,—one who has been ripened out of physical sensations, out of the half-way ground of the simple connections of thought, into the habitual and active play of his intuitive powers.

The words by which we designate the emotions are, for the most part, very loose in their application. Of these, the word feeling is the most general. It ranges through the three classes. The pains and pleasures of the body are feelings; equally so are the fears and hopes of the prudent, the delights of the artist, and the satisfaction of one obedient to moral truth. The word emotion, is applicable to the feelings of the two higher classes, hardly to those of the lower; while the word sentiment finds at least its fullest meaning in the third class only. We designate as sensations, physical feelings exclusively; as passions, intellectual feelings exclusively,—though only a part of them reach the intensity indicated by the term;—and as affections, the higher, the moral emotions exclusively. That, however, which is especially confusing in the language of the emotions, is the different states included under one word, like that of love. We love the food that pleases us, we love the wealth that gratifies desire, the scenery that delights the taste, the person whose character meets the approval of our moral sense. We have occasion, therefore, to put feelings covered by the same word, into entirely distinct classes, and to regard love as an appetite, a passion, or an affection, according to its several objects.

We shall give a chapter to each of the three divisions.

CHAPTER I.

The Physical Feelings.

§ 1. THE physical feelings are distinguished from others by arising directly from the body. They have a physical source and locality somewhere in the body, or, like nervous debility, are diffused through it. They are divisible as regards general quality, into pleasurable, indifferent, and painful feelings. By indifferent feelings we do not mean complex states of mingled pain and pleasure, but states declared to consciousness, but neither as yet agreeable or disagreeable. The three divisions, if we look at them in reference to action, may be termed the stimulative, the indicative and the repressive feelings. The condition of certain organs indicates a preparation, or want of preparation for activity. Thus an appetite gently aroused prepares the way for indulgence. Simply as an appetitive movement, as yet neither balked nor gratified, it is hardly an occasion of pain or pleasure, but merely points out, gives suggestion of, a line of gratification.

As we begin to indulge the appetite, a sensible, declared pleasure sets in, stimulating farther indulgence, and this continues till the present power of the sensibility is expended. Then a second indifferent, or indicative feeling succeeds, dissuading, without pain, from further indulgence. If this limit, however, be over-passed, positive discomfort follows, decidedly repressing activity. These three states may be regarded as a series of alternating cycles through which the physical feelings tend to move, and in one or other of which, when active, they remain for the time being. There is a farther connection between the three states, in the fact that they arise successively in one organ, or set of organs.

§ 2. The first of these sources of distinct physical feelings which we mention, are the special senses, the organs of sensation. The chief of these, at once recognizable, are touch, taste and smell. Sensations and perceptions should be distinguished, and these classed with cognitions, and those with feelings. Perceptions have with some clearness a *bi-partite* character; the object and the action directed towards it at once appear. The seeing, and the object seen, are necessary complements to each other; whereas by taste and smell we only indirectly, inferentially, and inquiringly reach the source, given and secured under another sense, that of sight. Evidently in sensation, we are engaged with the feeling; in perception with the source of the impression.

Perceptions also differ from sensations in having so little of a declared, local character, that, though physical in their source, they no more reveal their physical connections than does pure thought. Sensations, on the contrary, disclose themselves as a certain peculiar state of a given organ, and are therefore to be ranked as feelings. Of all the senses, touch occupies the most intermediate ground ; while its phenomena ordinarily present the phases of feeling, it may, in the absence of the higher senses of sight, of hearing, become so far intellectual as scarcely to direct attention to the sensation present as a sensation. It thus becomes the unobserved medium of knowledge, the matter revealed, being the only object consciously, obviously before the mind. The two offices are so intermingled in the organs of touch, that while this sense ordinarily performs the office of a special susceptibility, giving a new class of feelings, it may by cultivation come primarily to be a means of knowledge, yielding perceptions rather than sensations. Any sensation may be the occasion of a judgment, bearing the mind outward to a particular object ; the peculiarity of touch is, that by protracted and habitual use for this end, the sensational element is lost sight of, sinks from observation, and the perceptive element rises in its place, making this ordinarily over-shadowed sense, a not inefficient substitute for sight.

These special senses, all of them, stand closely connected with the intellect, and have thus been more frequently united with the organs of perception, and fallen into the first class of mental powers. The distinction now made seems, however, fore-shadowed in the physical fact, that the senses of sight and hearing are so immediately connected with the cerebrum, the seat and instrument of thought, that a removal of this destroys them, though leaving the other senses unimpared. Touch, taste and smell, however, while primarily feelings, are used constantly as means of discrimination and guides to action. They very frequently draw after them conclusions, set in motion the judgment, and thus return on the will through the mediation of the mind. This is the ordinary action of a pure, well-defined, special sensation. Taste may be so pungent or nauseating, as to produce a direct, involuntary action of ejection ; but odors and flavors are usually, in their effects on action, simply grounds of discrimination by which we are guided in accepting or rejecting the object before us, in assigning it a definite position among the things used by us. Our sensations thus start from the central, the perceptive, the indicative point, and then become either stimulative or repressive, according to their nature.

Sensations are also three-fold in their relations to enjoyments. From the midway ground of indifference, they pass into pain and pleasure. Their double office is here again very obvious. They are means of independent gratification as well as of guidance. They are sources of abundant, organic, physical pleasure, and find a primary purpose in this their direct character as feelings. In this connection, they act more immediately on the executive powers, stimulating the effort necessary for their gratification, and checking any movement that gives rise to pain. Sensations, then, are in a double sense stimulative by their direct character as feelings, by their indicative character, revealing to the intellect the nature of the objects about it. It is, however, in the first aspect alone, that they can be divided, as feelings, into the three classes, stimulative, indicative and repressive. Those sensations are chiefly indicative which, in reference to pleasure or pain, are indifferent. Things inimical, determined chiefly by the eye and ear, are recognized in part by touch, and sometimes by taste and odor. This discriminative use of the senses is an acquired one, and very much apart from the purpose which they subserve with all as avenues of enjoyment. Thus their perceptive and sensitive uses show a tendency to separation and mutual exclusion, though this relation hardly admits of the definite statement given it by Hamilton, that sensation and perception are in inverse ratio to each other. The facts are not of so measurable and mathematical a character, are more vital and mixed than this assertion recognizes.

§ 3. The sensations arising from the special senses glide easily into feelings of a distinct, yet of a less local and definite character, as the sense of pressure, of heat, and cold, or of an electric current. These again pass readily into others which indicate the condition of an organ, as nausea, irritation of the eye, lassitude, and its opposite the impulse of a super-abundant nervous power. This class of feelings it is not easy to enumerate. Some of them approach in character very closely the special senses, while others appear but rarely, and subserve a very limited purpose. There is, perhaps, no organ, or portion of the human body, which may not become the seat of a peculiar feeling, more especially a painful feeling, indicating difficulty, and demanding relief. As a class, the sensations which disclose states, have more frequent reference to some repression or modification of action, than to its excitation, and present themselves under the form of suffering, instead of enjoyment. The reverse is, however, many times true. Buoyant life declares itself in physical impulses, at first obscure, but leading when fully developed to the intense pleasure of sportive action. Redundant power tends to explosive effect, and renders such exertion very enjoyable.

Feelings which indicate states of the body or of its special organs, are for the most part present only as they tend directly to affect action, and through the will to secure either exertion, repression, or changed conditions. The feelings, or rather the nervous conditions that regulate involuntary action, do not usually come into consciousness. Respiration, in its safe and measured movement, is secured by nerves and muscles that act and react on each other automatically, with no direct cognition of the mind. Let, however, some unusual state arise; let the air be restricted, or become very impure, and distinct sensations follow, provoking in extreme cases the most violent exertion. The larger portion, then, of those sensations which spring from some unusual condition of our physical organs, are present to indicate a line of action; at least, to compel inquiry, and set the reflective powers to the work of guidance and correction. Thus are the nature and limits of the physical, physiological laws under which we live declared to us; the times of activity and repose, the forms and bounds of indulgence, and the necessity of remedial measures. As most diseases find their true remedy in some form of rest or of restraint, we see that the pains which indicate them are not only directly repressive of effort, but indirectly also through the increased advantage which rises from an appetite denied, from labor laid aside. On the other hand, the power to do begets corresponding effort, and is rewarded with a pleasure which in turn stimulates the body through the mind, and tends to make the exertion nutritive of the faculties to which it belongs. We cannot go to the extent of the view presented by Bain, which makes pleasure and pain automatic, the one stimulating, the other arresting action, much like the opening and closing dampers of a steam-engine. Such direct effects they frequently have, but more often incite or correct action through the intervention of thought and volition. Indeed pain may momentarily quicken action, and pleasure may ultimately exhaust the strength, and so slacken effort. The sensations stand in too living, too complex a relation to our vital, intellectual and voluntary powers to submit easily all their relations to a single statement. Pleasure and pain alike exhaust power, but the one with, the other without, compensation. An half-hour of intense suffering takes away not simply the strength—play would have done this in part—but leaves the nutritive powers depressed. The exertion of enjoyment, on the other hand, while expending the present store of power, re-acts favorably on the vital forces. Intense pleasure at its consummation trembles on the verge of pain, and intense pain, when not utterly exhaustive, passes back at its expiration into intense pleasure occasioned partly by contrast, and partly by the flowing in again of vital power to its normal channels.

§ 4. A third distinct class of sensations is the appetites. These again are closely united to those indicative feelings which declare the condition of an organ. They differ from these only in being more special, returning with regularity, and performing a constant and fixed service in the animal economy. We started with the special senses, sources of definite, local feelings, serving a free purpose of pleasure and discrimination. We glided from these into general sensations, chiefly distinguishable from them in serving a less constant and independent purpose. We now pass to appetites, specialized and regularly returning feelings, revealing not the general condition of an organ, but demanding a specific act of gratification. Both in the special senses and appetites, there is a definiteness and constancy of purpose, not found in the intermediate sensations, as well as a source of ever returning pleasure, almost independent of effort. Indeed, the appetite for food, as a means of enjoyment, so closely unites itself with taste and odor, as to yield with them a compound gratification incapable of practical analysis. An appetite is a returning physical feeling, tending to some definite act or state of gratification. The return in most of the appetites is at measured intervals; in others the spaces are more irregular. According to this definition, the desire for sleep is an appetite. Hunger and thirst are impulses recurring more fixedly; sexual appetite, one that is renewed less certainly.

An appetite in its first action, as yet neither gratified nor denied, is indicative: and indifferent as regards pleasure and pain. It is, indeed, the condition of the pleasure which is to arise from indulgence, but is itself hardly either a distinct enjoyment or a declared annoyance. One or other of these, however, it quickly becomes, according as its intimations are accepted or withstood.

Different appetites may be suppressed and modified with very different degrees of success, according to the purpose they subserve in our physical constitution. One is as imperative as the wants it indicates; another is, in the position it holds, very much the product of intellectual and moral forces. The appetites are physical indications and guides of action, and, in their healthy indulgence, uniformly give pleasure; in their denial, or excessive indulgence, as uniformly inflict pain. The pleasures and pains which accompany them are, carefully watched and collated, safe guides of action. They are, nevertheless, far from being sufficient, automatic forces, securing the results of physical well-being. While they are at first direct stimulants and immediate restraints, they are chiefly, in the human constitution, operative through a wise election and pursuit of pleasure, a sagacious avoidance of evil. The brute and the rational constitution seem to show an important distinction at this point; the one is wholly automatic in the restraint and control of appetite; the other leaves the checks chiefly to reason.

The purposes served by our sensations are various, frequently co-existent, and always concurrent. Of this, the special senses, the appetites and the feelings which accompany the active powers, are examples. A large circle of enjoyments are through them added to our physical organism, and a pleasurable life provided for. Immediately connected with this is a second purpose. A direct, physical stimulus is, through these feelings, administered to that nutritive and muscular action on which the well-being of the body depends. Pain abates, pleasure promotes effort. The one exhausts, the other stimulates, and, within certain limits, helps to renew the strength by which it is fed.

A third purpose of our sensations is found in the knowledge, otherwise unattainable, which they impart of the state of the body, the conditions and demands of its several organs. They thus become the basis of that reasoning by which we adjust action, food and remedial agents to our real wants; make an intelligent provision, and lay down wise precepts, for our immediate and future well-being. A fourth and somewhat more remote ministration of our sensations is to general knowledge. Through them, we come in contact in a new way with surrounding objects, take cognizance of a different set of qualities, and thus make more complete and perfect our classifications. There is a tendency, in thus making our sensations means of intellectual discrimination, somewhat to abate their force and character as feelings. Of this, we have sufficiently spoken. While sensation and perception are often closely blended, any increased distinctness of the one, tends to abate the immediate power of the other.

The relation of the physical feelings to health and activity is easily seen. This relation does not explain the feelings themselves. Unimpeded activity is pleasurable, but the seat—the source of the pleasure, is found in an original conformation of the physical man; as much so, we apprehend, as the enjoyment of a fragrant rose in the peculiar power of the special sense of smell. We are not to suppose that we have explained either pleasure or pain by referring them respectively to unrestrained, and to impeded activity. We are able to give some of the conditions, and some of the consequences of physical sensations, but their immediate causes in the organs themselves, we cannot give. The last and exhaustive analysis we cannot make. A feeling as a feeling is ultimately, and shall we not say, sufficiently known in itself.

Before passing to the intellectual feelings, we mark some border facts which prepare the way for the transition.

Irritability, which is often a physical state, and may always be more or less due to physical conditions, nevertheless does very much to determine the degree and character of the conditions present to the mind. There are inseparably mixed with their intellectual, provoking causes, immediate physical conditions, which often make them in degree, if not in kind, what they would not otherwise be.

What are termed natural affections, are also examples of transition facts. We suppose these words strictly employed to designate feelings aroused by physical facts, physical ties; not intellectually considered, but sensationally experienced. It may be doubted, whether there are any such affections in man. If there are, they are so lost in the higher feelings stirred by the same facts intellectually considered, that it is difficult to separate them. The animal is, for a time, passionately attached to its young. These affections seem to follow in a direct, physical way from the sensations present. The helplessness of the young apparently forms no ground of the emotion. The young of another animal may become the object of immediate and bitter attack. The substitution of another offspring for its own is successful only when the perceptive instincts of the parent are baffled and misled. Something of this direct attachment seems to appear in the human parent, though it is so overlaid and modified by feelings of a purely intellectual character, as to play no very important part in our constitution. Doubtless the tenderness of the mother does owe something of its quick, yearning, responsive action under the claims of the infant to the purely physical conditions of the relationship.

CHAPTER II.

The Intellectual Feelings.

§ I. THE intellectual are distinguished from the physical feelings by the fact of their dependence on objects and relations presented to the mind, and thus, in a secondary way, influencing the emotions. The sharp thrust of a weapon, brings instantaneous pain ; the abuse of an enemy arouses anger only as it is understood, and mentally contemplated. These feelings may also be divided, as regards emotional character, into pleasurable, indifferent and painful ; and as regards their relation to action, into those which accompany success, those which indicate a line of action, and those occasioned by failure, absolute or relative, partial or complete, and by causes tending to produce failure. The last division may be briefly and inaccurately expressed, by the words feelings of gratification, of direction, and of disappointment. The second central class demands the earliest treatment, as the other two flow from it on either hand. This class is chiefly composed of the emotions known as the desires. These may be termed the appetites of the mind, as they express its appetences, its longings, its objects of pursuit. They have been usually spoken of as direct, native feelings. Herein there seems to be some confusion of ideas. If they were direct, unreasoning impulses, they could not fall into the second general class of feelings, to wit: those which have an intellectual basis. That they are not spontaneous, immediate impulses, a little thought will be sufficient to show. As universally stated, they are directed toward abstract ideas, not toward concrete objects; they are desires of wealth, of power, of knowledge, not for wampum, for the ability to bend a bow, or to calculate an eclipse. Now a desire directed in the outset to a generalization, to an abstract quality, is an absurdity, since no such quality can be present to the mind except as the result of much comparison and many judgments. Neither should we avoid the difficulty by saying, that these desires fasten themselves with native, original force, on specific objects under each of the categories of desire. There are no specific objects which draw forth universal desire, and which can stand as concrete types, or representations, of the notions of power, wealth, honor. Specific objects, powers, become points of interest and desire, according as they are able to gratify certain native appetites or tastes. Possession is a matter of interest to the child only as the thing claimed stands in some relation to its sports by which it is capable of promoting its enjoyment.

Possession, without some connection with our pleasures, has no significance, either in early or later life. A square mile of territory on the frozen continent of the Antarctic ocean, has no power to awaken desire in any man. Now this discerning of the relation of things to our appetites, our active powers, our tastes, which makes them valuable, is an intellectual activity, receiving constant expansion as we grow older, and leading us to attach importance to the ownership of an increasing variety of things. The ignorant man cares not for a book, except as he can sell it; because the mental conditions which make possession important to him, have not been met.

Our desires, then, are secondary feelings uniformly evoked by the perceived relations of objects, of positive action to our primary, native feelings; our appetites below, and our tastes above. Without either the lower region of animal tendencies, or the higher region of spiritual impulses, desires would not exist; because those objects now included under the term wealth, or those possessions known as knowledge, would have no value, having no power to minister to our pleasure. The statement has been made only on the positive side ; of course we include the corresponding negative considerations. Objects may excite desire, because they enable us to escape pain. An action, however, which stands in no relation to either pain or pleasure, must be one to which we are wholly indifferent.

We have, then, no occasion to suppose, indeed no intelligible grounds for supposing, the presence of native desires in our constitution for certain abstract qualities, or for abstract qualities under a concrete form ; because first, the relation of wealth, power, knowledge, to our happiness is a sufficient explanation of our desire for them ; because, second, these desires come and go with this relation—the miser even not being able to prize that which cannot, under any conditions, be sold ; and third, because there is a difficulty in supposing generalizations arrived at by much reflection and constantly expanding, the direct object of a simple, primitive feeling.

The very notion and definition of a primitive feeling is rather the immediate action of some object or intuition on the emotional constitution. The secondary relation to our well-being, which things disclose through the intellect, are grounds of our secondary feelings.

In classifying the desires, we are then classifying the objects which draw them forth. Desire is an emotion essentially of the same character, whatever that be to which it attaches. The mind does not remain indifferent to those things and states which it sees to concern its enjoyments. This fact inspires a feeling towards them which we term desire. A desire is the inclination of the mind toward things which it sees to be the direct or indirect sources of pleasure. It rests back as a secondary feeling on those primary sensibilities to which the external world directly ministers. Now the variety of objects which gratify man, and the variety of their separate ministrations are so great, that it is not easy to give an exhaustive classification of them.

Those general words which divide, yet include the most of the things pursued by man, are wealth, power, honor, knowledge and virtue. They do not cover the entire ground. It is accurate, if not fitting language to say, I desire revenge. The heart also yearns for objects of affection, and that it itself should be made an object of love. When suffering pain, we desire its removal; when fearing punishment, we desire escape. Many of our secondary and more transient inclinations, are not included in these generalizations of the objects of pursuit.

The desire of happiness is sometimes added to the list. The objection to this, is, that this desire is a still broader generalization, including all the others. This desire embraces all our desires, is the utmost stretch of analysis and abstraction. Admit this, and there is no opportunity for farther division, classification,—all impulses are grouped under one general impulse common to each. The desire for existence is a secondary desire, dependent for its force on those other desires which make life pleasurable, valuable. To these secondary desires, there is no limit, as innumerable things may, at least for a moment, stand in the relation of means to the ends we are pursuing.

We regard desire, as a feeling, indifferent; neither pleasurable nor painful, at least in its earlier forms. When nourished into full strength, it may assume a more positive character. A desire for wealth, that is, as yet, neither gratified nor balked, while it becomes an immediate ground of pleasurable activity, while it gives direction and consort to the feelings, can hardly of itself be called distinctly painful or pleasurable. This is seen in the ease with which desire passes into pain or pleasure with any increase or decrease of the obstacles to its gratification. In the ordinary familiar balance of effort and reward, desire guides rather than vexes or excites us. When it produces pleasure, it is rather by the activity it inspires, the hopes it enkindles, than by its own nature as an impulse : when it provokes suffering, it does so by the unusual obstacles it encounters, by the disappointment of fruitless effort. A pure desire seems to be as simply indicative as any feeling can well be, to make way for the current of emotions that is sure to rush along in its trail.

The desires have different degrees of strength according to the minds in which they arise, and the objects toward which they are directed. The desire for wealth passes with a few into a passion, and becomes the most exacting of impulses, while, with others, it is so gentle an incentive as to control but few of their actions. Herein, again, is seen its secondary character. The mind that habitually forecasts the future, that brings coming enjoyments into clear contrast with immediate pleasures, is one in which the desires show their full strength. The conditions of their activity are fully met, and they soon come to rule with undisputed sway. One, however, in whom the primary appetites are exacting, and the reflective powers feeble, renders but wayward and intermittent obedience to the desires, and leaves the events of life to be fashioned by the objects in most immediate connection with the sensibilities.

The strength of desires also depends on the nature of the objects sought,—a farther result of their secondary characacter. The pursuit of wealth, of power, of honor, may, in rare instances, settle down into an exorbitant passion in minds in which the lower circle of vigorous, primitive sensibilities, is united with moderate reflective faculties, furnishing a clear, yet, nevertheless limited horizon of effort. In many cases these desires are relaxed by the disappointments which attend upon them, or the unsatisfactory nature of the results when realized. The desire for wealth is likely, under the force of habit, under the momentum of the mind, to pass into the blind passion of avarice, or to suffer abatement from the limited character of the good, wealth can confer. The desires for knowledge, for virtue, on the other hand, grow under success with a normal, a rational growth. Each acquisition is a stimulus to farther acquisition, and the satisfaction of possession increases every moment with possession. The mind more and more justifies its choice to itself, and congratulates itself on that which it has accomplished. The desire for wealth is like a stream that at length finds a precipice so high that in its leap it is lost in air, dissolved again in mist, and never resumes a peaceful flow ; while the love of knowledge and virtue, more tranquil currents, swell in volume, and roll on increasing waters to the ocean.

§ 2. On either hand, the desires give rise to a large class of feelings dependent upon them. We will speak first of those pleasurable ones which accompany success, and thus stimulate effort. Immediately consequent on a state of desire, inevitably incident to it, are the feelings of hope and joy in view of the prospect of obtaining the object sought. Indeed, hope is resolved, in analysis, into the feeling desire, and the intellectual condition, expectation. We would rather regard these as the occasion of the emotion than the very emotion, hope. Joy accompanies success, and passes through various stages, lying between tranquil satisfaction and triumphant exaltation. These feelings spring immediately from a free flow of the activities called forth by a successful desire, and in turn, greatly quicken their action. The emotional state thus becomes instantly complex, consisting of the immediate effect of anticipated pleasures, and the realized pleasure of fully employed powers. This has always been regarded as one of the most unalloyed forms of enjoyment—that evoked by the grasp of coming good by the mind as a certainty, together with the high exercise of its own faculties in securing it. The stimulated powers and feelings, not only yield the delight of successful action, but the imagination makes the most of the pleasure promised, and overlooks utterly the vexations and disappointments which too frequently embitter the actual enjoyment of it. This concurrence of the practical and imaginative faculties, leads to an exalted state of feeling, especially when neither experience has sobered, nor age made sluggish, the emotions.

A second class of pleasurable feeling arises in view of the relation of others to our success, our gratified desires. We are grateful to those who have aided us. We are sympathetically attached to those who share our triumphs, who enjoy our pleasures with us. Our feelings are made deeper, hence more pleasurable, by the impulse of kindred feelings on them. Emotional states, like electric conditions, intensify each other, and a movement once established tends to complete itself in part by the reflex influence of one mind on another. The love and complacency begotten by success are as manifest as the impatience and vexation that spring from failure. The moment of achievement, of gratification, is usually seized upon as propitious to those who seek either forgiveness or favor. The degree of this satisfaction in others depends on the intimacy of their relations to our success, but extends itself often in a feeble form to indifferent parties. It is expressed under various words according to its character and degree, as gratitude, good-will, good-fellowship, love, affection, attachment.

A third class of pleasurable feeling, comes from the connection of effort and success with ourselves. They are vanity, pride. These emotions are most influential over action, and constitute a large part of its reward. Vanity, the pleasure which the mind receives from the admiration, the favorable notice of others, exists with various conditions, and under very different degrees of intensity. In its moderate forms, it is a quiet incentive, and only becomes ill-grounded and foolish, when it leads to a neglect of real excellence and solid attainments, in favor of popular power and showy acquisitions. Within its legitimate sphere, it closely unites itself with that desire for the good opinion of others which the good man may well cherish. There are few feelings which sustain the inferior desires, as those for wealth and position, as constantly and effectively as this of vanity. Wealth owes its attractions, with most, to its ability to captivate and dazzle the public eye, to open gaping mouths, and bewilder feeble wits.

Pride arises from the same good opinion of one's self, and one's possessions, that characterize vanity. It is however accompanied with more independence of character, and does not, therefore, find its gratification so much in the admiration of others, as in its own admiration. Vanity loves parade, delights in the flow of popular sentiment, floats its gay shallop on the good opinion of others, and is stranded when public favor, like a shallow stream, is lost on some sand-bar. Pride, in its high opinion of itself, despises others, receives indifferently or contemptuously their admiration, and, like an ocean vessel, rides solitary on the heaving tide of its own conceit. Like vanity, it has a legitimate form. As just self-esteem, it furnishes strength and independence to character. It accompanies more frequently the second grade of desires, than those of power and knowledge. The food which the accomplishment of our desires affords to our own good opinion of ourselves, and our love of the admiration of others, is one of the most constant and certain, most secret and sweet, of the pleasures of success. In a modified form, these feelings enter into our highest moral sentiments. The various words by which we designate these feelings, derive their meanings in part from the different degrees of the same emotions, and in part from the supposed justice, or fitness, with which the feeling is entertained. Conceit, self-conceit, assumption, self-complacence, indicate a vanity or pride in advance of the grounds for it in our powers or possessions. Indeed, the words vanity and pride are also more commonly used to mark these excesses of feeling, than restrained and praiseworthy forms. Self-confidence, self-respect, personal pride designate the more measured and well-founded phases of these emotions.

§ 3. The feelings which accompany the failure of desire correspond to the opposite classes, but are more intense and more varied. Those which follow directly from the prospect of failure, or from failure itself, are fear, discouragements, disappointment, despair, all tending to repress effort, and to make the effort that is put forth peculiarly exhaustive. That the activity of the mind is an independent source of strength, is necessary to the highest, most successful development of purely physical strength, is indicated by the very different physical results which accompany efforts alike in intensity, but unlike in the satisfaction which accompanies them. Hope gives strength, discouragement at once takes it away. As physical life is an independent stimulus to the mind, so mental life is an independent stimulus to the body.

The second class of painful feelings, those excited toward others by opposition and failure, is especially full and varied. Envy, jealousy, dislike, antipathy, resentment, anger, hatred, malice, rage, revenge, are some of the words which express varied phases and stages of feeling, exasperated by the indirect or direct interference of others, by an opposition of attitude, or character, or effort. Envy and jealousy arise from the designed or undesigned displacing of ourselves in position, or in affection by others. They do not necessarily imply any fault on the part of their object, but merely an entrance upon ground we had coveted for ourselves. When this entrance is an intrusion, the feelings are proportionately more bitter. Antipathy, dislike, express the results of a sense of opposition in character which prepares us for opposition in action, and provokes in a milder form, by anticipation, feelings of repulsion.

Resentment, anger, hatred, malice, rage, revenge, mark the more violent outbursts of feeling toward those who directly thwart our efforts, who stand astride the path of our desires. These feelings, in their extreme form, so blind the reason as to become almost indiscriminate in their action; as to lead it to give vent to the pent-up passion on the first object that offers. The mind like an electric battery, charged to the full by the irritation and friction of chafing events, is ready to launch a bolt at the nearest point, to blast and splinter in mere wantonness of wrath.

It may be doubted, perhaps, whether these feelings of resentment are not in part pleasurable. As simple emotions we think not. They give rise, however, to secondary desires, desires of retaliation and revenge, and in the gratification of these we experience pleasure. Language recognizes this in such an expression, The sweetness of revenge. These feelings may also be blended with moral sentiments of indignation, and thus their true character be somewhat disguised.

Some have regarded it as a reflection on our constitution, that we should be capable of malevolent feelings. This perhaps it might be, if they were necessary, primary emotions, if, like the appetites, they found direct, inevitable expression. As secondary feelings, however, they depend for their character on the character of the person who entertains them. They arise under the general possibility of transgression, of wrong desires wrongly pursued, and thus are involved in the general problem of sin, and admit of the same remedy that transgression itself suffers. Right desires, in their method and measure right, may be attended only with right feelings. The holy will may ultimately reach to the correction of these products of the violent, the unsubmissive, the selfish will.

The last class of unpleasant feelings, arising from the relation to ourselves of baffled desire, is limited. They are certain forms of shame and humility. We are humbled by failure ; we are ashamed of the ill success which has followed our efforts. These emotions are disagreeable, and may become excessive, permanently weakening the incentives to effort. Humility and shame find their fullest play in the moral field. Like some of the other intellectual feelings, they are mere adumbrations of fuller emotions called forth by moral relations. It is the feelings now indicated in this second great class, resting primarily on self-interest, and especially liable to excess, that are termed passions. These emotions are frequently so strong that we *suffer* from them, that we seem to be their passive, afflicted subjects, rather than their responsible sources.

§ 4. A second limited class of intellectual feelings do not depend so immediately on the interest of the person entertaining them. These, like humility and shame, are chiefly anticipatory of the much fuller development of purely spiritual impulses. They are admiration, contempt, good-will, compassion. The highest, the chief object of admiration is character; though simple power, physical or intellectual, may draw forth the feeling. This emotion inclines to the class of pleasurable feelings, and this, we think, in proportion as it opens a line of emulative action. Wonderful powers shown in fields of effort entirely foreign to our own labors, by no means bestow, in the admiration they elicit, the same pleasure as do like triumphs in the familiar paths of our daily exertions. According, then, as admiration carries us from the mid-way point of indifference into successful effort, does the pleasure become declared and intense even. Let the feeling, by a contrast with our own weakness, discourage us, and it is painful rather than pleasant.

Contempt, on the other hand, tends to dissuade from

effort, is admonitory rather than persuasive, closes rather than opens paths for exertion. It is a painful emotion, except so far as, inflaming self-conceit, it finds, in the failure of others, the food of pride. A low, disparaging estimate of the powers of men, giving birth to contempt spiced with misanthropy, will, unless relieved by a marked exception in our own favor, depress action and enjoyment. Each newly discovered case of weakness increases the bitterness of the heart. This feeling slowly over-clouds the sky, and leaves the soul in a chill, benumbing, disheartening atmosphere, rendering it incapable of pleasure, and indisposing it to the effort by which the spell might be cast off. The contemptuous man takes home as guests, sarcasm, satire, unbelief, aversion. He abides in their companionship, lies down and rises with them, and suffers their corrosive breath to tarnish the brightness of every object. Contempt is the rust of the soul, which eats it up with increasing pain. Nothing can be intrinsically more diverse, or more diverse in their effects, than that intellectual contempt which feeds on the weakness of men, and that moral sentiment which scorns a mean action. The one is the recoil of the soul upward : the other, its gravitation downward, its cynical unbelief in goodness, its despair of strength.

Good-will and compassion are but feeble sentiments when disjoined from the moral nature. They are still pleasurable, still indices of action, impulses to a little desultory effort, but rarely have a deeper foundation than that of sympathy, which feebly transfers to us another's feelings; and plays but a secondary part among those towering and dominant passions which drink up the life of the soul. They are remote reflections, faint types of those strong affections, those profound sympathies which give to the higher, the moral nature its compass and power, which enable it successfully to confront the appetites and passions, outweighing the good they offer with a greater good.

§ 5. There are certain general conditions, by which the strength of the intellectual feelings is often strikingly affected. Novelty not only enhances the feelings appropriate to the occasion, it gives rise to a new feeling termed wonder. This is indeed a very vague and evanescent excitement, except as it directs inquiry and guides effort. It sounds the tocsin, sometimes of alarm, always of attention, to the mind, puts its faculties on the alert, and imparts pleasure according to the nature of the effort drawn forth. Wonder, therefore, is both a separate feeling, and also a condition on which the activity of the emotions often depends. The new is impressed upon us by our very constitution with a peculiar force, a distinct wave of sensibility, and is thus enabled to initiate a rapid, tidal flow of feeling, not otherwise possible. In early, and in uncultivated life, that which is novel is sought for its immediate emotional character. The grotesque, the odd, the extravagant, the new, the news, give fresh excitement, and the intrinsic value or worthlessness of the matter offered to the mind is overlooked. When the powers are more mature or more cultivated, wonder becomes a secondary, a briefly initiatory impulse, making way for the deeper satisfaction of recognized truth. When wonder fails to yield this pleasure, it drops away almost at once.

A second condition on which the degree of emotional activity depends, is harmony. Certain views and s ates unite easily, flow together and strengthen each other. Others stand in the opposite relation, and exist by mutual exclusion. Harmony is consistent with contrast. Indeed, this is one of the ways in which impressions are deepened and made complete. The intellectual view is made clear and decided by uniting like with like, and opposing like to unlike—by agreement and by contrast. The latter is often the more effective of the two methods of deepening an impression. Harmony, as a condition of feeling, includes the presence of what is concordant, and excludes objects discordant, lying in different parts of the intellectual and emotional field. It is opposed to distraction, to diverse emotions, and thus divided effects.

A third ground of increased feeling, is sympathy. A certain contagious force belongs to emotion. The swell of sentiment among masses, like the surge of the ocean, is heavy, forceful, dominant. It is difficult to maintain feelings which are not shared by those about us ; it is difficult to escape the influence of those which are prevalent. The minds of men flow into each other, and come to feel and propagate, with increasing power, the same influences. Sympathy, strictly so called, does not change the character of a sentiment, it only disseminates it. The inflammable nature of the feelings by which assemblies, mobs, armies are laid open to conflagration, each firing his neighbor, till all are caught up in one uncontrollable frenzy, is a very familiar fact.

A fourth condition on which the immediate force of the feelings depends, is association. This word covers most of the results of previous action on present intellectual states. It is what habit, indulgence are to the bodily appetites. Our feelings become grouped in memory by repeated experience, and on each recurrence, restore by suggestive power a large class of emotions and incentives with which they have previoustly consorted. Like feelings are thus sorted and consolidated into varied, powerful classes, which work together on the mind, one never arising alone, but uniformly having present for its aid, some of its familiar companions. We shall not understand the force of certain passions without comprehending the multiplied echoes which they find in the soul. We shall return to this point in a subsequent chapter.

The animation of the feelings is also frequently dependent on the power of imagination. Our intellectual emotions arise in connection with sensible objects, and the vividness with which these are present to the mind, will determine the degree of action in the accompanying sensibilities. The passionate and the poetic temperament are influenced by the images of the fancy. The clear and vivid pictures of the imagination arrest the attention, and arouse the passions, till they come baying along the trail of indulgence, like hounds in full sight.

The nature, character, and excitability of the emotions are diverse, but their activity at any one time depends, aside from direct influences, on these mental conditions. Arising out of intellectnal action, they are especially affected by the circumstances and conditions of that action. While the pleasurable feelings are evolved, for the most part, in connection with successful activity, and the painful ones in connection with baffled effort, we are not to suppose that this fact explains their very nature, or identifies action with enjoyment. It only indicates the relation of our emotions to the ends of life, but leaves them each to be understood in its simple, intrinsic character by experience.

CHAPTER III.

The Spiritual Feelings.

§ 1. The spiritual feelings are so called because they belong peculiarly to our higher nature. Intellectual action is spiritual action ; yet that which gives guidance and government to our interior, hidden life, is found in our intuitions. The intellect is instrumental under these; as, in the brute, it is simply a means to physical safety and gratification. Our spiritual feelings spring up, then, in direct connection with our intuitions ; those mental elements which make our life truly rational, which give to us a choice of ends, and liberty in the pursuit of them. The only intuitions which draw forth directly feeling, are those of truth, beauty and right. There is in the emotions connected with these regulative ideas, the action of the intellect, yet an action different from that presented by the last class of feelings. In these, it was the observed relation of things to our enjoyments, which was the ground of desire, with the attendant sensibilities. The mental action intervened between the remote appetites, taste, passion, and pointed out the means of gratification, and called forth a variety of emotions in prosecuting the labor presented. In the present case, the intellectual action precedes the intuition. Patient inquiry reveals the grounds of belief, the truth : a careful discrimination of qualities, of the symbols of expression, of complex relations, discloses the conditions of beauty : a thorough inquiry into the nature and results of action, its reflex and progressive effects, lay open its true character, and then the intuitive faculty comes in to complete and seal the work in the discernment of a new and a distinct quality—that of right. The proposition is said to be true, the statue is felt to be beautiful, the action is pronounced right, and forthwith there arise sentiments which find their spring in these ideas. These are the spiritual feelings. Their final, their immediate dependence is on the mind's intuitive action ; their secondary dependence, on our intellectual faculties. Our intellectual feelings, on the other hand, find their immediate source in mental action, in the conclusions of experience, and their ultimate ground in the appetites and tastes.

These feelings again are open to the same division into pleasurable, indifferent and painful emotions. This, as regards happiness, a chief and intimate relation of the feelings, must necessarily be the fundamental distinction of all the emotions. Their relation to action may be said to be secondary to their relation to enjoyment, since action itself is undertaken or withheld in view of its immediate or ultimate effects on the sensibilities. The feelings can only be classified by their external relations, since, intrinsically, they are all diverse, all simple original states, known in experience only. Of the external relations of the feelings, this relation to happiness is most essential, while that to action comes next in order, both as indicating an immediate purpose served by our sensibilities, and their secondary effects on our character and well-being. In their connection with action, the spiritual feelings assume a more imperative character than either of the other two classes. In them, they followed on to stimulate and gratify effort, or check and discourage it; here, they go before it as well to command as to forbid action. They cease merely to allure, and seek decisively to enjoin and prohibit different lines of conduct. The middle ground of indication seems narrowed to a point, and to be pressed closely on either hand by dissuasives and persuasives. The spiritual sentiments may be divided into those of persuasion and dissuasion. Their voice is always one of authority, though its authority need not be felt, so long as it is kindly and cheerfully accepted. Actual or contemplated resistance provokes a class of penal sensibilities; and obedience elicits feelings that have the positive character of approval and reward.

The weakest of these sentiments, and those therefore which least well represent the class, are the somewhat intangible, rare, and uncertain sensibilities which accompany the discovery, the recognition of the truth as truth. Truth is not a separate, regulative idea. It is included in that of resemblance. It is the recognized agreement of a proposition with the facts which it states. Much the majority of truths are received as truths with no emotion. Most of them are matters of interest only as they affect action,

—only in their relation to our desires, indicating success or failure, or revealing the line of conduct to be pursued. Truths, for the most part, are means possessed of no inherent, emotional force beyond their relation to ends.

This negative character of truth seems sometimes to disappear, and truth as truth to inspire a certain enthusiasm of mind, by which we feel that this is indeed the food of our spiritual nature. We may breathe the air ordinarily without thought, or sensible pleasure. Occasionally, we find it peculiarly invigorating ; we inhale great draughts, and bring our whole physical being into a more conscious and exalted state. Thus is it with the truth,—the daily breath of our intellectual life. We ordinarily overlook it ; at rare intervals we, in deep inspiration, feel its pervasive and subtle power, and rejoice in its possession. We travel along the valley, scarcely observing the objects about us, with no elation of feeling ; we pass some crowning summit, take in a wider range, and the before concealed wave of emotion becomes sensible to us ; we are lifted on its passing billow, as if a breath from another world had stolen suddenly across our path.

This is the kind of emotion to which we draw attention, —the enthusiasm sometimes felt in truth, more especially in those fundamental, far-reaching truths which seem to suddenly lift the veil of phenomena, of varied colors, and to disclose to us the frame-work of the universe ; the purposes which are running through it, and bearing it to its goal. This on-going of a divine plan, when recognized, startles and inspires the mind, lifts truth out of its daily, dry, instrumental ministrations, and gives us the sense of a new inheritance and possession in a universe whose conception we can thus lay hold of, whose secrets we can thus penetrate, whose wisdom and love we can thus interpret and feel. I care not how little, or how much of this sentiment we may have felt, how far it may be thought to be confined to the more poetic and penetrative temperaments; it is sufficient to draw attention to it as an enthusiasm for truth occasionally felt and avowed, finding expression in the collective use of the word truth, the truth, the truths, as if a certain concealed link and deep unity were to be found in all facts. We do this, too, in the face of those detestable facts, truths, which sin is forcing constantly upon our notice, as if after all, there were some profound fellowship, some one exaltation in all truths, rendering them *the truth.*

This sensibility to the truth, be it more or less clear, be it more or less deep, inspires pursuit, leads to faith in a profound, unfolding plan, and quickens the mind to discover the corrective laws, the compensatory statements for the defects and transgressions which lie on the surface of the world. This sentiment opens up a line of effort, inspires enthusiasm, sends faith in advance of reason, and rejoices in the slow displacement of accredited by apprehended facts, of statement by disclosure, of trust by sight, of intuitive belief by the light of comprehensive principles. It is little more than the exaltation and joy of our spiritual faculties as they enter on, and begin to occupy their inheritance—an inheritance which we are pleased to call that of eternal truth, though on the shifting surface of changing events, everything seems most transitory—of blessed truth, though most horrible and terrible facts are daily evolved before our eyes. Yes, the sense and the revelation of deep principles that undergird the world with abiding strength, and gather it up in the embrace of an exalted, a blessed purpose, are with us; steal in upon us in our exaltation, and yield the repose which a belief in its ultimate triumph inspires. There is unlocked in our language and our nature, a belief in truth, central, adamantine, giving safe, benignant support to the universe of God.

In like manner, we carry over to the false, the untrue, a

farther concentration of opposition and rejection in the word falsehood. We personify it as a distinct principle or power of mischief, believe in its weakness, and rejoice in in its ultimate overthrow. No matter what may have been their character, few of any party have ever espoused falsehood as such, few have not felt that the confession of it would be the admission of ultimate failure. We recognize the vague way in which these words, truth and falsehood, are frequently used; yet, nevertheless, we claim that there is in this tendency of the mind to recognize the inherent opposition of the true and the false, the ultimate, necessary victory of the one over the other—a latent belief in fundamental principles and forces, which it is the vain, temporary effort of falsehood to cover up and counter-work. This embrace of the real, as ultimately involving the ideal, and to pass in evolution from excellence to excellence, is the fruit of the mind's discovery of truth and error, its hearty acceptance of the one and the rejection of the other; its satisfaction in the eternal plan of God.

§ 2. The next group of intuitive feelings, though of a more manifest character, and more prevalent, has yet much of the same subtlety, the same choice of persons and times. Indeed, these are features of the whole class of emotions of which we are speaking. It has, doubtless, been one reason of the difficulty with which the spiritual feelings and the intuitive ideas, on which they are immediately dependent, have been recognized—that they are not, like the physical feeling, universally present with approximately equal power, but in many scarcely seem to exist at all, and in their full intense forms to be confined to comparatively few. Yet the reason of this is obvious. They are each of them dependent on previous culture, on a faithful, special, discriminating action of the understanding. The beauty of the world is not seen, or at least is but very partially and inadequately seen, without an inquiry into its structure and relations, without a discernment of the thought, exquisite perfection of idea and workmanship involved in it. No more is the right understood without a broad survey of conduct, the tracing of actions to their consequences; without rising above the immediate current of the stream, to see whence and whither its flow. The intuitive feelings, therefore, can only be strong and clear in the more penetrative and reflective minds. They do not thereby cease to be universal or characteristic when their appropriate conditions are met.

The esthetical emotions arise solely under the previous action of mind. Disorder, absolute and complete, can furnish no beauty, nothing to be admired, nothing intrinsically to be delighted in. Order, arrangement, is the first step toward beauty, is the first simplest product of taste. But this order is the product of thought. This arrangement will present itself as beautiful in proportion to the number and variety of the ends it meets, and the ease and accuracy with which these separate purposes are fulfilled. A little formal order imposed by mere utility, simple convenience in the classification of material, is not sufficient, or sufficiently significant to excite and to satisfy the taste. It is not till more feeling enters into our plan, more variety, skill and precision of adjustment, that the elements of beauty begin to be clearly revealed, and the mind takes an additional delight in the work, aside from each and all of the ends subserved by it. Gardening, architecture, music, are the arts least imitative,—the arts in which the beauty present is most immediately the result of the combining power of the human mind. In each of these, mere order produces scarcely a sensible effect. It is not till the plan discovers high appreciation of the resources at the disposal of the artist, and great power and pleasure in combining and developing them—not till the product becomes thoroughly emotional, and in its scope and variety betrays a mind and heart alike active, that it begins in turn to command our emotion, and impress us, as the case may be, with the grace, symmetry, harmony, force of the conception.

Here, then, beauty throws us into appreciative sympathy with the thoughts and feelings of a worker; of one who executes well and powerfully, and delights in such execution —one with whom perfection is a thing esteemed, sought after, and includes far more than the immediate subordination of the means employed to a useful, physical end. It is this effort of the mind, without neglecting utility, to lift each of its works out of the mere routine of labor, off from the simple plain of service into an emotional region, —to make it in its excellence, in its skillful or affectionate or grand handling, a source of independent, superior, constant pleasure, that is the source of beauty, and of its command over the heart. Not merely work, or good work, but superior, expressive, emotional work is its aim. The esthetical feelings cause us to delight in such labor, and to go, as far as may be, to every undertaking crowned with garlands.

If we pass to the beauties of nature, equally do we find that it is thought, aptness of arrangement, skill of workmanship, labor performed with infinite love and faithfulness, that arrest the mind and gratify the heart. In proportion as many adaptations, many powers are gathered into a brief compass, and with a perfect finish and relation of parts united in one organic whole, are we climbing with slow gradations, with a thousand steps of varied progress from the lowest life to the highest, from the plant to man, delighted with the goodness of the thought, the kind and abundant ministration of the faculties to the well-being and excellence of the final product. In each advance of beauty, there is more expression, because there is more and more perfect, and more and more beneficent labor, till, in man, we find the highest condensation of power and regard, service, compactness, symmetry, finish, in their most perfect forms.

Everywhere, then, it is the labor of mind and heart, the births of thought and feeling, the rational products of high intelligence and love, that arouse the sensibility of beauty; and we are so constituted that we are not, cannot, be indifferent to these qualities when perceived by us. A cold, intellectual apprehension does not exhaust them. They elicit a certain regard, assume a certain prominence of position, which we designate as beauty, and the pleasures of beauty. Such enjoyment on our part is a crowning sympathy with excellence; such perception, an additional incentive to high attainment. They are the thirst of an aspiring spirit for that which is beyond, which is above, for that which it knows it can grasp and enjoy. They take all barrenness, all deadness from simple intellectual movement, breathe through it desire, cause it to draw back the curtain between us and the ideal world, and fire us with the zeal of pursuit.

While the specific character of esthetical emotions is very pronounced, their minor differences are very great. The same fruits have not all the same flavor. The most exquisite and characteristic tastes complete the circle, with an endless division and change of quality. In works of nature, plants, trees, landscapes, birds, beasts, men; in works of art, painting, statues, poems; in varied objects, and in their yet more varied combinations, we find a constant change of predominant qualities, endless degrees of power, and ever shifting methods of expression. Hence arises in esthetical sentiments every shade of form and force, from impressions scarcely perceptible to those which wholly occupy the soul—overpowering emotions breaking out upon it like a flood. The flow of these enjoyments in the sensitive mind, may be compared to the movement of music, now gay and cheerful, now common-plaçe, now low and sad, now mysterious, now wild, now sublime, gliding from phase to phase of emotion, with perfect ease and inexhaustible felicity. The scope, body, variety of feelings which are either in whole or in part of an esthetical character, are in sensitive, poetic temperaments very marked. A large share, both of their gentler as well as more exalted pleasures, spring from this source.

The form of action which these emotions prompt is manifest. They always afford a mild, often a powerful stimulus to painstaking, emulative and refined action. They promote the finish, the perfections, the beauty of every product of the hand or of the mind. They reveal themselves in the physical results of labor, and certainly not less in character. The restraints and checks of esthetic sentim ents are experienced constantly in manners and social customs, and, if the taste is keen and just, in the more deep, personal, spiritual traits of action. Indeed, nobility, magnanimity, the symmetry and proportion of robust, thorough, healthy virtue, can hardly be reached without a large infusion of this esthetic insight, which discerns, delicately and completely, the formal as well as the intrinsic bearing of conduct. The dependent, complementary relation of the esthetic to the ethic sense cannot be doubtful. Some may strive to make of the first a detached law of action, but it only performs safely and to the full its office, as it accepts the higher law, and aids in its complete application. Perfect beauty in man, its highest subject, is the strong and varied and delicate development of moral power—the infusion of all the members and means of life with this inner, true life of the soul—the flowing outward in limb, lineament, and language of those manifold forces and susceptibilities that spring from wholesome, healthy, physical forces, in the handling of a supreme, spiritual power. Taste rightly developed can no more fail to distinguish morality from immorality, to work under the one and against the other, than it can fail to discriminate between life and death, health and disease, exalt the first, and hide the second in its deformity. Beauty stands in the same relation to action as right; like it, enjoins and forbids, rewards and punishes. It blows a more silvery trumpet, its notes are less clear, penetrating and decisive than those which break sternly forth from the lips of ethical law, yet they wind their way into many remote places, and persuasively bend into cheerful and perfect order, the otherwise unpliant recruits of virtue.

§ 3. We have now reached the feelings which are more central and characteristic, in the class to which they belong, the moral sentiments. The emotions just spoken of would lose much of their character were it not for their interpenetration by those of the moral nature. It is this filtration of the higher sensibilities downward which gives adherence and authority to the recognition of truth, to esthetical feelings, which of themselves simply have little binding force. The only imperative voice in man's nature, is that of conscience, of moral intuitions; all other authority is but the echo and reflection of this. In one view of the subject our moral nature may be said to be our entire nature; since a moral quality and moral relation are imparted to all thoughts and actions, by the presence of this supreme, supervisory power. In a more familiar use, our moral nature includes these emotions which more directly spring from it. Conscience, the perceptive faculty, which, in an indivisible act, sees the right and feels the sense of obligation, is the centre of our moral constitution. Without it, we should have no affections, moral sentiments; with it, we find the whole atmosphere of our being irradiated, and a thousand colors revealed in objects, tangible, indeed, in the darkness, with odor and with flavor, but with no direct avenue of approach through the physical night to the intellectual day. Light does not more modify, I may say etherealize matter, multiplying a thousand fold its intelligible signs, crowding them in from all quarters and all distances on the astonished mind, than does a moral perception affect our estimates of character, deepen in meaning, and broaden in time, the relations of actions.

The fundamental moral feeling from which all others spring, is that of obligation. This, as regards pleasure and pain, is indifferent. It may give place to one or the other, according to the attitude assumed toward the duties designated. The blended, the indivisible nature of the intuition, and the accompanying sentiment should be carefully marked. A sense of obligation, a mere feeling, with nothing to which that feeling attaches, by which it is evoked, is theoretically unintelligible, and practically unservicable. An intuition of right on the other hand, which does not instantly assume the force and pressure of duty, loses its character and slips from the throne of the mind. Intrinsic quality and exterior form, the intellectual and the emotional elements, are inseparably blended, and give us a command, whose unquestionable authority, like one born to rule, is in the immediate fact, in tone, attitude, outspoken power.

If obedience follows the intimations of our moral sense, there sets in a deep and deepening current of pleasurable feelings, of reward. The force and intensity of these emotions will depend very much on the degree in which the judgments which sustain the action of conscience, which prepare the way for its decisions, have been cultivated; on the relative force which the moral sentiments have secured in our constitution by obedience. Ethical, like esthetical feelings, are very dependent on cultivation. The reason of this is obvious, since in neither case are we dealing, as in external perception, with a direct, immediate faculty, but with one acting on the previous intellections, the previous conceptions of the mind, and therefore limited in its scope and correctness to them. It is evident that the character of phenomena should be judged by instances in which they are most manifest and complete, not by cases in which they are obscure and furtive. A powerful moral nature makes itself at once felt in the pleasures it pours in upon the obedient mind, of such degree and quality, that the appreciative heart prefers them to all others, and purchases them at any price of suffering which can be exacted of it. Yet these enjoyments are of a tranquil rather than of a violent kind; a deep sense of satisfaction in the choices made, a thorough contentment in actions done, an inner approval which anticipates a like outward acceptance on the part of the wise and just.

The feelings which follow disobedience, though more irregular and unequal in their action, often dilatory and partial, when compared with those of approval and reward, yet frequently assume a strong, clear, undeniable character. Shame, guilt, remorse, willful opposition, and sullen despair, may, in turn, hold sway, and make themselves as distinct as, and more bitter than, any other feelings which the heart ever experiences. For reaching this result, more or less time may be required. Repeated disclosure of the disasters of transgressions, the accumulation of physical retributions, a revelation of pervasive law, hemming in and baffling the disobedient, may be needed to instruct the moral judgments, and awaken the moral sense. When, however, a pause is given to the career of sin, when reflection and the intuitive results of reflection can no longer be averted, the force and direction of moral emotion are as certain as the pain or pleasure of sense, when things bitter or sweet are on the palate. The pains of indigestion may follow more slowly than disgust from food in itself offensive; but the consequences are no less of a distinct and undeniable character.

Moral sufferings may be postponed in more ways, and longer than many other emotional issues of action; yet the development of causes ripens them none the less certainly to their results. The whole history of the race, renders the positive character of the moral sentiments as undeniable as the physical consequences of an unwholesome diet. The fear, the cowardice, the apprehension, the boldness, the approval, the confidence; self-condemnation, self-gratulation; the reproaches of conscience, the dismay, the despair attendant on wickedness achieved, the composure of assured conviction, the calm anticipation of suffering, the triumph over it, fill the records of history, are the staple of dramatic and heroic fiction. Heathen and Christian literature alike, breathes in its more profound and earnest moods, one spirit.

Says Juvenal:

> "But tell me, why must those be thought to 'scape,
> Whom guilt, arrayed in very dreadful shape,
> Still urges, and whom conscience, ne'er asleep,
> Wounds with incessant strokes, not loud but deep,
> While the vexed mind, her own tormentor, plies
> A scorpion scourge, unmarked by human eyes."

The history of martyrs especially develops the moral forces in man, since, on these feelings, the struggle has turned. The cruel tossings of such a mind as that of Cranmer, clear, conscientious, yet timid and distrustful, between fear and conviction, discloses as certainly as any thing can disclose the nature of the forces at work, unless it be the varying sympathy, the alternate charity and condemnation of succeeding generations, in view of the momentary overthrow and ultimate triumph of the moral sentiments in the fearful, bold martyr.

§ 4. Personal qualities are greatly modified by the moral nature. Meekness, humility lose all servility, are consistent with the utmost strength, and firmness softens down without weakening the outline of character.

Still more is this true of our feelings towards others. These, in the conscientious temperament, receive almost their entire force from the moral sentiments. The affections, a distinct class of sensibilities, are our emotions toward others as moral beings. Admiration, love, sympathy, benevolence, forgiveness, charity, patience, indignation, contempt, shame, are feelings, which, though they may bear the same name with certain intellectual emotions, are very different from them. Love a passion, and love an affection, the indignation of anger, and the indignation of a violated moral sense, are alike diverse sentiments in their relation both to enjoyment and to action. The first may as easily prey upon happiness as promote it; the second cannot fail of being productive of pleasure.

In the moral sensibilities, the sharpness, the bitterness of the selfish element disappear, and the benignity, composure, patience of a moral impulse take their place. It is the intermingling of the kinds of feeling, and of the words applicable to them, which confound the character of action, and the classification of this department.

The direction in which the moral sensibilities find fullest play is that of religious sentiments. The relations and duties designated as religious are those which, by the feelings, the results involved, are fitted to act most powerfully on the conscience and affections. The religious emotions, therefore, seem at times to overshadow other forms of ethical action, since their intensity and scope bear some proportion to the interests involved,—to the ennobling, greatly stimulating presentations of the divine attributes. The foundation of religion is ethics, yet the ethical form is often swallowed up in the deep, spontaneous play of the religious affections. If we consider the permanent issues of happiness, of joy and peace, as settled in our own constitution by the moral sentiments, and the relation of our action under them; if we remember that nothing in our fellow-men is of more abiding interest to us than their character, than the moral purposes indicated, and line of conduct adopted : and, above all, if we bring to mind that the deepest, the supreme play of feeling is towards God, chiefly known to us as a moral being, we shall see that this class of sentiments now presented, are at once the most varied, the most full, the most central and powerful of our emotions. So pervasive are they, that they give coloring to intellectual feelings which they cannot rule, enter in a fragmentary form where completeness is denied them, and are brought in to intensify or modify or disguise sentiments intrinsically at war with them. The exact shades of approval and condemnation, of contentment and restlessness, of belief and unbelief in them, are as endless as are the relations which men's actions assume to virtue.

Their authority, their retributive connection with pleasure and pain, the undercurrent of fear or hope, of repose or alarm, of conscious virtue or acknowledged guilt, which they cause to flow through the soul, obviously assign them the highest rank in the highest class of feelings.

CHAPTER IV.

Dynamics of the Emotions.

§ 1. We have spoken of the three classes of feelings ; the physical, the intellectual, and the spiritual. We wish now to see them more collectively in their relations to each other, in the formation of character and the control of action. The first class spring immediately from physical conditions, and, including incidental occasions of pleasure, have primary reference to physical well-being. At points they transcend this object. Taste, touch, smell, are means of simple, intellectual distinctions ; yet, it remains true, that the senses which are the avenues of feeling, the appetites, the sensations, indicating special physical conditions, all have primary reference to health, to guiding action, in nourishing and maintaining the vigour of the body. Even here, it can hardly be said, that, "All pleasure arises from the free play of our faculties and capacities ; and all pain from their compulsory repression, or compulsory activity." Much less is this generalization of Hamilton's applicable to the remaining classes of emotion.

It is the unhealthy and the healthy action, the unwholesome repression and the wholesome repression, that give pain and pleasure respectively, and this not always at once, but as an ultimate consequence. Pain enters frequently to arrest action, and not as the consequence of arrested action. Mere activity, voluntary though it may be, does not necessarily give the conditions of enjoyment : these must depend on its relations to health. Neither does repressed exertion, involuntary though the restraint may be, define the conditions of physical suffering. Overlooking the mental vexation of such constraint, the physical consequences may be agreeable. Physical pleasures seem to depend on the relation which activity and repose have to health, and not on their relation to the will of the agent. Some forms of disease provoke voluntary, fitful, restless, yet painful effort. The exertion, or the want of it, by no means explains the accompanying pain or pleasure. These are ultimate facts ; we know through experience their general connection with physical well-being. Our pain and pleasures come in this way to impart a direct stimulus to appropriate effort for the maintenance of the body, still more to instruct us as to its condition and wants, and thus, in a secondary way, guide our action. They also subserve the purpose of intellectual discrimination, and of gratification.

The second class have relation to success, are pleasurable

and painful in proportion as this intellectual end is secured or lost. Unsuccessful activity, no matter how free and spontaneous it may have been, is always, in the intellectual feelings which accompany it, disagreeable, often intensely painful. Our physical and our intellectual enjoyments may not always harmonize. Effort in itself wholesome, may fail of its object and occasion disappointment; and exertion crowned with the most flattering success, may bring severe infliction of physical penalties. The mind institutes its own ends, and afterwards finds pleasure, or experiences suffering, by its prosperity or failure in the pursuit of them. As the primary relation of the intellectual emotions is to success in the ends aimed at, the pleasure and pain in this direction experienced, act as stimuli to sagacity, and faithfulness in the choice and use of means. This is an instrumental, an intermediate field, and its enjoyments are of a secondary, intermediate character.

Spiritual pleasures have reference to the choice of ends, to the marking out of lines of conduct,—to obedience to higher, alternative impulses. These again may often fail of concurrence with intellectual enjoyments. We have the satisfaction of success in the attainment of ends which we should never have chosen, and the moral rebuke may thus set in at the point at which the intellectual pleasure is most complete. Physical health and spiritual health are ultimate, and the secondary intellectual enjoyments cannot avert the consequences of failure as regards either of them. Spiritual enjoyments and sufferings come in to enforce obedience,—obedience to the law of spiritual life. They stand in the same relation to this, that physical pleasures do to the lower life of the body. They are simple, ultimate, with the approval of the moral sense sustaining them. With self-established authority, the conscience legislates for the whole man, and according as its commands are wisely understood, and wisely applied, the minor physical and intellectual enjoyments are gathered up in these supreme pleasures of the soul.

Our enjoyments are not thus simply the fruits of activity, they are of such a character as to define its limits, and direct it to appropriate objects. The law of life in the whole man is indicated by them. The ends to be pursued, the limits to be set to activity, even in its right directions, are pointed out, with the accompanying injunction laid upon us of a skillful choice and use of means.

§ 2. The three classes of feelings now referred to, have a successive, rather than an equal and simultaneous hold on the mind. The physical feelings are most immediate, direct, importunate in their claims. The intellectual life is awakened through the physical life, in some sense follows it. The sensations, the appetites, the states of the body, are early and decided means of good and evil—means independent of thought, with a necessary and irresistible appeal to the sensibilities. The intellectual feelings, as secondary, involve a previous action of mind, are not strong except in connection with considerable anticipation, forethought, a somewhat broad survey of the relations of actions. For this reason, the desires do not set in in a deep, strong current, except in more advanced minds, or in the more civilized states of society. In a barbarous community, the immediate impulses are chiefly animal; in a civilized community the desires come to rule the leading classes, while the appetites still bear sway in the lower ranks. The spiritual feelings are yet more tardy in their full development. For anything like broad, decisive action of our higher intuitions, there is requisite much previous reflection. As beauty involves the union of inner power with perfect form, there must be, for its due perception, a deep, discriminating insight into both. As the universal sway of morality arises from a clear perception of the dependence of individual and general well-being on the form and spirit of conduct in its every manifestation, it is not till faithful observation, and protracted reflection have disclosed the character and issues of action, that the ethical impulse can find very complete application. In the outset it is likely to be confined to a few negative precepts, cutting off the individual from gross violations of the right. Ten commandments expounded in the most barren way may seem its limits. Only the latest culture can open these into the pervasive precept of universal love. The most enlightened communities, therefore, as yet present a very partial government of the spiritual sentiments. When the artistic sensibilities have been awakened, they have hitherto affected but limited classes, and this in a partial, one-sided form, sometimes even in direct violation of the moral sentiment which underlies all high acts. The religious emotions also have been restricted in their action, and fragmentary in their character. The spirit and the force of a higher life have not, in their completeness, been grasped, and we have had an ethics more or less at war with esthetics—a rugged force, which could not yet discriminate and command all the elements requisite for its own most perfect expression.

§ 3. Were it not that communities—that successive generations of men, achieve a collective growth, which the individual is able to receive inductively from them, starting at the point they have already reached; this order of development in the feelings would make the condition of mankind comparatively hopeless. But the growth of society reveals very clearly this progress from the physical to the intellectual feelings, and in an incipient form is disclosing that farther movement by which the artistic and ethical sentiments, under the perfect, harmonious rule of the higher impulse, shall take the supreme position amid the powers and pleasures of the human heart.

When any one feeling begins to predominate in the individual or the community, many things concur to strengthen its hold. Take, as an illustration, such a desire as that for wealth. It soon becomes a strong current, plowing for itself a deep bed, walled on either hand, and not readily changed. The desire by repetition returns easily, as an habitual one. Surrounding objects and pursuits are more and more contemplated in their ability to gratify this feeling, and therefore by their presence more uniformly bring it uppermost in the mind. Kindred pursuits draw together parties in whom the desire is already developed, and by emulation and the confirmation of like judgments, they inflame it in each other. Thus a large commercial city seems a very maelstrom of economic currents, and every individual, a separate particle spinning round and round under the same feverish impulse, and waiting to be swallowed up by the same insatiable lust. The brood of feelings also warmed into life by a parent desire, unite at once in the same clamorous and importunate cries. Vanity, pride, the satisfaction of success, the fear of failure, all quicken effort, and occupy the heart, when for a moment, the original impulse relaxes. The circle of secondary desires is momentarily enlarged as the means of gratification are placed within their reach, and the wealth acquired is often less and less able to meet the claims laid upon it, by feelings which, without law or limit in themselves, become monstrous and ravenous in proportion to the food given them. Thus external and internal circumstances are increasingly shaped to the ruling feeling—grow up more and more under it, institute claims in harmony with it, confirm the judgments which sustain it, and weaken and remove to a distance, adverse emotion. From this household of dependents, from this pressure of a prevalent opinion, from this confirmed and consolidated conviction of the soul itself, it is difficult to find an avenue of escape. If we substitute an appetite for a desire, though there is less warping of the judgment, there is in its place a peevish, persecuting habit, not easily to be worn out or resisted. From this confirmed movement which the feelings for the time-being assume, it becomes necessary that the forces which work for progress, should find concentration, and also, that long periods should be allowed them in which to possess and fortify the ground they may be able to win. The overthrow of one class of feelings, and their permanent replacement by another, in a community, is a truly gigantic work, requiring often the slow eradication and correction of a protracted and varied experience.

§ 4. The feelings involve, equally with the thoughts, an expenditure of power, of vital force. The stronger feelings therefore cannot long last. They must be relatively brief. Intense grief is followed by comparative apathy; exciting pleasures by depression of spirits, and vehement anger by relative indifference. Hence it happens that those who are most violent in their feelings are most fickle —the rush of the mind in one direction, soon provoking the return gale. The evenly happy life must be fed by the milder, more sustained sentiments; and the peace, the rest of the soul is found in the balance and correction of its feelings, one by the other. The moral sentiments yield superior repose, not from their own nature alone, but also from the restraints and rule to which they subject all vexing and exorbitant emotions. Esthetic pleasures are among the most peaceful, since they are among the most harmonized and proportionate of the sentiments. An overwrought moral sentiment is sure to provoke corresponding distortion and discomfort in the spiritual life.

The chief difference between play and labor seems to be that the one gives vent to a superabundant power and life in a direction in which it spontaneously flows, and the other demands, in view of a reward, exertion to which the physical or intellectual state does not prompt. Labor approaches play in its character in proportion as the effort becomes spontaneous. Now success stimulates the feelings, and the quickened feelings arouse the active powers in the direction of their gratification. Hence it happens, that those whose labor is abundantly rewarded often take so keen a delight in it, as scarcely to be willing to turn aside for so-called play. The true amelioration of labor is success, the success which expresses power and enhances it, which makes the movement of realization easy and sportive. Drudgery is not so much labor as poorly requited labor. Hence labor that is undertaken under the prompting of strong desire, is much more easily endured than the same exertion when coerced; since incidentally the pleasurable feelings find play, and enliven and make easy, the effort. Self-directed and prosperous labor, then, will, in proportion as these elements of liberty and power enter into it, assume the character of play, and the ultimate lifting up of the burden of toil will be found in a more spontaneous and successful movement, that is, in one more thoroughly intellectual. Exactly in the degree in which the higher power is present and prevalent, do we already see the servitude of labor removed, and it made the desire of the mind. Virtue must assume this easy, irrepressible character which belongs to the physical putting forth of animal life, before it can lay aside the harsh aspect of toil and struggle, and present the beauty of angelic strength—strength that is no more burdened by the load laid upon it, than the hero of the ring with his own muscle.

§ 5. The feelings of the animal, if the view we have presented of his endowments is correct, are almost purely physical. His courage is physical courage; his fear, physical fear; that is to say, these states are imposed upon him directly by external objects. The one is the rushing in of nerve power, prompting to conflict; the other, the desertion of the seats of strength by the energies of life—an immediate provocation, an inclination, to flight instead of attack. Memory, giving rise to association, may indeed, in the higher animals, start trains of feeling and thus of action, aside from the power of the object which is more remotely their cause. Yet these feelings are comparatively limited. Little apprehension is shown except in the presence of danger, and then not according to its real nature, but its sensible form. The alarm manifested by many animals assumes a direct, instinctive character,—the appropriate action evidently follows the sensitive impression without any intervention of judgment. The young of the partridge hide themselves instantly on the first intrusion. Barn fowls are filled with immoderate and universal alarm as the shadow of the hawk glides by them. The actions of the lower creation assume generally this direct dependence on sensations, with an occasional intervention of the intellectual element of association.

Having now the emotions completely before us in their relation to the mind, and to each other, we are better able to decide on the merits of that theory which recognizes but two classes, resolving the spiritual feelings into the intellectual. This will hardly seem possible, if we fairly estimate all that belongs to the intuitive emotions. These higher sentiments so percolate downward, so tinge secondary feelings, giving them a new character and value, that it is difficult to analyze out the purely physical sensibilities, and to see how far these, with the action of the mental faculties upon them, can be made the foundation of our rich, emotional endowments. When, with the utilitarian, we undertake honestly to construct our entire spiritual constitution from these purely physical elements, we have a heavy labor laid upon us. Not only must the primary sense of truth, of beauty, and of obligation, be laid aside, all the affections which spring from them must be dismissed, and also that esthetical or ethical quality or flavor which inevitably penetrates intellectual emotions, whose staple is physical pleasure. A rogue will pride himself on a certain honor, whose fiber and force are found in single threads of morality. A clown is vain of possessions, whose excellence consists largely in beauties hidden in great part from him.

Do this work of analysis thoroughly, separate carefully out all but strictly physical feelings, and we shall find remaining very inadequate elements, to be transformed by intellectual combination into the varied and profound sensibilities of a truly developed nature. The natural feeling of tenderness must be made the material out of which this vast superstructure is reared. Yet, in the powerful and growing consent of appetite and purely selfish impulses, how quickly and wholly would this feeble sentiment be swept away. How hopeless the effort to stay the actual forces of mischief in the world, not only with no sense of obligation in the mind, but no admiration of virtue, no perception of the beauty of excellence as such, no delight in any form of intrinsic merit, but always and everywhere, a cold, gross, sensual judgment of actions and their results; —the pleasure of compassion rated coolly at its scale-mark in a selfish mind, and with nothing farther to commend it, except as it can be shown ultimately to make way for physical indulgence.

Grade these pleasures of the body, give them each their numerical value, put the occasional play of natural sympathy with them: let the intellect honestly, closely adhere to them; add, subtract, involve, evolve, at pleasure; and forecast in the long reaches of its calculations such periods as it pleases, and how infinitely short, after all, must its promises to a line of right, that is, sagacious action, fall short of those deep, instant, noble impulses which our sense of beauty and of virtue bestow. Virtue is useful because it holds in its right hand peculiar and unmeasured rewards, because it is virtue. It is not virtue because it is useful, because it is laden with baskets filled with fruits plucked from the trees, of a sensual paradise.

BOOK III.

THE WILL.

§ 1. We have now to speak of the powers of volition—the centre and source of free activity. Willing is distinguished from thinking and feeling in its positive and peculiar character, by a reference to consciousness—to that experience in which its phenomenal nature is laid open. It, moreover, bears a different relation to action from that of either of the other two, and this may be pointed out. It stands in the last, the most immediate connection with effort. Exertion is prompted by feeling, is anticipated and guided by thought, is initiated and maintained by volition. While the motive lies back in the emotions, the final determination and executive impulse of free action are found in the will. The intellect is instrumental, secondary, intermediate in its office. It presents objects to the feelings, and inquires into the means of their easiest, safest, gratification.

The voluntary powers are simple as compared either with those of thought or feeling. Our emotions present by far the most numerous, complex and varied features of the mind. Our intellectual faculties are relatively few, yet exceedingly subtle in their inter-dependence and action. Our voluntary powers are yet more simple, and offer their chief difficulty in intrinsic character, in the problem of liberty. There are certain anticipatory forms of vital action, of which we shall speak, though not properly voluntary. Next we shall consider executive volitions, and later, the highest form of volition, choice, determination. The first division of volitions is into primary and executive volitions. Primary volitions may be farther divided into ultimate and desultory volitions. This last distinction, however, is not one which takes hold in the least of the character itself of the determination, but is only one which marks its relations in action. The ultimate choice is that which presents the most remote objects of pursuit in reference to which other volitions are intermediate and secondary. As we meet among these intervening volitions, some that overlook for the moment the claims of the primary purpose, and are not therefore in reference to it, executive, we term them desultory choices. They differ not in intrinsic character from ultimate choices. The ground of division is found in their relation to the individual, to his line of action.

CHAPTER I.

Vital Action anticipatory of Volition.

§ 1. WE are not to understand from the caption of this chapter, that any form of simple vital action contains the germ of true volition, of choice. This prior, unconscious action is nevertheless so closely united with the secondary, dependent forms of voluntary effort, known as executive volitions, that we shall not be able to understand these, without some general apprehension of the mechanism they employ, and its methods of play, under simple, vital forces.

Life, we hold to be a superior, independent power, working pervasively, yet under one harmonious plan or impulse in all parts of the living body. This life,—this pre-eminent, peculiar and inscrutable power, whether we regard it as the immediate presence of the Divine hand, or as a distinct existence, is *the* maker—the indispensable architect of that most strange and marvelous of structures, a living thing; be it plant, shrub, tree, insect, bird, beast, or man. Molecular, chemical, electric, thermal forces are the means employed; but these as much fail to explain the form and relations of the final product, the wonderful manner of its putting up and repair, as do the stone, mortar and timber, the digging, the hewing, and the heaving, the plan and proportions of a cathedral. The exact thing to be accounted for is that on which these blind forces cast no light. How came they to work in these marvelous relations to each other; how to institute these unusual and strange conditions of various and complete life, a power which they nowhere else exhibit? We explain the action within the chemist's retort, by the chemical properties of the material present, but the retort itself, the application of the heat, the proportion of the ingredients, the experiment as an experiment, must find a solution in a new, an intelligent agency. Account as we will for changes that go on in the blood, that there should be veins, arteries, such a fluid as the blood, and the needed power to propel it; these and like adaptations which make up the living agent, meet with no explanation in simple, molecular forces. Yet these forces always and everywhere intervene between the inscrutable agent and the phenomenal result. Under a phenomenal form, they are the second point reached back of the first—the complete, the massive product. Molecular movement is to the living structure, what the mechanical transfer of stone and timber is to the edifice. Many of the changes by which the animal structure is built up and renewed, take place locally, by an action there instituted. But as the parts of the body are reciprocally interdependent, the changes of one part must be correlated and harmonized with the state, the wants of other parts. This transfer of vital sympathy and force is chiefly affected by the nervous system, which is also the instrument of the will—of the mind. An intricate net-work of nerves lies over the surface of the body, spreads through its members, and is gathered in certain lines and centres of nervous communication. The character and office of the nervous system are compactly stated in the following quotation, taken, by Bain, from *Quain's Anatomy :* "The Nervous System consists of a *central part,* or rather a series of connected *central organs* named the *cerebro-spinal axis,* or *cerebro-spinal centre ;* and of the *nerves,* which have the form of cords connected by one extremity with the cerebro-spinal centre, and extending from thence through the body to the muscles, sensible parts, and other organs placed under their control. The nerves form the medium of communication between these distant parts and the centre ; one class of nervous fibres, termed *afferent,* (in-bringing) or *centripetal,* conducting impressions toward the centre,—another the *efferent* (out-carrying) or *centrifugal* carrying material stimuli from the centre to the moving organs. The nerves are therefore said to be internuncial in their office, whilst the central organ receives the impressions conducted to it by the one class of nerves, and imparts stimuli to the other, rendering certain of these impressions cognizable to the mind, and combining in due association, and towards a definite end, movements, whether voluntary or involuntary, of different, and often of distant parts." "The nervous system is made up of a substance proper and peculiar to it, with enclosing membranes, cellular tissues, and blood-vessels. The *nervous substance* has long been distinguished into two kinds, obviously differing from each other in color, and therefore named the *white* and the *grey,* or cineritious." The collective mass, made up of the Cerebrum, the Cerebellum the Pons Varolii, the Medulla

Oblongata and Spinal Cord, constitutes the nervous centre, the Cerebro-Spinal Axis.

"It would appear, then, that the cerebro-spinal centre, or the brain and spinal cord taken together, is an aggregate of distinct nervous masses or parts, each made up of a mixture of white and grey matter. The grey matter is the vesicular substance consisting of cells or vesicles: the white matter is the fibrous substance, being made up of fibres bundled together. The grey matter is a terminus; to it the fibrous collections lead, or from it commence. The fibrous matter contained within any of the cerebral masses is placed there as a means of communicating with some portion or other of the layers, or other collections, of grey substance. Beginning with the spinal cord,—which we have seen to be a rod or column of white matter or fibres, enclosing a slender core of grey substance;—if we trace the fibres of the cord upwards, we find them continuing into the medulla oblongata, the first and the lowest portion of the brain. Of the whole mass of fibres entering the medulla oblongata, the larger portion pass up into the pons Varolii and the cerebellum: while a part terminates in the grey substance of the medulla itself; and from that grey substance other fibres take their rise and proceed onward, in the company of the through-going fibres of the cord. Thus the emerging white matter of the medulla oblongata is partly the fibres that entered it as a continuation of the cord, and partly the fibres originating in the grey central matter of the medulla, replacing, as it would seem, those that terminated there. From the pons Varolii, where we come next, the white fibres advance in various directions, intersecting with transverse fibres connecting the two halves of the cerebellum, and passing upwards towards the cerebrum proper. The fibres thus going upwards constitute the crura, peduncles, or stems of the cerebrum, and seem destined to terminate in the grey matter of the convoluted surface of the hemispheres.

But in passing through the ganglia of the brain—the thalami optici, and corpora striata—the arrangement described above is repeated ; that is to say, while part of the fibres proceed through the ganglionic masses, the rest stop short in the grey substance of those masses, which grey substance gives origin to other fibres to pass out with those that had an uninterrupted course through the bodies alluded to. Both sets together—those passing through and those originating in the grey substance of the corpora striata, or thalami optici, constitute a portion of the white or fibrous substances of the hemispheres, spreading out and terminating in the grey matter, or cortical layer of the convolutions. They are the first of three classes of fibres, described above, as constituting the white matter of the cerebrum, that is to say, the ascending or diverging class.

"Whatever number of central masses we may calculate as interposed between the spinal cord beneath, and the convoluted surface of the cerebrum, the manner of communication between them is found to be as now stated. The fibres passing between one intermediate mass and another, are partly transmitted and partly arrested. Wherever grey matter exists, there is the commencement or termination of white matter. The fibres that enter the cerebellum from the medulla oblongata, terminate in whole or in part in its outer layer of grey substance, and in that substance a new set of fibres originate to pass to other parts of the brain, as the corpora quadrigemina, the hemispheres, etc., and from one half of the cerebellum to the other. The fibres spreading out, as already mentioned, in the hemispheres toward the convoluted grey surface, will have had very various origins. Some may perhaps have come all the way from the extremities of the body, passing by the spinal cord, medulla oblongata, cerebellum, pons Varolii, thalami optici, etc. ; others have originated in the grey matter of the cord, passing without a break through all the intervening centres; a third class may have had their rise in the grey matter of the pons, a fifth in the cerebellum, a sixth in the corpora quadrigemina; others in the thalami optici, or corpora striata; besides other more minute sources.

"The arrangement may thus be seen to resemble the course of a railway train. The various central masses are like so many stations, where the train drops a certain number of passengers and takes up others in their stead, whilst some are carried through to the final terminus. A system of telegraph wires might be formed to represent exactly what takes place in the brain. If from a general terminus in London, a mass of wires were carried out to proceed towards Liverpool, and if one wire of the mass were to end at each station, while from the same station new wires arose, one for every station, farther on, a complete and perfectly independent connexion could be kept up between any two stations along the line. Calling the stations A, b, c, d, E, there would be from A, the London terminus, the wires Ab, Ac, Ad, AE; from b, would arise, bc, bd, bE; from c, cd, cE; and from d, dc, dE. The mass of wires formed on the road at a point between c and d, would be A E, or the one through-going wire, bE and bd, cE, and cd; five wires in all, which would be the number sustained throughout. This system of telegraph communication would be, so far as appears, the type of nervous communication among the various masses strung together in the cerebro-spinal axis or centre."—*Bain, page* 29.

The nerves are divided into two classes, the spinal and the cerebral; the one passing into the body along the spinal cord, the other directly from the brain. The nerves go forth in pairs from the spinal cord, passing out on either side between the vertebræ. Of this class, there are thirty-one couples. Each of these nerves is divided at its root, into two portions termed the anterior root and posterior root. These portions subserve distinct purposes. The function of a nerve is to transmit impression, influences, or stimuli from one part of the system to another. The nerves originate nothing; they are exclusively a medium of communication. Yet the nerve is an active rather than a passive conductor. It strengthens the current as it passes along. The conveying structure is the fibrous, the white matter of the nervous system. A different function, that of originating influence, is reserved for the grey matter. Distinct nerves are devoted to each distinct office of transmission, and are divided into two classes according as they convey feelings inward, or the stimuli to action outward.

The cerebral nerves are composed of nine pairs; four, of pure sensation, terminating in the special senses, and five motor nerves.

§ 2. The spinal cord is the means of sensation and of movement through the entire trunk and extremities. If this cord is cut, sensation and the power of movement by the *will*, are lost in the parts below the point of separation. The power of movement nevertheless remains under local irritation after the division. Superficial irritation will cause a spasmodic movement, accomplished by a reflex action of the spinal cord alone. Movements closely resembling voluntary action, of which the individual is unconscious, and which he cannot control, will, under these circumstances, take place in the limbs. Careful experiments show that a circle of nervous action is completed through the spinal cord, independently of the brain. The statements here briefly made are only those which have received careful experimental confirmation. The spinal cord, by virtue of its grey matter, is itself secondarily a nerve centre. Including in the spinal cord the medulla oblongata, continuous in structure and functions with it, we find that they, independently of the cerebrum, of feeling or volition, of consciousness, originate and sustain many movements. They seem in opposition to the cerebrum, to be the seat of unconscious, involuntary action, to institute and harmonize the automatic action of the body. Of this sort are most of the movements connected with digestion. After the food has passed the lips, been tasted and masticated in the mouth, and thus been fully subjected to inspection and voluntary action, it goes through the remaining processes of digestion, dilution, assimilation, without further consciousness or voluntary action. The contractions of the throat, the peristaltic movement of the stomach and intestines are accomplished by nervous stimuli transmitted from the medulla oblongata. This portion of the nervous system, it is also thought, chiefly sustains the muscular action in breathing. This is complex and rhythmical, nicely alternating in the states indicated, and in the muscular action induced. To receive and combine the indications of the actual state of the lungs, and to distribute to the muscles the appropriate stimuli, so far as the movement is stated and involuntary, is thought to be a portion of the office of the medulla oblongata. This action is, moreover, capable of being modified, arrested, or quickened by voluntary effort.

In the same way the support and harmonizing of the muscular movements generally are referred with sufficient proof to the cerebellum. By far the larger part of this action is involuntary and unconscious, though voluntary stimuli can reach and modify it. A portion of this sustaining influence of the voluntary muscles is known to be received from the spinal cord alone, to wit, that which gives them always a certain tension or tone, distinguishing them from lifeless flesh, and maintaining them in readiness for instant effort. That the harmonizing and co-ordinating of muscular movement are due to the cerebellum, is shown by proof briefly presented in the following passage from Todd and Bowman, page 50.

"Animals deprived of the cerebellum are in a condition very similar to that of a drunken man, so far as relates to their power of locomotion. They are unable to produce that combination of action in different sets of muscles which is necessary to enable them to assume, to maintain any attitudes. They cannot stand still for a moment, and in attempting to walk, their gait is unsteady, they totter from side to side, and their progress is interrupted by frequent falls. The fruitless attempts which they make to stand or walk, are sufficient proof that a certain degree of intelligence remains, and that voluntary power continues to be enjoyed."

The cerebrum, on the other hand, is directly connected with all voluntary and conscious action. We present its functions in the words of Bain, to whom we are especially indebted in this connection. "Experiments have been made with a view of determining the characteristic functions of this cerebral mass, so large in the human brain, although dwindling to the most insignificant dimensions in the lowest vertebrate animals, namely, reptiles and fishes.

"The convolutions are the portions most accessible to operations. The hemispheres have been seen above to consist of an outer layer of convoluted grey matter, and an interior mass of white, fibrous, or connecting matter. When irritation is applied to the hemispheres, as by pricking or cutting, we find a remarkable absence of the effects manifested in the other centres. Neither feeling nor movement is produced. This makes a very great distinction between the hemispheres and the whole of the ganglia and centres lying beneath them.

"Pressure from above downwards, produces stupor.

"The removal of both hemispheres in an animal has the following results:

"First: Sight and hearing are entirely lost.

"Second: Consciousness, including both Feeling and

Thought, seems utterly abolished ; so that whatever bodily activity may survive, the mental life is extinct.

"Third : All power of moving for an end, all forethought, purpose, or volition, is entirely extinguished. This is an inevitable consequence of the preceding fact. For without feeling and the memory of feelings and ideas, there can be no voluntary action. The simple act of seizing food implies, besides the power of sight, the feeling of hunger, and the mental association of the appearance of the food with the satisfying of the feeling.

"Fourth : The power of accomplishing many connected movements still remains. The actions of flying or walking may be sustained after the loss of the hemispheres, but in that case a stimulus from without is necessary in order to commence the action. As a matter of course, the automatic actions, those that we have seen to go on in the decapitated or anencephalous animal may still proceed.

"Fifth : The sensibility of the skin, and taste, and smell, would appear to remain in a greatly impaired form. Such sensibility, however, cannot be of the nature of true sensation, for to have a sensation is to feel. It may consist in some mode of reflex stimulation, operated through the other centres. By operating energetically on any nerve of sense, we may excite reflex movements extending over almost all the muscles of the body.

"Hence it appears that the hemispheres of the brain are indispensable to the exercise of our two highest senses, and to feeling, volition, and thought."—*The Senses and the Intellect, page* 57.

§ 3. We are now prepared to understand that vital, nervous action which is not voluntary but anticipatory merely. Its first most simple form is that of reflex action—superficial irritation returned directly from a nervous centre as motor stimulus. This, detached nervous ganglia accomplish in animal life, and the divided spinal cord in man. An advance on this is seen in continuous, vital movement accomplished by a special nervous centre like the medulla oblongata, wholly involuntary and beyond the cognition of the mind. A farther progress is seen in that mixed action which is chiefly involuntary, and sustained by a nervous centre as the cerebellum, which is not the seat of consciousness, but is intimately connected with a second nervous centre, as the cerebrum, from which it receives voluntary influences. That we should understand this blending of the automatic and the voluntary is indispensable to a right apprehension of the will. At this point, physical inquiry has been very fruitful in its influence on philosophy.

We are not to regard the nerves as mere dead lines of transit, along which the nerve-fluid, or nerve-power glides, but at once as means of generating and transmitting it. Says Bain, page, 63: "The conducting power of nerve fibre is attended with nervous waste, and the substance has to be constantly renewed from the blood, which is largely supplied to the nerves, although not so largely as to the vesicles.

"If now we compare this liability to waste and exhaustion, with the undying endurance of an electric wire, we shall be struck with a very great contrast. The wire is doubtless a more compact, resisting and sluggish mass; the conduction requires a certain energy of electric action to set it agoing, and in the course of a great distance becomes faint and dies away. The nerve, on the other hand, is stimulated by a slighter influence, and propagates that influence with increase, by the consumption of its own material. The wire must be acted on at both ends, by the closure of the circuit, before acting as a conductor in any degree; the nerve takes fire from a slight stimulus, like a train of gunpowder, and is wasted by the current that it propagates. If this view be correct, the influence conveyed is much more beholden to the conducting fibres, than electricity is to the copper wire. The fibres are made to sustain or increase the force at the cost of their own substance.

"The nerve force is propagated more slowly than an electric current through a wire. The rate has been estimated at about two hundred feet a second as an average. It is to be remarked, that a nerve is not a simple conductor, but is supposed to consist of a countless number of molecules, each of which has playing round it an electrical current, or currents, which are an obstacle to the simple or direct propagation. There is always a certain delay in passing through the nerve centres; a reflex movement occupies from one-thirtieth to one-tenth of a second under favorable circumstances, which is more time than would be required for transmitting an influence through the same length of nerve without interruption. When the stimulus is weak, a proportionally longer time is required to produce the corresponding movement. We may hence infer that what is called nervous excitement is a quicker rate of the nervous current. The obvious facts bear out this view."

These then are the means by which an external force is received, modified and distributed in centres, by which an internal state directs and secures the succeeding steps in vital movement; by which an inner impulse of the mind is made in muscular effort to reach the external world; or by which these vital and mental forms of effort are inseparably blended.

CHAPTER II.

Executive Volition.

§ 1. We are to distinguish executive from primary volition. Primary volition is frequently termed choice, and there is no objection to the word, if we carefully exclude from it the intellectual weighing of reasons, the balancing of inducements which often accompany it. The choice, the volition, is not in these, but in the act which brings them to a conclusion. A choice initiates, determines upon a series of acts in reference to an object or end to be reached by them; an executive volition regards the performance of these acts thus determined on.

The primary volition is the true seat of freedom, since subsequent acts flow necessarily from it. This choice may indeed be reconsidered, but so long as it remains in force, so long as it is a purpose of the soul, the acts included under it, flow directly from it, fixed thereby in their character. An alternative is presented to the first volition, not to those later volitions by which it is completed. These may be looked upon simply as the directed and prolonged force of the first, as much so as the repeated shocks of the ricochetting cannon-ball are the results of an impulse received at once and in the distance.

Executive volitions, therefore, have comparatively little interest. It is only of importance that we distinguish them from primary acts of will, and prevent confusion by seeing their relation to these. They are successive points from which fresh executive impulse is given to a series of actions whose existence and purpose have already been determined. Some have striven to separate widely between volition and choice. The division is a secondary one, covered by this distinction between executive and primary volition or choice. These secondary volitions springing out of consciousness, though properly phenomena of mind-become inseparably blended with those automatic, unconscious movements, by which most vital action, and the larger share even of what is termed voluntary action, is sustained.

§ 2. The voluntary and conscious region of action is evidently very much more limited in the lower animals than in man. We might expect this, from the much larger relative development of the secondary, nervous centres, as compared with the cerebrum—the seat or instrument of conscious activity—in the one case than in the other. A command of limbs, a power and discipline of muscle, which with man are the result of protracted training, are spontaneous in the young of animals. No conscious, tentative effort, seems to lie back of their powers. They develop themselves rather spontaneously, with the precision, certainty and rhythm of automatic, nervous life. Sensations, feelings, do their work directly, and though as feelings they enter consciousness, they seem to depart thence with an automatic, rather than with a voluntary impulse, with the decision and certainty of a self-sustained movement, rather than with the hesitancy and uncertainty of choice. With primary volitions, secondary volitions would seem also to disappear, and the conscious and unconscious feelings—or, more properly, the feelings and unrecognized physical states—to blend with each other in securing fitting muscular stimuli.

In man, in connection with choice there enters into action a large element of both conscious and voluntary stimuli, and these mingle with, and modify, and are sustained by, the voluntary action of lower nervous centres. Indeed, the acquisition of skill seems very much to consist in transferring the nervous impulse from the conscious to the unconscious centres, or at least, in sustaining the one by the automatic action of the other. The distinct, conscious, voluntary impulse of each effort in the combined movement is lost, and the changing conditions developed by the progress itself of action,—be those recognized or unrecognized—with increasing, self-poised force sustain it. Here, we would look, so far as we should look at all, for the sub-conscious region of Hamilton and others. It is in the case of the will found in purely physical phenomena, which transpire chiefly in the lower nervous centres, or, if in the cerebrum, in it simply as a nervous centre, and not as the agent and instrument of mind. Here the physical and the mental are closely united, inseparably blended with each other, and muscular education lies largely in substituting involuntary for voluntary connections—in establishing an independent movement which the mind may at any moment modify or correct, but is not called upon momentarily to sustain. Thus we quicken or check inspiration, though the ordinary action of the lungs proceeds independently of the will. Again, we wink when we will, yet wink constantly also under a purely vital impulse. The movements in walking are also instances of this interlacing of the voluntary and involuntary—the slow displacement of the one by the other. A walk determined on, the mind may busy itself with other things, and the muscular play be unconsciously sustained. If, however, any portion of the way presents peculiar difficulties, attention is renewed, and a voluntary stimulus quickens the muscles to the needed effort. The leap made, the embarrassments overcome, the automatic movement again sets in.

There is, perhaps, no more complete example of self-sustained, nervous action, reached as the result of protracted, voluntary effort, than that of reading. In fluent enunciation, the organs of speech are modified each minute, so as to express several hundred distinct sounds. These rapid and precise changes go on unconsciously. There is no direct, voluntary impulse back of them. So far is this true, that it is entirely possible to read intelligibly with no conscious recognition, not only of the meaning of the words, but even of the letters which compose them. One, in moments of abstraction, may find himself at the foot of the page, with no proof of having passed over its contents, except the attention of others, and the point reached by the eye. Such reading, while it transpires, is as involuntary, is as unconscious, as purely automatic, as the inhalation of the breath which makes it possible. Nor is the sensible effect of the images present to the eye on the muscles of the throat in guiding and propelling them, any more surprising than the declaration each instant, at the nervous centre, of the state of the lungs, and the correlative return of stimulus. Executive volitions, then, are greatly modified by the interplay of voluntary and involuntary action; by the ease with which the second displaces the first, and yet can be restored at option to its former character. There seems to be four kinds of vital movement; those always automatic beyond the reach of the will; those primarily automatic but capable of modification by volition; those at first voluntary but passing by repetition into direct unconscious connections, and those exclusively voluntary. Of this last class, the examples are comparatively few, and belong chiefly to those desultory actions which have no opportunity to settle down into habit; that is, to receive stated support from involuntary excitement. Yet, even these actions are only relatively voluntary. It is doubtless impossible to find any complex movement which is wholly supported by executive, voluntary effort. Even when we utter our own thoughts, though attention and purpose are constantly present, a share of the muscular movement, that imparting motion to the lungs for instance, is of an involuntary kind. In struggling to give a difficult sound from a foreign language, the effort seems for a time to approach independent, voluntary exertion, and is often, for that reason, very unsuccessful.

CHAPTER III.

Primary Volition, or Choice.

§ 1. We have now reached that central point on which all volition rests. Every form of action, previous to this, is but a more subtle play of physical forces, a modified case of cause and effect. In choice alone, we find the home of liberty, the source of power, the unconditioned support from which hangs all the chain of linked events.

Some divisions have been made in choice, which have value in practical morals, but little interest in philosophy. They mark the relation of choices to the action and character of the person whose they are, and not any inherent difference in the volitional acts themselves. Thus, an ultimate choice is one which has reference to the most remote, or at least, the most general and inclusive ends of action. Thus a choice of virtue, right, holiness, is of this nature, since it at once sets a limit and law to all other volitions, made secondary in their relations to this. A choice of pleasure to be pursued directly and everywhere, is of this character. Such choices have more frequently a theoretical than a practical existence. The pursuit of pleasure usually arises under detached, limited choices fastening to some object at no great remove in advance. The universality of such volition is of a quasi, not of a formal character. Even the choice of virtue is doubtless often made by a specific surrender to a given duty, rather than by a broad forecast of the entire field of effort,—is the settling the struggle of life under an example, instead of a general principle.

Desultory volitions are also spoken of; that is, volitions which spring up one side of the leading line of action, directly or indirectly at cross purposes with it. Thus one whose general pursuit is that of pleasure, gives way transiently to the claims of right, and one usually obedient to duty, for a time, turns aside under some peculiar temptation. Of these choices, practically there are many ; and while their moral bearing is most important, as choices, they present no points of particular interest. Life is more frequently expended under the impulse of general choices,—not assuming the character of a single, ultimate choice, though as certainly as those choices, throwing action into one direction—and under desultory choices, bending without reversing the current of the soul. Thus actions flow onward, submitting to a gravitation they may not have recognized, and yet, in never-ending circuits and turnings, betraying the influence of the passing hour.

§ 2. Passing, then, these distinctions in the relations of volitions rather than in their character, we have only to consider simple choice, the primary act of the will,—the source of spontaneous power. We shall speak first of what is involved in this notion of free-will, choice, and later, of the proof of its existence. As liberty is a primary, simple notion, we must define it by cutting it off from other things, by denying of it those qualities which have become attached to it from abroad, reflected upon it from the physical connections of the world below it, and then leave it to be understood and accepted by the intuitive grasp of the mind alone.

Liberty is not, as some would have us believe, found in the absence of outside coercion. If this were liberty, the plant would be free in its growth ; since this proceeds under no mechanical, external impulse, is the result of the action of inner forces. When we say that man is free, we do not, in the higher use of the word, mean to affirm that he is not bound or imprisoned. The ordinary significance of language makes this point sufficiently plain.

By the word choice, we intend to cut off all efficient

forces, that is all physical forces, external or internal, mechanical or vital, from any control over, or direct effect upon the action which is so designated. The commencement of the line of effort which springs from a primary volition—a volition, as we shall concisely term it—is absolute and complete.

We do not affirm hereby anything concerning the exact manner in which the train of physical forces is set in motion by volition, but only that it does, of its own power, initiate the actions, the physical movements, which follow. These may lie in store for it, ready to be used, but the will liberates and controls them. The will, then, in the first place, stands above and beyond the range of all causation, even in its most subtile forms, presented by nervous energies and influences. It descends upon and uses these, is not evolved by them.

By the limitations now given, all reflex action, all automatic action, under the play of the senses and appetites, are, as physical states, excluded from the realm of liberty, are but the higher forms of physical action. Equally are those executive volitions which have received their impulse from above, those acts which follow directly an intellectual weighing of means, a balancing of probabilities, a deliberative movement which is a simple gathering and eddying of executive force looking for a new avenue, the best avenue, for advance, cut off from the freedom which attaches to choice. Having reached a point wholly unaffected by force, physical force, we are to inquire what are the conditions of liberty. The inducements to action in the will, lie before it, not behind it; they are motives, not causes. There is no opportunity for choice, for liberty, unless there are two or more of these, or as by successive rejection they at length assume the typical form, unless there are two motives or lines of influence. Neither is there proper opportunity for choice unless these two are distinct motives, subcordinate to distinct ends. If the relation is one of means simply, purely, it is not an act of volition, of choice, but one of intellectual estimates, of judgment. As the word choice is applied both to selection and election, both to the purely mental act deciding on adaptations, and to the volitional act deciding between courses of conduct with different and independent moral characteristics, we easily confound the two. These motives, then, must be present, and so present as to furnish a true alternative of action,—not a seeming one. Ten dollars as opposed to five dollars, as detached, single considerations, constitute to each other no sufficient, no true alternative. They are exactly of the same kind, and, in ordinary states of mind, there is no basis of action on which the less can be preferred to the greater, since that which gives value to five dollars, gives double value to ten dollars; and to feel the first inducement without feeling the greater force of the second is simply to disclose a defective estimate, or an abnormal state either of the mind or of social wants. In all cases of which this is a type, there is no proper freedom. The mind can only choose the less valuable, the less desirable of things like in kind, by adding to the smaller inducement a distinct, factitious consideration, as that of evincing independence, or the exhibition of eccentricity. If, then, all motives are resolvable at bottom into impulse, and measurable on one standard, we assert that there is no real liberty, but only that semblance presented by an intellectual inquiry into the intrinsic value of things, not bearing their sale-mark on them.

§ 3. There is necessary to liberty not only two motives, but motives unlike in kind, resting back ultimately on different principles, revealing different forms of good and phases of character. In other words, there is no choice without the moral element which can alone oppose itself to all varieties of physical good, and present a distinct ground of action, a reward, incommensurable with any sensual pleasure. The esthetical element indeed, as infused with ethical sentiment, may furnish a secondary feature in that contrast of action which gives a basis of choice.

Two such motives being present, the question returns, What is their relation to choice? We answer: they influence the will, without in any sense controlling it, determining it; here we have reached the final, inexplicable thing, liberty. The will can, by its own power, take either of the two lines of action, to the rejection of the other; can feel motives to any degree, yet refuse to yield to them. The will, with spontaneous independent power, initiates the one or the other of the two courses of action before it. Here is neither fatality nor chance, causation nor fortuity. The will feels, without submitting to motives, and discloses in itself a true beginning of action.

§ 4. There is one view of liberty which needs to be guarded against, and in the rejection of it, we shall have defined sufficiently the conditions of choice. It is this. The will always does yield to the strongest motive, not of necessity, but as a fact. In the first place, this theory incurs all the difficulties of the view, that the will does yield to either of the two motives by an impulse or decision resting in itself alone, without its advantages. By motives in this discussion, we understand not simply their outward, objective element, but the inner, subjective one as well, all in short that makes them motives.

Influences are influences only through the susceptibilities on which they play, the desires they evoke. The one theory affirms that these motives may be spoken of as stronger and weaker, and that in each case of choice that motive prevails, though not necessarily, which is the strongest. The other theory asserts such a distinction of motives is impertinent, and the will itself, in its freedom, is the sufficient and entire reason of the volition that follows.

The mind, in the act of choice, is no more ruled by its own states than by external conditions. If it were, liberty would as certainly disappear, as if, in the outset, we placed the will within reach of the physical forces. We should do with two steps what we had refused to do with one. The present state of the sensibilities would be determined by previous states, and these by constitutional endowments and external circumstances, and thus the threads of influence, the lines of causation, be at length lodged elsewhere than in the will. Each volition would be the fruit of conditions, which it itself had not determined, and thus be as certainly interlocked with the flow of forces as is the mill-wheel which revolves in the stream. The one theory evades this result by saying, that the stronger motive does control the will, yet not necessarily. The choice may be, though it never is, against it. The other denies the applicability of the conception, greater and less, and affirms an absolute, unqualified freedom, finding and seeking no explanation in the force of motives.

This admission, that the will may choose the line of action supported by what is termed the weaker motive, involves philosophically all the difficulties of the view which represents it as alike independent of both incentives, and making either a true alternative to the other. There is no philosophical obstacle to supposing that the will *does* sometimes do what it is admitted that it *may* do. The statement of an action as possible involves the concession of grounds sufficient to render it intelligible, if it should actually transpire. No law of mind can be violated by the happening of that which these laws suffer us to regard as possible. We must rely on special reasons, not on general principles to establish the impossibility in given cases of that which we have granted to be a theoretic possibility. We can find, therefore, in philosophy alone no sufficient reason for saying in the same breath, that a thing may be, and denying that it ever will be. The last assertion must rest on some special, empirical reason; since the first assertion sweeps the ground of philosophy and says, that there is nothing to prevent it. Our philosophy, then, as philosophy, is no more encumbered with the assertion, that the will does choose, than with the declaration, it may choose, either alternative. The general principles which admit the one statement, will cover the other. The fact, that an admitted possibility never does become actual, must be established, if established at all, on special reasons peculiar to each case. If there were a general principle or law against the action, it would not remain possible.

Moreover this theory establishes an inductive law, of the strongest possible character, against itself. Admittedly, the weakest motive, so termed, never is chosen. There is an absolutely uniform line of action in innumerable and most diversified cases. No law of induction is established on stronger grounds. Yet, when we are just about to reach the conclusion, that what, under no circumstances, is or ever will be, is an action excluded by the very nature and method of the forces at work, we are suddenly bidden to face around with the very unexpected assertion, the choice under discussion is one that may constantly be made. On what ground does this odd inversion rest? Not on that of experience, of induction, for this line of argument prepares the way with well-nigh irresistible power, for exactly the opposite statement. Not on philosophical principles, for, as previously shown, these principles would, if unrestricted by experience, unmodified by special reasons, show that what may at any time happen, probably, under the inexhaustible variety of circumstances presented by human life, will happen. This assertion, then, that the will may, but never does, choose the weaker motive, grounds itself neither on experience nor philosophy. It is a self-destructive affirmation under either view of it.

§ 5. Again, to what a mere shadow does it reduce liberty. We are free by virtue of a power never put forth. If we could not accept the rejected alternative, we should not be free; yet, one of the two alternatives always, before choice, stands in such relation to the will, that it never accepts it. The action of the will is practically as fixed by antecedent condition as any line of causation. One might as well claim that a python should walk, on the ground of certain rudimentary limbs said to be hidden under its skin, as to annex all the fearful consequences of sin to such a hypothetical power as this—a power that has never found exercise, subserves no practical purpose, and is only possessed of a metaphysical existence. To sustain the ponderous chain of sin, its interlocked links reaching through all eternity, its galling weight crushing the life of myriads, —by so theoretical and fanciful a support, can certainly never subserve the purposes of actual government.

Farther, a will of this sort, is wholly superfluous. If motives have superior efficiency, and this efficiency is always yielded to, why should any volition intervene? There is a power present, able to secure action, and that does secure the action that actually follows. Why should not this surplus of power, this over-balance of influence, be left in an immediate, precise, inevitable way to reach its own results. Are we to insert another wheel, in itself of no practical account, only that we may band to it the moral universe, and assert responsibility? If so, let us, in the name of virtue and honesty, give it some other office than that of simply propagating, bearing inward, a power already existing in completeness in the motive. To deal thus subtly with one's moral judgments, to practise upon them with these evanescent distinctions and cunning subterfuges of words, itself, I had almost said, approaches wickedness.

§ 6. Whence springs this distinction of motives into stronger and weaker, but from a false analogy with the forces

U OF M

of the physical world? We are not to attach to the word influence a definite, measurable power capable of numerical comparison with like powers. If our pleasures were all referable to one sensorium, something of this sort might be admissible. But they are not. A moral gratification can be expressed in no terms of greater and less with a sensual indulgence. Were it not for our higher, our moral, our rational nature; were we wholly physical, the conditions of liberty would indeed disappear. We might weigh the claims of the senses, assign a numerical value to indulgences, and trace the rise and fall of motion along this new meter of the appetites. But nothing of this is possible, no approximate estimates of pleasure are possible, when the moral nature enters into the calculation; when the supreme claims of conscience afford a full and fair alternative to every degree and form of self-indulgence. We should have no occasion for freedom, were it not for the self-imposed law of the moral nature, and in issuing a command, it also gives the conditions of that liberty which enables us to obey it. There is no such final reference of motives to the same or like sensibilities, by which we are able to pronounce them greater or less. There is no common term or point between mere pleasure and duty. We cannot take the pleasure of a glass of wine from a sense of obligation, and give a numerical remainder.

But if there is no antecedent standard by which motives may be measured, it is a mere circle of words to call that the strongest motive which does prevail, and then to repeat the assertion made, in the form, the will always chooses the strongest motive. There must be antecedent measurement, and there is no such measurement, or our language means nothing.

This view overlooks the office of the moral nature, the transcendent purchase and power that it gives to choice. It confounds simple, intellectual discrimination between en-

M 10 U

joyments, or, still worse, a certain automatic adjustment and balance between animal impulses with choice. Liberty keeps aloof from this lower region. It reposes on extended wing in the upper air of our rational, intuitive powers and emotions. There is, and of necessity must be, a moral character to every true act of choice, since the higher impulses must enter to break up and rule out these mathematical estimates of greater and less, these automatic adjustments of influences essentially one.

The sense of guilt which accompanies a moral struggle, sustains the view we have presented. If the guilty party could feel, that he had yielded to the strongest motive, that a balance had been cast up between motives, and he had accepted the largest sum proffered, the sense of condemnation and shame would be very different from what it now is. In proportion, however, as the transcendent, unmeasurable character of virtue is present to the mind, are the accompanying moral struggle and the subsequent sense of guilt, strong and bitter. The more declared the sin, the more clear the knowledge of the high nature of the things rejected. It is the increase of light and motive, not their decrease, which evokes the forces of moral retribution. The mind is not allowed to say to itself, to console itself, with the assertion, that at the time and under the circumstances, it actually chose the strongest pleasure, the highest good. Its infinite folly, its unaccountable guilt are enforced upon it, not its sad mistake, its grave misjudgment.

§ 7. Against the notion of liberty, absolute and complete, now presented, it may be urged, that it admits of no control, that its action cannot be anticipated, and hence provided for. Now liberty is limited to the alternatives before it. It cannot choose anything but only one of two things, and it is unsafe to give the opportunity of choice, when we are not ready for the acceptance of either of the things offered. Liberty is simply a larger field of activity, the opening of two lines of activity instead of one, and this is often found very easy, even for man in his control and management of his fellows. It does, indeed, make of government an higher art, but does not, in skillful hands, take away its perfect efficiency, all the efficiency contemplated.

Liberty provides for less, recognizes less, of a certain sort of efficiency, than does slavery. The inevitable, mechanical movement of necessary forces is, indeed, lost; but there is substituted a nobler movement, because it is a freer one, manageable in a different measure, and on different principles. Those who prefer the clang and ceaseless ongoing of machinery, may not be pleased; but the product itself, nevertheless, is every way superior.

Moreover, will is constantly declaring itself of its own liberty, establishing a movement and revealing a character, more and more manifest to those who have to deal with it. The virtue of a virtuous man does not cease to be free, nor the vice of a vicious man, because the choice of each is not momentarily altered. A free action remains free, no matter how far pursued, and those impulses of the rational life once revealed, become more and more declared and fixed in these directions. The conduct of a perfectly virtuous being is among the most calculable forces in the whole universe, and this without the least loss of freedom. We manage events readily which turn on moral evidence, yet the connections are not absolute, are not seen by us to be certain. There is the same difference between causation and liberty, as between demonstration and evidence, proof and argument. Each subserves a feasible, practical purpose.

It may be farther objected, that liberty so defined is synonymous with chance. It is not. The ground of action—and there remains a most adequate and complete ground—is simply transferred from the motives to the will, from the outside to the inside, from secondary and causal agents to a primary and independent one. We must, indeed, give up all hope of conceiving this under forms of the imagination, or, of the understanding, through analogical judgments; but let alone, it is just as intelligible, as red, or sweet, or hard, or as causation itself, which, for some inscrutable reason, seems to be thought by many to be so perfectly translucent, so fluid and penetrative a notion as to be the only proper solvent for everything else. If we could get over the futile feeling that everything must be like something else, a habit of mind confirmed by physical inquiry, we should have no more theoretical, than we have practical, difficulty with liberty, claiming hourly its fullest consequences from child and adult, from friend and foe.

§ 8. What are the proofs of the existence of the power of choice as now defined? Our analysis, our rejection of this and that explanation as insufficient, have proceeded on the claims of an intuitive notion. This we have striven to preserve from statements which would limit or destroy it. We have denied the conclusion which seemed incompatible with perfect freedom, which furtively subjected the mind once more to the same forces which drive the world. Our proof of the existence of this power is not found directly in consciousness. If it were, the question would hardly admit of dispute. The evidence of consciousness is negative rather than positive. We are conscious of the presence of motives, that is, antecedent feelings; we are conscious of volition, these are phenomenal; we are not conscious of the connection between the two, this is not phenomenal. We are negatively, indeed, aware of no restraint; our volitions seem to be, what we affirm they are, free. But consciousness does not directly settle this question, for the sufficient reason, that freedom is not a phenomenon, but the ground or condition, or form of a phenomenon, and hence it does not immediately arise in consciousness, but is only inferable from what is there present.

The occasion of this inference is found in our moral nature. Laws are constantly imposed on our actions by ourselves, by others, and our moral sense justifies them. The record of history and of individual life everywhere presents them, and hourly, momentarily demands them. Now no law, no command can be imposed on a being that is not free. The only law to which such a being can be subjected, is a physical law, working in, under, through it. A moral law above it, before it, is an absurdity; and, if followed by punishment, is most cruel, unless it is based upon the power of obedience, unless the individual can conform to it.

Hence those who are consistent with themselves, who logically accept the consequences of their own doctrines, utterly subvert the phenomena, the facts of the moral world, and give an entirely new rendering of them as a consequence of their denial of liberty. Says Bain, in *The Emotions and The Will:* "Under a certain motive, as hunger, I act in a certain way, taking the food that is before me, going where I shall be fed, or performing some other preliminary condition. The sequence is simple and clear when so expressed; bring in the idea of freedom, and there is instantly a chaos, imbroglio, or jumble. What is to be said, therefore, is that this idea ought never to have come into the theoretical explanation of the will, and ought now to be summarily expelled." Again, "the word choice is one of the modes of designating the supposed liberty of voluntary actions. The real meaning, that is to say, the only real fact that can be pointed at in correspondence with it, is the acting out one of several different promptings. When a person purchases an article out of several submitted to view, the recommendations of that one are said to be greater than of the rest, and nothing more needs really be said in describing the transaction. It may happen for a moment the opposing attractions are exactly balanced, and decision suspended thereby. The equipoise may even continue for a length of time, but when the decision is actually come to, the fact and the meaning are that some consideration has arisen to the mind, giving a superior energy of motive to the side that has preponderated. This is the whole substance of the act of choosing. The designation, liberty of choice, has no real meaning, except as denying extraneous interference." In the same line, he continues, "The term responsibility, is a figurative expression of the kind called by writers on rhetoric, 'metonomy' where a thing is named by some of its causes, effects, or adjuncts, as when the crown is put for royalty, the mitre for episcopacy, &c. Seeing that in every country where forms of justice have been established, a criminal is allowed to answer the charge made against him, before he is punished, this circumstance has been taken up, and used to designate punishment. We shall find it conduce to clearness to put aside the figure, and employ the literal term. Instead, therefore, of responsibility, I shall substitute punishability; for a man can never be said to be responsible, if you are not prepared to punish him, when he cannot satisfactorily answer the charges made against him." In another passage, he gives concisely his notion of the method of moral suasion. "There is one form of stating the fact of ability that brings us face to face with the great metaphysical puzzle. It not uncommonly happens that a delinquent pleads his moral weakness in justification of his offence. The school-boy whose animal spirits carry him to a breach of decorum, or whose anger has made him do violence on a school-fellow, will sometimes defend himself by saying he was carried away, and could not restrain himself. In other words, he makes out a case closely allied to physical compulsion. He is sometimes answered by saying, that he could have restrained himself if he had chosen, willed, or sufficiently wished to do so. Such an answer is really a puzzle or paradox, and must mean something very different from what is apparently expressed. The fact is, that the offender was in a state of mind such that his conduct followed according to the uniformity of his being, and if the same antecedents were exactly repeated, the same consequent would certainly be reproduced. In that view, therefore, the foregoing answer is irrelevant, not to say nonsensical. The proper form, and the practical meaning to be conveyed, is this: It is true, that as your feelings then stood, your conduct resulted as it did; but I am now to deal with you in such a way, that when the situation recurs, new feelings and motives will be present, sufficient, I hope, to issue differently. I now punish you, or threaten you, or admonish you in order that an antecedent motive may enter into your mind, as a counteraction to your animal spirits or temper on another occasion, seeing that, acting as you did, you were plainly in want of such a motive. I am determined that your conduct shall be reformed, and therefore every time that you make such a lapse, I will supply more and more incentives in favor of what is your duty."

Here is consistency. Mr. Bain has determined that there is no freedom; nay, that the notion is an invalid and absurd one, and hence he pushes his theory right over the convictions of men expressed in the most unmistakable, universal and constant use of language. He says to himself, the line of my road lies through yonder hill, and he buries his engine up to the furnace in the soil in the vain effort to drive it through. As we have undertaken only the easier and more modest task of explaining, instead of overthrowing, the universal facts of mind, we must needs believe that the world, wise and ignorant, have not whistled to the wind in talking about freedom, choice, responsibility, and in constructing the frame-work of private, social and religious life upon them. In the above theory, there is the entire transformation, the utter overthrow of the very familiar facts of hourly life, that seek our explanation. The language we apply to them is all wrong. There is no proper guilt or punishment, virtue or reward. There is no law, as we use the word in social and ethical discussions; all is ultimately resolvable into physical force. The man indeed, like the brute, can be reached on two sides instead of one. He can be pushed, guided from behind, and, through the mirror of the mind, can be invited, influenced by things yet before him. As, by ingenious reflection, rays that do not directly fall upon the object, are thrown upon it, so forces not yet realized, are flung by anticipation, by the reflection of thought on the mind, and become present powers working vital results in the brain. To lay a command, therefore, as conscience does, and furnish, for its execution, no forces, promise no pleasures, threaten no pains, as the immediate results of obedience or disobedience, is, according to the above view, absurd, is to furnish the plan of a noble edifice, and provide no workmen to put it up. There is, on this theory, no more moral law than when I flourish a whip in the face of a restive ox, or apply it to his tough hide. The actions are essentially one; the first brings the anticipation of pain, and the second, actual pain.

In the passages quoted, there is an undersigned confession that the author can make nothing of true moral phenomena, of moral law, and has, therefore, put in their place a gross caricature, at war with the form and language of our daily life. We do treat the brute and the man very differently, and the more diversely, as we are the more intelligent. We furnish an influence, an incentive for the one, we claim its existence in the other. We provide for obedience here, we demand it there; we give the sharp intonation here, we simply state the law in its imperial power there. We accept as complete the service which fear has brought here; there we despise it, as no solution of the claims of right on the soul. Bain gives the theory of brute life, we are striving to give that of rational life. If a true, moral command is ever uttered from within, or from without, rightfully to man, liberty, the power to obey it, is implied therein.

§ 9. The second portion of the proof of liberty, without which the first would be incomplete, is the fact, that the mind does spontaneously, inevitably place this notion of liberty back of human, responsible action as its explanation. Our conclusion is the conclusion of the race; just as certainly, universally, inevitably as in any judgment whatever, made by us. We no more necessarily refer an effect to a cause, than we do responsibility to liberty; and responsibility we universally claim of others. It remains to be shown, that any man has ever lived, who has not believed in the guilt of his neighbor; it is axiomatic in practical morals, that guilt is commensurate with power. Every excuse and apology presuppose it. The full form, then, of the proof of the existence of freedom is found in the double fact, that we universally lay moral claims upon others. and that we justify ourselves in so doing, by attributing liberty to them. There is a large class of familiar and undeniable facts which the mind constantly, pertinaciously explains by an assertion of its power of choice. The difficulty of philosophers in analyzing it, their perplexities over it, their escape by denials of it, are no more proofs against it, than the like treatment of the mind's action in a dozen other directions. The spontaneous, certain, ever-recurring action of the mind is the proof we have of liberty, and the only proof we have for anything our faculties offer us. We see and see again, till we believe that we see. We think and think again, till we accept our thought.

CHAPTER IV.

Dynamics of the Will, and of the Mind.

§ 1. The will is so nearly single, that little is to be said of the form of its activity. There is but one line of exertion, the executive volitions resting back on a choice. This endures as a permanent impulse, and finds execution in mingled, voluntary and vital action. From what has been said, it is evident that animals are destitute of freedom, of all proper power of choice. Their action is the unconscious, involuntary resolution of feelings and physical states into muscular impulse. The feelings which arise in consciousness are as directly and automatically connected with action as those physical states which never there present themselves, but, in the darkness and concealment of a purely vital force, accomplish their purpose.

The will is strengthened chiefly by use, and that not alone by its own activity, but, perhaps, even more by the restraint and check thus imposed on the passions and appetites. Those, allowed control for any length of time, assume so domineering and persistent a form, that the will regains only with the utmost diffculty, the ground that it has lost. This minor anarchy of the soul is, of all forms of confusion, the least susceptible of a remedy, as aid cannot come from abroad, and the chronic weakness of the powers that offer resistance to the mob of impulses, and establish authority over them, speedily passes beyond all cure. Some sudden shock of the moral nature, in rare cases the awakening of a strong desire, is the only spring of hope.

In speaking of the activities of the mind as a whole, we are to remember, that these bear by no means the same proportion to each other in different individuals. Not only are specific, intellectual endowments and feelings diverse in power, the three classes of activities present various degrees of development. In one, intellectual effort absorbs the mind ; in another, the emotions are the chief seats of action ; while a third is possessed of a will that lapses into stubbornness, through the inefficiency of the thoughts in its guidance. Moreover, different temperaments cause essentially the same faculties to exhibit very different degrees of force. The nutritive and the nervous systems are most intimately associated with the mind. Great impressibility and power in the nervous organization ; the same impressibility with less power ; a preponderance of the nutritive functions giving a full animal life ; nervous power well-balanced and well-sustained by the nutritive system, are distinct, physical conditions, which greatly modify the measure, hopefulness, and satisfaction of intellectual efforts, resting back on natural endowments of mind very nearly the same. As the body is at once the medium by which impressions reach the mind, the source whence the strength for their consideration is secured, and the instrument by which its practical and theoretical conclusions concerning them are expressed, the importance of the physical conditions of mental activity cannot easily be over-stated, nor be too carefully inquired into. These researches, however, pertain chiefly to physiology. It is our task to trace the strictly mental interplay of the faculties, a dependence, not the result of purely physical connections.

§ 2. Thought, feeling and volition, express the order in which action occurs, the line along which any influence brought to bear on the mind, passes through its faculties.

Yet these three steps, though usual, are not all necessary. Through sensation, feeling may be directly occasioned, and activity immediately follow from it, yet this is of an involuntary character. Thought accompanies, unites feeling and volition, points out the present relation of things, and guides them to the right use of means.

While the first movement is in the direction now indicated, there are reflex influences of an opposite character. The feelings affect strongly the thoughts. They direct attention to pleasing objects, fasten the faculties upon them, and thus intensify the emotions already established. The candor and fairness of the judgment are lost through this influence of the feelings, withdrawing attention from facts displeasing to them, and minutely and laboriously searching out those which maintain and justify their action. Unusual intellectual and moral development is required on the part of one possessed of strong feelings, to reach even ordinary impartiality, and to give any considerable weight to reasons for action opposed to the inclinations. The intellect thus becomes the instrument of the feelings, using all its acuteness, its power of representation, perversion, and one-sided argumentation in behalf of conclusions already reached by the heart. When the intellect is thus the sagacious counsellor, the cunning attorney of the emotions, the distortions of truth are proportioned to its strength, and the most powerful thinking is productive only of misleading sophism.

The feelings, in the same way, frequently engage the will, and the man becomes obstinate, headstrong, willful in the line of action indicated by them. There is no defence against this, but that quick moral sense, which responds with an adequate alternative to the selfish suggestions of the mind, and introduces a calm consideration of the claims of duty into each case. The only sufficient resistance to this domination which strong feelings, headlong desires are sure to assume over the intellect and the will, through the one evoking all the imagery which influences passion, and the reasons which justify it, and through the other imparting a haste and momentum to action which at once clear the way of all ordinary obstacles, and render the onset easy and retreat difficult, is afforded by the moral nature calming feeling, soliciting candor, and holding the will in the leash of duty.

Government in the mind is not than self-evolved, is not the spontaneous inter-action of forces graded to their tasks, but is found in the direct, authoritative claims of a law-giving power. The order of the mind is moral, not natural; one of command and obedience, and not of self-poised powers; one to be discerned and pursued, not one to be developed. The disorder of transgression discovers itself, not in faculties lost, not in addition to, or subtraction from, the original powers of the mind, but in that disproportionate developmeut among them which is the fruit of anarchy, of usurpation on the one side, and overthrow on the other.

§ 3. If we look at the influences at work on any one mind, at any one time to make it what it is, there seems to be in it very little power of resistance or modification. The thoughts take such partial and justifying views of action, so blind themselves to the future results, and even the immediate consequences of conduct, so misrender and misinterpret facts; the feelings so reward and maintain indulgence, cast such disfavor and so repulsive an atmosphere over every form of restraint, choke up the path of reform with so many imaginary difficulties, and find the accustomed way so open, so easy, so inevitable; the will submits so easily where it is wont to submit, is so reluctant to open a new conflict, and so weak to resist the impatient, persistent, and domineering passions and appetites, that swarm in troops around it at every suggestion of change, that much modification of character established in its springs and conditions of action seem to us impossible. Indeed, only the breaking in of an earthquake power is able to alter and redirect the channels in which the activities of the soul are flowing.

If, however, we look at long periods, we see that there

is a supreme control of the will over the mind. Single changes that in the outset are alien to the general movement, prepare the way for others. New thoughts give rise to new feelings, and these slowly displace the old ; the activity induced in fresh pursuits establishes and strengthens the will, and sets gradually at work varied reflex forces, giving different external and internal conditions, new feelings, motives and rewards of effort. At length, the mind accepts spontaneously the changed form of life, the old channel is deserted, and a complete transformation is achieved. There is a momentum in mind which prevents its movements becoming wayward and fitful, and yet there is present a force which can slowly and certainly bend them in any direction it chooses.

§ 4. The feelings are plainly most central and important in the constitution of the mind. Here is the seat of pleasure, of enjoyment, of all good. Thence spring the motives which influence the will, which offer its alternatives, and thither return the fruits of choice—fresh gratifications with accompanying incentives to effort. The intellect is scarcely less instrumental to the emotions. It multiplies its resources that these may be nourished ; it fills it canvas with figures that these may be profoundly moved. The emotions are sooner or later endowed with all the treasures of thought, and the painter, the poet, all who can accomplish this transfer most quickly, skillfully, perfectly, become the chief artists in human society. The merchant, the inventor, labor for grosser forms of transmutation, the artist for higher, the true hero, for the highest. He alone lifts thought into the moral sublimity of an actual life, that is integral with the triumph of order—the ample victory of the law of freedom in the universe of God.

As the impulses to action spring from the feelings, and the fruits of action return to them ; as the value of knowledge is found in the pleasure, power, guidance, it affords, it is evident that happiness must depend on the predominant emotions. Out of the heart are the issues of life. The physical feelings, the appetites, are primitive sources of pleasure; yet they are necessarily intermittent, and can be made safely to occupy but a small part of the time which falls to us. Moreover, their permanent enjoyment depends on physical vigor, and this must be maintained by that temperance, by that well-regulated activity which sets these enjoyments still further limits. It is only on the condition of making the appetites secondary, incidental sources of good, that they can at all maintain their position as safe and just means of pleasure.

The intellectual feelings, the desires, are, indeed, capable of incessant activity, yet fail of conferring a sufficient and permanent good. There is not that repose in them, that perfect reaction of gratification on the appetitive desire which arrests it in complete indulgence. These intellectual impulses become rather increasingly exorbitant in their claims, fling us ever forward in search of the unattained, and leave us restless and unsatisfied with every acquisition actually secured. If we check the desire, we are immediately thrown back on other sources of good; it fails any longer to maintain our active powers, and call forth our hopes. We must once again put to ourselves the question, What are these grounds, these sources of independent pleasure, of which at length, with the means in our hands that wealth, power, and rank confer, we are to avail ourselves in reaching complete and permanent happiness? If, on the other hand, we steadily inflame and expand the desire, we are fed on promises never realized, we are driven from one round of activity to another. We spread a feast, but have no time to partake of it, or, beginning to partake, are disappointed in its quality. The good is not in it we thought to be there, and we are driven to the hopeless expedient of still farther enlarging our board, enriching our service, and multiplying our viands. It thus not unfrequently happens, that the appetites decrease in the ratio in which the means of their gratification increase, and, at length, under this ever-returning experience, we discover that desires are wearing us out with unrequited labor; that the coin is indeed paid into the hand, but that it has lost its purchasing power; that we have served for Rachel, and that Leah has been given us.

The rational feelings, on the contrary, yield adequate and supreme pleasure, for several reasons. The higher intuitions call forth emotions which are of a primitive and permanent character; unlike the appetites, they may accompany our every action with subdued pleasure, or with the swell of buoyant emotion. They may give way to outside, incidental enjoyments, and yet return to us as the undertone of a steady and protracted harmony. Moreover, there is repose in them. The taste, the ethical sense are filled with the satisfaction which beauty and virtue afford; without stimulating an excessive activity, they momentarily reward it. It is not a good in advance, so much as one in possession, that gives to the contemplation of beauty, of physical and moral excellence, a supreme and abiding pleasure. The concurrent reward and stimulus of the faculties, take from them the intense thirst of desire, the restless, insatiate longing of intellectual emotions, expanding the circle each instant, and finding it forever made up of the same futile pleasures in greater multiplicity.

Again, the rational gratifications increase in scope and in purity of tone. They arise from intellections which, with the growth of mind, become broader, more varied and more just. They yield, therefore, to the esthetical and moral sense, more extended, harmonious, and profound impressions. No one exhausts art, no one measures the resources of virtue, nor makes barren to the contemplation those plans and that providence which are working the world up, with all its stubborn and refractory materials, into a perfect and permanent product of religious art.

These pleasures owe their high character also to the extent in which they combine and blend all the activities of the triple powers of man. The intellect is most active in preparing the conditions, in giving the grounds of esthetical and ethical intuitions, while the intuitions combine inseparably perception and emotion. To see the beautiful and the good is to feel their power. Nor is the will inactive. Under the surface of the mind, fully occupied with these noblest objects of contemplation, there flows a steady purpose to conform all action to them, never to mar them, to win them by becoming a part of them. Here is doubtless the secret of the repose, the rest of art and virtue, that they remove all conflict from our powers, and blend them in satisfied and indivisible activity. This is not asserted of art as divorced from virtue, but of art as the highest embodiment of rational life, of virtue.

CHAPTER V.

The Relations of the System here offered, to the Prevalent Forms of Philosophy.

§ 1. THE inquiries of broadest outside and inside interest as regards any system of philosophy are : How does it unite the intellectual and physical world? Which, if either, does it absorb in the other? By what laws does it hold the balance between them? What is with it the pregnant, ontological principles? The philosophy now offered strives to maintain, so far as man is concerned, physical and mental phenomena on an independent basis ; so far as God is concerned, centres and absorbs them both in Him. It thus endeavors to explain the constant, the familiar facts of experience, not as a vision, delusive in its form ; but as the substantial, sufficient frame-work of knowledge. It does not by thought abolish that which called forth thought, but retains entire the phenomena it seeks to explain. Indeed, it is difficult to see on what ground the reasoning of a few is to be accepted, which overturns fundamentally the conclusions of the many concerning facts of which each is independently cognizant. To yield our faith to such theories seems to be a surrender of the trustworthiness of our faculties, since, with almost perfect unanimity and endless reiteration, they have reached results exactly opposite to those thus offered. Nor is it an answer to this statement to say, that such a submission of the philosophical to the common mind, precludes progress. It does not preclude the addition of new facts, a more careful analysis of old facts, with the correction of opinions that is sure to follow. It does cast suspicion on a movement which pre-supposes the entire error and deceptiveness of all spontaneous convictions, which denies the validity of every conclusion but its own, and will not go to the common mind for the facts even that seek statement and explanation ; for the facts without which there could be no philosophy. Such theories shake centrally the structure of knowledge, and lead to a complete distrust of those faculties which have been so signally, so universally, so completely wrong in directions wholly open to their action. To make one, two, three mistakes, and retain confidence is possible, to affirm that everything hitherto has been a mistake, is to reflect the most gloomy uncertainty on our present conclusions, which have no other verification than that they are the last results of faculties hitherto always at fault.

That a system of philosophy lies, in the main, in the line of recognized conclusions, gathering up, harmonizing and expounding them, furnishes the same evidence of its truth as that afforded to a physical theory by the fact, that it easily includes and explains the facts under discussion ; or to a social theory, by the fact, that it recognizes and makes clear, events of hourly occurrence. Nor is it sufficient to give alleged reasons why men have been mistaken ; universal and complete mistake is an impeachment of the mind whose consequences cannot be evaded.

We postulate in the system now presented, the trustworthiness of all our faculties in their careful, corrected, legitimate exercise ; and accept as proof of a faculty or power, steady, reiterative action in any direction, yielding fruits of knowledge. What we see and hear, we accept as seen and heard, because our faculties are self-consistent and persistent in the affirmation. They renew the impressions in the same form on each like occasion. For a like reason we accept the conclusions of judgment. If we reached a different result each time we reviewed the proof of a proposition, we should trust no one of our conclusions. We believe what we believe, because the mind, on repeated inquiry, on repeated investigation, arrives again and again at the same convictions. Thus is it with memory. We are uncertain when we find inconsistent and changeable impressions arising ; we are certain when the faculty restores the same image on each occasion. We start with no *a priori* theory as to what faculties the mind can have. We recognize as a fact that it does do what it seems to do, and take as a sufficient and ultimate proof of its power to do, and do correctly anything, to impart and impart correctly any knowledge, the observed fact, that it does do this repeatedly and consistently. We cannot, therefore, accept the existence of the notion of causation, and recognize the constant use which the mind makes of it, and at the same time affirm it to be wholly illusory and deceptive. The admitted fact establishes by and of itself, a power of mind to discern and employ this notion, and is thus an ultimate and sufficient proof of the correctness of such a notion, of the value of the service rendered by it. We should as soon say, the mind insists that it sees, insists that it thinks, but the idea is fanciful; as to say, the mind persists in assigning causes, but it has no ground for such assignment. The simple fact, that it does persistently assign them, is all the proof we require, is all the proof we are resting on in any department of knowledge.

We postulate, then, the assertions, that the mind does what it does by virtue of a power of doing it, and that the habitual, enumerated conclusions of a power are evidence, sufficient evidence, and the only possible evidence of its existence and their own truth. If the mind supplies ideas, discusses, uses them, in a steady uniform office; ideas which the senses alone cannot reach, then this fact is satisfactory proof, that these ideas, like sensation, colors, tastes, sounds, rest back on a distinct faculty, and are sufficiently verified by that faculty. The philosophy here presented, bridges the chasm between mind and matter, not by direct sensation, but indirectly, by intuitive ideas, whose presence gives occasion to the discussion, and makes it intelligible to us. In pronouncing so authoritatively, as some do, that matter is cut off hopelessly from mind, that there can be no communication between them, they seem to contradict their own statement; since the mind is dealing with matter in the very affirmation by which it declares matter to be unapproachable. It is not, then, with the idea of matter, that the mind finds difficulty. This it works with in all its theories, and discovers nothing in it self-destructive, or destructive to the notion of mind. Whether, however, this idea, so manageable within the mind, has any outward thing that corresponds with it, is a question of simple proof, and if such proof be present, yields no new perplexity. If the mind can in thought handle things so unlike itself as natural objects, it can also recognize their actual being on sufficient evidence. But it is said, there can be no such evidence, for such evidence implies not an ideal, but an actual influence of matter on mind. Is there, then, a clear *a priori* impossibility, that there should be found in the phenomena of mind such traces of the influences of matter, as to furnish the grounds for an inference of its existence. To the ordinary mind this question presents not the least difficulty. To it, sensations, perceptions, are plainly such traces. But, says one who has longer contemplated the problem, is not space the condition of all material being, and is not this the one form which has no actual relevance to acts of mind? Is not consciousness the essential characteristic of thought, and does not this in turn exclude altogether physical forces. How then shall a material force strike within consciousness, or how shall a mental activity leave it to appear in space? Here undoubtedly our powers of explanation are at fault. The inquiries put us, lie too deep in the secret nature, the unphenomenal nature of things to admit of that phenomenal statement or explanation which is sought for. Indeed, in the very language in which our queries are urged, we have over-leaped the limits of clear thought. In speaking of a mental activity as *leaving consciousness*, or a physical force as *entering it*, we have subjected to the conditions of space that which is wholly foreign thereto. Yet these embarrassments should be no ground of disquiet, since, sooner or later, whatever path we take, we reach the unphenomenal, and thus the inexplicable. The how of pure thought is as unintelligible as the how of pure matter, and the inter-dependence of the two is no more obscure than the manner of the existence of either. The nature of thought is as unknown to us as any thing can be. We discover easily the relations of things that lie in its light, but what that light is in which they are seen, what is the sub-phenomenal nature of the activity whose product we retain as a judgment, is wholly inscrutable in the sense of being capable of a phenomenal rendering. When we reach the bounds of events, we also reach the limits of a certain form of explanation. Yet we cannot avoid confronting the less plain and penetrable forms of existence that lie beyond, without a flat denial of them, and such a denial leaves our visible world wholly afloat, and is itself the source of greater perplexities than those it seeks to escape. Moreover that space is not directly or indirectly penetrable by the activities of mind, is a proposition whose conditions are too obscure to suffer it to be ranked as an *a priori* conception. Were it not for our belief in the actual existence of the external world, and our connection with it, there would be no problem, since ideally the mind moves freely in space. If matter did not exist, if powers to apprehend it did not belong to us, there would be nothing to call forth the question which perplexes us. The very query itself thus becomes proof of the fact.

We are not alone in an inability to solve ultimate problems, pertaining to matter beyond the bounds of experience. Indeed, an experience that should commence with a complete knowing, that should even know how it knew, would be an eye that saw itself, an ear that heard itself. Consciousness is not such an organ. It reveals thought, not the nature of the thinking powers; its phenomenal, formal character, not the very essence of the act itself. All that we claim is, that there is no *a priori* impossibility discoverable by us, making a transfer of influence from mind to matter, from matter to mind, an absurdity. Our last traces of physical force in the movement inward are found in the brain, our first traces in the movement outward are also met with at the same point. Thus far only can the eye trace material changes; here is it first able to pick them up. How the last nervous impulse is linked to the play of consciousness, or how a pure volition breaks forth and liberates a physical force without itself becoming such a force, we cannot explain. We only affirm that our ignorance is so complete as to cut us off as perfectly from a denial of the possibility of such a transfer, as from an exposition of it. We simply do not see, that the realms of space and consciousness anywhere over-lap, or even touch each other. We are profoundly ignorant of the nature of any connection between the two. We therefore satisfy ourselves with denying the existence of any *a priori* proof against such a dependence; while experience, under the spontaneous interpretation which the human mind everywhere gives it, constantly affirms it as a fact.

In the ideal world, the mind freely contemplates physical being and forces. It moves at liberty among them, regards them as modified by its own activity, and is, in turn, modified in its thinking by them. It thus far recognizes no incompatibility between the two realms; but is prepared to accept those actual relations which give occasion to these ideal ones. If an *a priori* necessity, ingrained in mind, divided the two fields, how could the mind so easily escape it in its own spontaneous movements? It does not, cannot regard lines as at once parallel and intersecting; a relation of space as equivalent to one of time; how, then, can it practically accept the communicability of matter and mind, and theoretically pronounce it impossible?

§ 2. An increasingly prevalent form of philosophy, held crudely by some, is that which swallows mind up in matter. In its most logical, yet most naked and repulsive forms, it resolves all thought into the mere action of nervous centres, induced in a purely physical way by physical forces, forces directly inhering in matter. We have hardly sufficient respect for this system to treat it with patience. It is for the most part the product of scientific inquiry, a study of the laws of the material world simply. While often affecting great contempt for *a priori* systems, and claiming experience as the only source and test of truth, in its philosophy—by courtesy so called—it presents an example of the most unreasonable and absurd *a priori* method anywhere found in the progress of knowledge.

The momentum, the entire organum, the scheme of inquiry and instruments of thought, with which it approaches the intellectual world, have been gathered in departments utterly alien to the one to be contemplated. Far from being ready for independent inquiry, ready to accept new facts under their own laws, philosophers of this school approach the science of mind, with the antecedent, the *a priori* conviction, that physical laws reign everywhere, that there is the same fixed dependence of events in the realm of thought as that which they have found in matter. They thus, with the blindness of a limited system, and the willfulness of a restricted one, push up the stream of causes as far as they can go, and then deny that there is anything beyond. As this theory fails, not merely to explain, but even to accept, the new and very diverse phenomena of consciousness, to analyze and expound them within their own field, under their own forms; and feebly substitutes for them some connected, but very different phenomena, to wit those of the nervous centres, we feel at liberty, giving its scientific inquiries due praise, to pass it very lightly as a philosophy. It deals with shadows and not with substances, with the external conditions and accompaniments of mental activity, and not with the inner forms and laws of those activities. Under that fatal certainty which causes equivalent errors to follow each other in opposite extremes, it strives to stand outside in space and expound consciousness, as formerly the hasty philosopher inclosed in consciousness constructed his outside, *a priori* facts.

The last gate which this school suppose themselves to

have opened, at which the powers of the physical world are to rush in and submerge those of mind, is that known as the correlation of forces. All material forces are convertible and indestructible. Hence it is concluded, that those which are at play in the living and nervous organism mutually replace each other, can receive no accessions, and must evolve from within themselves all the most subtile and the most palpable of the activities of rational, human life. Accept this relation of forces in the body, and we yet need, for the full explanation of the facts, the independent, spontaneous power of mind. I am content to believe, that every thought, feeling, volition involves the expenditure, the modification of a physical force in some form present to the body; that the mind avails itself of a stream of forces that flow incessantly though its physical organization, into this dips its wheel, and with it works out its purposes. This admission by no means closes the argument.

We have here a telegraph, we discover that the electric, chemical, thermal, mechanical forces liberated are so far equivalent as to induce us to believe that they are perfectly so. We stand in an office; we behold an intelligible cypher rapidly appearing on the ribbon before us; does the equivalence, the indestructibility, the convertibility of the forces in the mechanism we have investigated, explain the message we have received? We may say, that nothing has been lost or added to the sum of forces concerned in the transfer of these words. Very well, the words in their intelligibility still seek solution. These are explained by the constant interference of a higher power, a remote operator, above the circle of self-balanced forces which have transferred the motion from the indicating to the inscribing index. Now, I may never see the hand that plays the remote key, but I cannot fail to believe in its existence, nor in the independent, intelligent character of the force that presides there. I know not how the key is touched, by which the self-poised, nervous forces of the brain are set in motion ; but in the product wrought out, I do see unmistakably the evidence of such initiation, guidance, arrest. How the conditions, under which nervous forces are used, in evolving intellectual and physical phenomena, are secured, is not plain, but the existence of such conditions is as thoroughly proved as that of the telegraph operator. The continuity and equality of the forces in the nervous circuit, if fully established, does not weaken or embarrass the conviction. It simply leaves us where it found us, ignorant of the way in which the mind employs the current of material forces ; these still yield the clearest evidence of being at some point of their circuit intersected by another and higher circle of influences. To say, that the only force which can modify physical forces must itself be a physical force, betraying its presence among them as a new, additive power, is not merely to affirm what we do not know, but is to make the assertion that the intelligence and spontaneity of the products momentarily evolved by these nervous centres, do not indicate like qualities in the ultimate agency, an assertion in flat contradiction of the principles of reasoning on which we habitually proceed.

How little this form of philosophy can accomplish is evident from the fact, that it itself must admit, that some kinds of matter are intelligent, self-conscious, spontaneous, and others are not. Thus having laboriously swallowed up mind in matter, it is compelled to re-include under matter, distinctions in every way as perplexing and inscrutable as those displaced. The facts remain, and either matter is self-conscious, or that which is self-conscious is mind. Words rather than ideas, are thus offered as explanations in this deceptive resolution of two distinct elements into one. If an adversary of this theory chooses to add the farther affirmation that this self-conscious matter is also free, the point can only be fairly settled by re-opening the entire discussion ; for it is antecedently no more improbable that matter is free, than it is that matter is intelligent, conscious. The forces concerned in intellectual action are either conditioned from within to all the facts of mind, and we are remitted to consciousness to determine what these facts are in their entire complement ; or these forces are conditioned to their action from without. If we accept the first statement, we have recognized two kinds of forces or activities utterly distinct from each other ; if we accept the last, we have used two words, and called one set of forces appearing in space, material ; and the same forces arising in consciousness, mental ; thus either denying or overlooking the distinctions between them. What possible explanation is there in this ? Does not the fundamental differences between matter and mind, open to all our faculties, remain as before ? It would be well for philosophers to remember that theories cannot reflexively wipe out facts, and that those of mind are of the most primitive and undeniable character. What is included among them must be found by inquiry within the mind itself. If either of the two classes of facts are to be merged in the other, physical ones necessarily yield to those of mind, as in their nature secondary, and as being known only as they appear in consciousness. As the material world is at best reached mediately, inferentially, it cannot logically displace the very faculties that know it. The knowing must have precedence of the thing known. If either is to be found to contain the other, it must be the first the second, not the second the first.

Materialism does not always assume the crude form now controverted. It has sometimes a more mixed and subtile character, one in which it is partially blended with idealism. Mr. Mill, while deriving all knowledge from experience, and declining to recognize any intuitive elements, nevertheless leaves the existence of matter in doubt. Sensations and perceptions are accepted apparently in an ideal form, and the outside world of realities, which lies back of them, is left unapproached. Such a system is beset with more difficulties than either materialism or idealism. Sensations, whose existence and influence lie wholly within the mind, can with less reason be made to control and give form to the mind, than matter conceived as wholly outside and independent of the intellectual powers. Indeed it is not easy to see how a perception can occupy this anomalous position, on the one side giving law to the mind, on the other, cut off from all known, exterior dependence, and resting back on the very faculties whose form it controls.

This system exhibits the same partial and defective analysis which belongs to all materialism. Space and time are evolved from experience, though they are the conditions of experience. They are made to spring from sensations, though themselves utterly beyond sensation. Those ideas, on the other hand, that are admittedly in the mind, yet admittedly beyond experience, are pronounced delusive. Of this character is that of causation. Breaking this cord of connection, the external world swings loose from this philosophy. There lies against it concisely these difficulties. Claiming experience to be the source of knowledge, it elaborates a system far removed from ordinary conviction, and subversive of many of its most cherished opinions. It knows nothing of matter, while mankind know this chiefly. It gives sensations, perceptions control over the mind, while the opinions of men divide control between outside and inside conditions. It makes delusive the notion of causation, which above all has universal sway in the practical world.

It denies moreover the necessity of any ideas whatever, while the whole history of pure mathematics, of reasoning, show the contrary. It is compelled to refer to experience the recognition of such facts as this, that straight lines, parallel through a portion of their extent, are so through their whole extent. Its analyses are inadequate, and it rejects without ground or reason, the ideas for which it can find no place in its system. It saves those notions which it can deceptively evolve from experience, and those it fails thus to explain it rejects. That is to say, it makes its method the test of the facts, and not the facts the test of its method.

§ 3. The next system of which we shall speak, is also a mongrel one, that presented by Hamilton. Its most striking feature is, that it makes matter itself the direct object of perception, and thus, losing one occasion for intuitive ideas, accepts a part of them, perverts a part, and neglects a part. Among those resolved into powerlessness, are causation, liberty and the infinite. We need only to speak of its central characteristic, the direct perception of matter. Against this there holds, we believe, the very generally accepted axiom that nothing can act save where it is. The introduction of the adverb where, shows this statement to be limited to physical forces, since these alone appear in space, alone have locality. Physical forces must be where they are exercised. This will hardly be denied by any one. For a force to show itself as a force where it is not, would be for it to be and not to be, at the same point at the same time. Mind, thought, have no reference to space, and hence it conveys no very intelligible idea to say, that the mind must be, a thought must be where it acts. Their objects of consideration may come from any quarter, and any distance; conclusions may strike out into the most remote regions, and such words as come and go, near and distant, have only a figurative signification. Now perception, till the brain is passed, is a thing of physical forces, and each organ and nerve can only be affected by that within it, not by that without it. It is against the above axiom to say, that I feel the stone, meaning thereby that the sensation is outside the organ—conversant, less or more, with the very essence of being in the stone. The organ is affected by what is within itself; till the contour of its own forces, states is penetrated, the object might as well be miles, as inches, or fractions of an inch distant. Physical effects lie as content in each organ of sense, and are as localized within it, as is the object without it. If, then, these physical changes of condition which accompany perception, sensation, were known to, that is perceived by, the mind, the very object, the source of these, would not thereby be directly known or perceived. But these states are not perceived, we know nothing about either the eye, the ear, or tongue, in seeing, hearing, tasting. Sensation, perception, enter consciousness, and lose at once special relations and organic force. When we have reached the last movement, the last physical change in our nervous organism, we have not reached the first thing that the mind is conscious of in sensation. No organ of sensation is revealed by its own sensations, but by other sensations of other organs of which it is made an object. If, then, the mind knows the object at all in perception, it is not directly by the movement inward from the object, since this finds arrest, change; when from it, as a cause, there passes a nervous affection, as effect or content, into an organ of sense; and this again meets with a most inexplicable change, when, from a nervous wave passing through a nervous centre, there is a transfer to consciousness, and the true content of the mind, a sensation, a feeling, lies within it, divested of local relations. We might as well say, that the first ball is in the second ball moving after concussion, as to say, that the very object of perception or any portion of it, is in this its latest effect. No, the second ball moves through a change within itself; the organ becomes a condition of perception through a new condition of its own nervous substance.

It is, then, by an outward movement of the mind, that matter is known, and this is not perception, this is not sensation, but inference, conclusion, the interpretation of sensations. Through the notions of existence, and causation, and space, the mind establishes, arranges the external world. Sensations, till interpreted and expounded by judgment, are the crudest possible conditions of knowledge. This theory, it may be said, is also contradictory of universal belief. Doubtless the part played by the judgments, the intuitions, in the action of the senses is very generally overlooked; but the validity of these perceptive conclusions is not generally denied by us. A little observation shows us, that processes which we had regarded as simple, are indeed complex, the apparent simplicity arising only from the ease and rapidity with which they are performed. The common mind does not pronounce, is not prepared to pronounce, on the method of knowledge, what it affirms is the fact of knowledge.

If it be said, that the act of perception itself is the result of an outward, not an inward movement, that it takes place at the exterior tip of the nerve, not as the consequence of physical effects traced to the nerve centres; we say, that the mind must either pass perceptively beyond its own positive organism, which presents special and local sensations, beyond the sensational organ, or the perceptive act is still within the human body, and thus without, and removed from, the object perceived. Moreover, such a theory neglects the obvious ministration to perception of all the chain of nervous influences, beginning at the centre and passing outward. If these are instruments, means to sensation, they must intervene in time between the presence of the object and the perception of it. While pure mental actions, like intuitive judgments, are without local relation, perception, in its physical conditions, comes within space; and these, that they may remain conditions to perception, must be antecedent to it; that is, the inscrutable transition from a nervous state to a feeling follows the inner, nervous current. Of an outer nervous current, there is no proof. The mind has therefore no other, no further physical, that is no further perceptive connection with the object than that in which these several conditions of the organ intervene between the mind and the object.

§ 4. The last system of which we shall speak, is Idealism, in its pure form. Idealism, with many minor differences in the manner of its presentation, has peculiar excellences and defects. It seizes the most fundamental, the truly germinal element of the universe, and evolves all else with consistent logic from it. It does not humble mind under the laws of matter, but makes it the source and law of all things. As all existences, all known existences, must at some point, in some way, enter consciousness, or be productive of phenomena there, it is evident that idealism has no occasion to lose or overlook any part of knowledge, any known thing. Neglecting that intuitive, inevitable, inferential action of the mind by which it recognizes the objective validity and relations of the various sources of its perceptions and sensations, idealism is able, by limiting the attention to the phenomena of the internal world alone, in part independent, and in part the shadow, of external things, to trace the inherent relations among these, and develop a purely ideal system of purely ideal objects. Herein, there is opportunity for great subtlety, profoundity, consistency, and even breadth of thought; since everything, outer and inner, finds representation here. If the images of all the objects and events of the external world were brought to the eye of a spectator on a transparency, it is plain that he might form a very inclusive, and, in some of its aspects, correct philosophy concerning them. Consciousness is such a screen, and the philosopher, confining his attention to this, may evolve a very harmonious system.

Idealism, more signally than most other theories, fails of being a science, a knowing as actual of that which is conceived as theoretical. It matters little, that the inherent connections are necessary, unless the premises from point to point of the argument are verified as real. The difficulties of idealism are much the same as those of the *a priori* proof of the existence of God. An ideal conclusion is evolved from ideal premises, but as the last do not take hold of the world of facts, no more does the first. Philosophy is not merely philosophy, but a science as well. It possesses inductive, united with deductive, elements. It resembles mixed rather than pure mathematics. It does not start with definitions of ideal objects, but with facts. Idealism, on the other hand, while contemplating thought, contemplates it as thought merely, in its form and formal relations rather than in its actual, phenomenal character and force. It deduces the individual from the general. It inquires, not so much, what is given actually and practically with independent testimony by the several faculties of mind, as what can be evolved from the mere fact of thought.

The result is, that no system is as far removed from general belief and faith as idealism. None so signally fails to recognize and expound the phenomena of mind either under the form they actually assume, or are thought to assume in experience. It seems rather a field of intellectual gymnastics than of sound, sober inquiry concerning things, corrected and guided each instant by an observation of facts.

Idealism starts with assuming the least possible. It would commence with nothing if it could. It accepts only sensible activity known in consciousness. It must not even say, "an action," lest there should thus be implied something which is active. From this it proceeds to develop matter and mind, activity and divided activity, recognizing itself in consciousness, opposing to the naked knowing, the consciousness of knowing. Thus it moves onward, spinning a world out of its own bowels, and with little more of actual correspondence of results to the notions of men, to that which is in and about us, than there exists between the threads of a spider's web, and the actual forces which hold the world together. Yet the idealist relishes his own system none the less, for being so stuffed and trussed with the ego.

Science, or scientific philosophy, does not inquire how little it may assume, but how much it may consistently accept; at how many points it has reached ultimate facts. If the idealist is at liberty to regard the connections of thought not as fanciful and chimerical, but, as they seem to be, logical and coherent; in short to accept thinking as thinking, as a valid and reliable act; if he is at liberty to assume memory, do not these necessary assumptions involve the fitness, the right, and the necessity of still farther assumption? Are not these, portions of a set of powers, and if the philosopher avails himself of two, can he do better than to avail himself of all? Does he trespass any more on sound principles in using the entire group, than in using these? Indeed, does he not act absurdly in employing thus adroitly a part, and neglecting the remainder, equally fitted for another and specific purpose? Should it be one's object to see how much can be done with the least possible means, or to see how much can be accomplished with all available means? Having a clue, an indication, ought not he, as a thinker, to follow it as far as it will carry him, and does it not carry him logically to a faith in all his faculties, since he must have a faith in a part of them? Possibly, he can hop a little distance painfully on one foot; is it therefore, wise—practically, philosophically wise for him to sling up the other? Under this line of thinking, the scientific philosopher at once sets to work to determine by observation and analysis all his faculties, and accepts the testimony of them all, as each necessary to the right understanding of the peculiar and independent facts rendered by it.

Thus the idealist, regarding himself by pre-eminence the philosopher, and the less cunning but more wise inquirer, begin at once to diverge. The one constructs a system of remarkable connections, subtile and sagacious, but altogether airy and unsubstantial; the other acquires classified knowledge, with many lines of causation and deductive relations in it; often presenting, indeed, inscrutable points, yet always having the ring and firmness of facts. Idealism is ideal; science, the philosophy we seek, is actual.

§ 5. The system we have now presented, aims fully to recognize the different, independent kinds of knowing. Each of these is ultimate, and, therefore, inexplicable under other forms of knowing. To carry one faculty into the province of another, is to displace that other, and with it the information it is fitted to give. Knowledge, in its last analysis, has always a certain mystery about it; perhaps for the very reason that we can go no farther. There is a mystery in a color, as green; in a taste, as sweet; in an odor, as fragrant; in a judgment, pronouncing the stone to be hard; in every intuition, as that of a cause, of liberty, of the infinite. We must not expect to expel mystery, but to reduce it to a minimum, and place it at the right points.

One of the chief labors of the philosopher is to keep independent faculties, so recognized on adequate grounds, from devouring each other; from making incursions into fields alien to them, from refusing to accept at all what has not been submitted to themselves, and received their peculiar seal. The imagination and the understanding, belong especially to these intrusive faculties, while the intuition of cause, having swept through the entire physical world, is ever bent on a raid into spiritual realms. To be ready to recognize, in their unrestricted forms, the facts of consciousness as revealed in the mind, in language, in history; to analyze these repeatedly, cautiously, without bias and perversion, for the discovery of the simple activities or faculties they reveal; and afterward to hold fast to every affirmation of these faculties, is the duty of the wise cultivator of mental science. We have, in this discussion, developed a little love for the word science above that of philosophy, because of this inductive element it so obviously includes.

The independent validity both of causation and of liberty has been recognized. Each idea is present to the mind in the spontaneous explanation which it offers to a certain class of facts. They divide the universe of events between them. In the one moiety or portion, we have necessity, in the other, liberty; in the one, movements already conditioned by the forces at work, in the other, movements then and there conditioned by the power that initiates them. The authority, the proof of these two notions is exactly the same. The mind, by its own penetrative, explanatory strength, supplies them as the ground or condition of the facts before it. In these relations to each other, liberty is primary, and causation is secondary. Causation marks dependence, a dependence which, on its own level, can find no arrest, no matter how far we trace it. Events, follow them backward, forward, on either hand, are conditioned one upon another; forces are already at work accomplishing the tasks assigned them. But a first, an independent, an unconditioned force nowhere appears. Causal action, therefore, necessarily presents a fragmentary and partial character. Of it alone, there can be made up no whole, no universe; since the more we have, the more we demand to explain what we have. The events before us, like the section of a river, must flow into and flow out of the horizon. We can reach no beginning and no conclusion, nor even find diminution as we go backward, or increase as we go forward. The boundaries of our vision enlarge themselves in all directions, but are always illusory, never found.

Liberty, on the contrary, to the extent of the events which spring from it, affords a complete commencement. We need go no farther back. An arrest is found in it, and the causative events which flow thence are explained by the form, impetus, and direction, which it has imparted to them. Causation is necessarily finite in its manifestation; since it inheres in a power already put forth, and conditioned to a given number and form of products. Liberty rests back on the agent, never goes forth from him, and partakes, in its possibilities, of the breadth and the limitations of his faculties. It commands more than the actual, to wit the potential of being. Infinite power can inhere in a free personality, and in no other form of existence.

Causation is closely connected with space. It may be questioned whether it ever acts in any other connection. It inheres in forces, and these are physical, put forth from personality, into separate, spacial existence. The phenomena of mind which involve cause and effect, do so through material dependencies. The mind's own action would seem to be either always spontaneous or free, that is its spontaneity is revealed under the three forms of thought, feeling and volition. Liberty, in contra-distinction, remains always in consciousness. We can only choose consciously. Matter can only be the source of force, of causative action. Mind is the source of spontaneous and of free action; of spontaneous action, that is action springing independently from it, though often evoked by conditions not supplied by it; of free action, that is action held within, but not bound to, any one of the conditions which are its occasion. In physical forces, there is virtually but one force. We contemplate only the effective force, the force out of equilibrum, and passing into equilibrum by the very activity induced. In spontaneous, intellectual life, there is also virtually but one condition, voluntary action. These two conditions, as far as man is concerned, shape combinedly and independently the world of facts.

Liberty, again, lies back of all all causation, because the whole flood of forms in which and with which human liberty plays, springs from the choice of God, is but the executive power with which he momentarily sustains and accomplishes his purposes. Here we reach another, for the present, ultimate fact. We know not how the mind affects these secondary physical forces, that in the human body play beneath its touch? No more do we understand how these imperishable and uniform forces on which the universe is buoyed, of which it is fashioned, go forth from the will of God. Yet their wholly finite, dependent, necessary character compels the reason thus to refer them, thus to centre them, in an independent, self-sufficient source; and therein to complete, to round off the conception of the universe in time as in space. A cord of great length is no more self-supporting, no more explicable in itself, than a shorter one. The only idea which is, as it were, spherical, self-centered, demanding nothing, suffering nothing outside of itself, is that of an Infinite, Personal God, a sufficient source of all things; whose spontaneity and liberty require no explanation, and bring explanation to all beside. On this ground, and on this alone, the reason accepts the idea, as one by which it does see, as a sun that does spread its light through the whole heavens, leaving nothing which is not sought out by its rays. The final proof of truth is the fact of light, the very fact of light admitting no controversy and no denial to those who receive it—to whom it gives the power to become the sons of God. The real efficiency of every word is found in the disclosure of itself as the light which comes down from heaven.

THE END.

www.ingramcontent.com/pod-product-compliance
Lightning Source LLC
LaVergne TN
LVHW010156110826
845151LV00002B/530
* 9 7 8 1 4 2 5 5 3 6 6 7 1 *